Engraved by H.W. Smith from an original picture by Copley in the possession of Dr. John C. Warren.

HISTORY

OF THE

UNITED STATES,

FROM THE

DISCOVERY OF THE AMERICAN CONTINENT.

BY

GEORGE BANCROFT.

VOL. VII.

BOSTON:
LITTLE, BROWN AND COMPANY.
1858.

PREFACE.

The period of the American Revolution of which a portion is here treated, divides itself into two epochs; the first extending to the Declaration of Independence; the second, to the acknowledgment of that Independence by Great Britain. In preparing the volume, there has been no parsimony of labor; but marginal references to the documents out of which it has mainly been constructed are omitted. This is done not from an unwillingness to subject every statement of fact, even in its minutest details, to the severest scrutiny; but from the variety and multitude of the papers which have been used, and which could not be intelligibly cited, without burdening the pages with a disproportionate commentary.

From the very voluminous manuscripts which I have brought together, I hope at some not very distant day to cull out for publication such letters as may at once confirm my narrative and possess an intrinsic and general interest by illustrating the character and sentiments of the people during the ten or twelve years preceding the Fourth of July, 1776.

At the close of the sixth volume of this work, some imperfect acknowledgment was made to those from whom I have received most essential service while making my collection of materials. I shall hereafter have occasion to recur to that subject; at this time I desire to express my sense of the friendly regard of many persons in various parts of our country, who have sent me unpublished documents, or historical pamphlets and monographs, such as the liberal and inquisitive are constantly publishing. Whatever can be obtained in the ordinary way through the booksellers, I have no need to solicit; but I am and shall ever be grateful to any person who will forward to me at New York any materials which cannot be obtained except through private courtesy.

NEW YORK, March 31, 1858.

CONTENTS.

CHAPTER I.

AMERICA, BRITAIN, AND FRANCE, IN MAY, 1774. May, 1774.

CHAPTER II.

NEW YORK PROPOSES A GENERAL CONGRESS. May, 1774.

CHAPTER III.

VOICES FROM THE SOUTH. May, 1774, continued.

CHAPTER IV.

MASSACHUSETTS APPOINTS THE TIME AND PLACE FOR A GENERAL CONGRESS. June, 1774.

CHAPTER V.

BOSTON MINISTERED TO BY THE CONTINENT. June—July, 1774.

CHAPTER VI.

AMERICA RESOLVES TO MEET IN GENERAL CONGRESS. July, 1774.

CHAPTER XIV.

HOW CATHOLIC EMANCIPATION BEGAN. October, 1774.

CHAPTER XV.

THE GOVERNOR OF VIRGINIA NULLIFIES THE QUEBEC ACT. October—November, 1774.

CHAPTER XVI.

THE FOURTEENTH PARLIAMENT OF GREAT BRITAIN. October—December, 1774.

CHAPTER XVII.

THE KING REJECTS THE OFFERS OF CONGRESS. December, 1774—January, 1775.

CHAPTER XVIII.

CHATHAM LAYS THE FOUNDATION OF PEACE. January 20th, 1775.

CHAPTER XIX.

THE PEOPLE OF NEW YORK TRUE TO UNION. January—February, 1775.

CHAPTER XX.

PARLIAMENT DECLARES MASSACHUSETTS IN REBELLION. Jan. 23—Feb. 9, 1775.

CHAPTER XXI.

THE SPIRIT OF NEW ENGLAND. February, 1775.

CHAPTER XXII.

HAS NEW ENGLAND A RIGHT IN THE NEWFOUNDLAND FISHERIES? Feb., 1775.

CHAPTER XXIII.

THE ANNIVERSARY OF THE BOSTON MASSACRE. February—March, 1775.

CHAPTER XXIV.

PUBLIC OPINION IN ENGLAND. March, 1775.

CHAPTER XXV.

VIRGINIA PREPARES FOR SELF-DEFENCE. March—April, 1775.

CHAPTER XXVI.

THE KING WAITS TO HEAR THE SUCCESS OF LORD NORTH'S PROPOSITION. April—May, 1775.

CHAPTER XXVII.

LEXINGTON. April 19th, 1775.

CHAPTER XXVIII.

TO CONCORD AND BACK TO BOSTON. April 19th, 1775.

CHAPTER XXXII.

EFFECTS OF THE DAY OF LEXINGTON AND CONCORD, continued: TICONDEROGA TAKEN. May, 1775.

CHAPTER XXXIII.

EFFECTS OF THE DAY OF LEXINGTON AND CONCORD IN EUROPE. May to July, 1775.

CHAPTER XXXIV.

THE SECOND CONTINENTAL CONGRESS. May, 1775.

CHAPTER XXXV.

THE REVOLUTION EMANATES FROM THE PEOPLE. May, 1775.

CHAPTER XXXVI.

CONGRESS OFFERS TO NEGOTIATE WITH THE KING. May, 1775.

CHAPTER XXXVII.

MASSACHUSETTS ASKS FOR GEORGE WASHINGTON AS COMMANDER IN CHIEF.
June 1—17, 1775.

CHAPTER XXXVIII.

PRESCOTT OCCUPIES BREED'S HILL. June 16-17, 1775.

CHAPTER XXXIX.

BUNKER HILL BATTLE. June 17, 1775.

CHAPTER XL.

THE RESULT OF BUNKER HILL BATTLE. June 17, 1775.

THE

AMERICAN REVOLUTION.

EPOCH THIRD.

AMERICA DECLARES ITSELF INDEPENDENT.

1774—1776.

AMERICA DECLARES ITSELF INDEPENDENT.

CHAPTER I.

AMERICA, BRITAIN AND FRANCE, IN MAY, 1774.

May, 1774.

CHAP. I. 1774. May.

The hour of the American Revolution was come. The people of the continent with irresistible energy obeyed one general impulse, as the earth in spring listens to the command of nature, and without the appearance of effort bursts forth to life in perfect harmony. The change which Divine wisdom ordained, and which no human policy or force could hold back, proceeded as uniformly and as majestically as the laws of being, and was as certain as the decrees of eternity. The movement was quickened, even when it was most resisted; and its fiercest adversaries worked together effectually for its fulfilment. The indestructible elements of freedom in the colonies asked room for expansion and growth. Standing in manifold relations with the governments, the culture, and the experience of the past, the Americans seized

CHAP. I. 1774. May. as their peculiar inheritance the traditions of liberty. Beyond any other nation they had made trial of the possible forms of popular representation; and respected the activity of individual conscience and thought. The resources of the vast country in agriculture and commerce, forests and fisheries, mines and materials for manufactures, were so diversified and complete, that their development could neither be guided nor circumscribed by a government beyond the ocean; the numbers, purity, culture, industry, and daring of its inhabitants proclaimed the existence of a people, rich in creative energy, and ripe for institutions of their own.

They were rushing towards revolution, and they knew it not. They refused to acknowledge even to themselves the hope that was swelling within them; and yet they were possessed by the truth, that man holds inherent and indefeasible rights; and as their religion had its witness coeval and coextensive with intelligence, so in their political aspirations they deduced from universal principles a bill of rights, as old as creation and as wide as humanity. The idea of freedom had never been wholly unknown; it had always revealed itself at least to a few of the wise, whose prophetic instincts were quickened by love of their kind; its rising light flashed joy across the darkest centuries; and its growing energy can be traced in the tendency of the ages. In America it was the breath of life to the people. For the first time it found a region and a race, where it could be professed with the earnestness of an indwelling conviction, and be defended with the enthusiasm that heretofore had marked no wars but those for religion. When all Europe slumbered over questions of liberty, a band of exiles, keeping watch by night, heard the glad tidings which promised the political regeneration of the world. A revolution, unexpected in the moment of its coming, but prepared by glorious forerunners, grew naturally and necessarily out of the series of past events by the formative principle of a living belief. And why should man organize resistance to the grand design of Providence? Why should not the consent of the ancestral land and the gratulations of every other call the young nation to its place among the powers of the earth? Britain was the mighty mother who bred and formed men capable of laying the foundation of so noble an empire; and she alone could have formed them. She had excelled all nations of the world as the planter of colonies. The condition which entitled her colonies to independence was now more than fulfilled. Their vigorous vitality refused conformity to foreign laws and external rule. They could take no other way to perfection than by the unconstrained development of that which was within them. They were not only able to govern themselves, they alone were able to do so; subordination visibly repressed their energies. It was only by self-direction that they could at all times and in entireness freely employ in action their collective and individual powers to the fullest extent of their ever increasing intelligence. Could not the illustrious nation which had gained no distinction in war, in literature, or in science, comparable to that of having wisely founded distant settlements on a system of liberty, willingly perfect its beneficent work, now when no more was required than the acknowledgment that its offspring was come

CHAP. I. 1774. May. of age, and its own duty accomplished? Why must the ripening of lineal virtue be struck at, as rebellion in the lawful sons? Why is their unwavering attachment to the essential principle of their existence to be persecuted as treason, rather than viewed with delight as the crowning glory of the country from which they sprung? If the institutions of Britain were so deeply fixed in the usages and opinions of its people, that their deviations from justice could not as yet be rectified; if the old continent was pining under systems of authority which were not fit to be borne, and which as yet no way opened to amend, why should not a people be heartened to build a commonwealth in the wilderness, which alone offered it a home?

So reasoned a few in Britain who were jeered "as visionary enthusiasts;" deserving no weight in public affairs. Parliament had asserted an absolute lordship over the colonies in all cases whatsoever; and fretting itself into a frenzy at the denial of its unlimited dominion, was blindly destroying all its recognised authority in the madness of its zeal for more. The majority of the ministers, including the most active and determined, were bent on the immediate employment of force. Lord North, who recoiled from civil war, exercised no control over his colleagues, leaving the government to be conducted by the several departments. As a consequence, the king became the only point of administrative union, and ruled as well as reigned. In him an approving conscience had no misgiving as to his duty. His heart knew no relenting; his will never wavered. Though America were to be drenched in blood and its towns reduced to ashes, though its people were to be driven to struggle for total independence, though he himself should find it necessary to bid high for hosts of mercenaries from the Scheldt to Moscow, and in quest of savage allies, go tapping at every wigwam from Lake Huron to the Gulf of Mexico, he was resolved to coerce the thirteen colonies into submission. The people of Great Britain identified themselves, though but for the moment, with his anger, and talked like so many kings of their subjects beyond the Atlantic. Of their ability to crush resistance they refused to doubt; nor did they, nor the ministers, nor George the Third, apprehend interference, except from that great neighboring kingdom whose vast colonial system Britain had just overthrown.

All Europe, though at peace, was languishing under exhaustion from wars of ambition, or vices of government, and crying out for relief from abuses which threatened to dissolve the old social order. In France, enduring life belonged to two elements only in the state—the people and monarchical power; and every successive event increased the importance of the one and the other. It was its common people which saved that country from perishing of corrupt unbelief, and made it the most powerful state of continental Europe. The peasants, it is true, were poor and oppressed and ignorant; but all Frenchmen, alike townspeople and villagers, were free. There was no protecting philanthropy on the part of the nobility; no hierarchy of mutually dependent ranks; no softening of contrasts by the blending of colors and harmonizing of shades; the poor, though gay by temperament, lived sad and apart; bereft of intercourse with

CHAP. I. 1774. May.

superior culture; never mirthful but in mockery of misery; not cared for in their want, nor solaced in hospitals, nor visited in prisons; but the bonds had been struck alike from the mechanic in the workshop and the hind in the fields. The laborer at the forge was no longer a serf; the lord of the manor exercised jurisdiction no more over vassals; in all of old France the peasants were freemen, and in the happiest provinces had been so for half a thousand years. Only a few of them, as of the nobles in the middle ages, could read; but a vast number owned the acres which they tilled. By lineage, language, universality of personal freedom, and diffusion of landed property, the common people of France formed one compact and indivisible nation.

Two circumstances which increased the wretchedness of the third estate, increased also their importance. The feudal aristocracy had been called into being for the protection of the kingdom; but in the progress of ages, they had escaped from the obligation to military service. In this manner they ceased to be the peers of their sovereign; and though they still scorned every profession but that of arms, they received their commissions from the king's favor, and drew from his exchequer their pay as hirelings. Thus the organization of the army ceased to circumscribe royal power, which now raised soldiers directly from the humbler classes. The defence of the country had passed from the king and his peers with their vassals to the king in direct connection with those vassals who were thus become a people.

Again, the nobility, carefully securing the exemption of their own estates, had, in their struggles with the central power, betrayed the commons, by allowing the monarch to tax them at will. Proving false to their trust as the privileged guardians of liberty, and renouncing the military service that had formed the motive to their creation, they made themselves an insulated and worthless caste. All that was beneficent in feudalism had died out. Soulless relics of the past, the nobles threw up their hereditary rustic independence to fasten themselves as courtiers upon the treasury. They hung like a burden on the state, which they no longer guided, nor sustained, nor defended, nor consoled. Some few among them, rising superior to their rank, helped to bear society onwards to its regeneration; but as a class their life was morally at an end. France could throw them off as readily as a stag sheds its antlers. They had abdicated their political importance, which passed to the people. The imposts which they refused to share, and which in two centuries had increased tenfold, fell almost exclusively on the lowly, who toiled and suffered, having no redress against those employed by the government; regarding the monarch with touching reverence and love, though they knew him mostly as the power that harried them; ruled as though joy were no fit companion for labor; as though want were the necessary goad to industry, and sorrow the only guarantee of quiet. They were the strength of the kingdom, the ceaseless producers of its wealth; the supplier of its armies; the sole and exhaustless source of its revenue; and yet, in their forlornness, they cherished scarcely a dim vision of a happier futurity below.

Meantime monarchy was concentrating a mass of

CHAP. I. 1774. May.

power, which a strong arm could wield with irresistible effect, which an effeminate squanderer could not exhaust. Instead of a sovereign restrained by his equals, and depending on free grants from the states, one will commanded a standing army, and imposed taxes on the unprivileged classes. These taxes, moreover, it collected by its own officers, so that throughout all the provinces of France an administration of plebeians, accountable to the king alone, superseded in substance, though not always in form, the ancient methods of feudalism.

Like the army and the treasury the establishment of religion was subordinate to the crown. The Catholic church assumes to represent the Divine wisdom itself, and as a logical consequence, the law which it interprets should be higher than the temporal power. The Gallican church owned allegiance to the state; and when it was observed that Jesuits had inculcated the subordination of the temporal sovereign to a superior rule under which the wicked tyrant might be arraigned, dethroned, or even slain, Louis the Fifteenth uprooted by his word the best organized religious society in Christendom; not perceiving that the sudden exile of the Jesuits and their schools of learning, left the rising generation more easy converts to unbelief. The clergy were tainted with the general scepticism; they stooped before the temporal power to win its protection, and did not scruple to enforce by persecution a semblance of homage to the symbols of religion, of which the life was put to sleep.

The magistrates, with graver manners than the clergy or the nobility, did not so much hate administrative despotism as grasp at its direction; they themselves had so scanty means of self-defence against its arm, that when they hesitated to register the king's decrees, even the word of Louis the Fifteenth could dissolve parliaments which were almost as ancient as the French monarchy itself.

For the benefit of the king's treasury, free charters, granted or confirmed in the middle ages to towns and cities, had over and over again been confiscated, to be ransomed by the citizens, or sold to an oligarchy; so that municipal liberties were no longer independent of the royal caprice.

France was the most lettered nation of the world, and its authors loved to be politicians. Of these the conservative class, whose fanatical partisanship included in their system of order the continuance of every established abuse, had no support but in the king. Scoffers also abounded; but they did not care to restrain arbitrary power, or remove the abuses which they satirized. One universal scepticism questioned the creed of churches and the code of feudal law, the authority of the hierarchy and the sanctity of monarchy; but unbelief had neither the capacity nor the wish to organize a new civilization. The philosophy of the day could not guide a revolution, for it professed to receive no truth but through the senses, denied the moral government of the world, and derided the possibility of disinterested goodness. As there was no practical school of politics in which experience might train statesmen to test new projects, the passion for elementary theories had no moderating counterpoise; and the authors of ameliorating plans favored the unity of administration, that one indisputable word might abolish the complicated

CHAP. I. 1774. May.

usages and laws which had been the deposits of many conquests, or the growth of ages, and found a uniform system on principles of human reason.

At this time the central power, in the hands of a monarch infamous by his enslavement to pleasure, had become hideously selfish and immoral; palsied and depraved; swallowing up all other authority, and yet unconscious of the attendant radical change in the feudal constitution; dreaming itself absolute, yet wanting personal respectability; confessing the necessity of administrative reforms, which it was yet unable to direct. For great ends it was helpless, though it was able to torture and distress the feeble; to fill the criminal code with the barbarisms of arrogant cruelty; to reserve for exceptional courts every accusation against even the humblest of its agents; to judge by special tribunals questions involving life and fortune; to issue arbitrary warrants of imprisonment; to punish without information or sentence; making itself the more hateful the less it was restrained.

The duty and honor of the kingdom were sacrificed in its foreign policy. Louis the Fifteenth was a tranquil spectator of the division of Poland, and courted the friendship of George the Third of England, not to efface the false notion of international enmity which was a brand on the civilization of that age, but to gain a new support for monarchical power. For this end the humiliations of the last war would have been forgiven by the monarch, had not the heart of the nation still palpitated with resentment. Under the supremacy of the king's mistress sensual pleasure ruled the court; dictated the appointment of ministers; confused the administration; multiplied the griefs of the overburdened peasantry; and would have irretrievably degraded France, but for its third estate, who were always rising in importance, ready to lift their head and assert their power, whenever in any part of the world a happier people should give them an example.

The heir to the throne of France was not admitted to the royal council, and grew up ignorant of business and inert. The dauphiness Marie Antoinette, in the splendor of supreme rank, preserved the gay cheerfulness of youth. She was conscious of being lovely, and was willing to be admired; but she knew how to temper graceful condescension with august severity. Impatient of the stateliness of etiquette, which controlled her choice of companions even more than the disposition of her hours, she broke away from wearisome formalities with the eager vivacity of self-will; and was happiest when she could forget that she was a princess and be herself. From the same quickness of nature, she readily took part in any prevailing public excitement, regardless of reasons of state or the decorum of the palace. Unless her pride was incensed, she was merciful; and she delighted in bestowing gifts; but her benevolence was chiefly the indulgence of a capricious humor, which never attracted the affection of the poor. Faithful in her devotedness to the nobles, she knew not the utter decay of their order; and had no other thought than that the traditions of centuries bound them to defend her life and name. But the rugged days of feudalism were gone by; and its frivolous descendants were more ready to draw their

CHAP. I. 1774. May. swords for precedence in a dance at court, than to protect the honor of their future queen. From her arrival in France, Marie Antoinette was hated by the opponents of the Austrian alliance; and even while she was receiving the homage of the court during her first years at Versailles, a faction in the highest ranks calumniated her artless impulsiveness as the evidence of crime.

On this scene of a degenerate nobility and popular distress; of administrative corruptness and ruined finances; of a brave but luxurious army and a slothful navy; of royal authority, unbounded, unquestioned, and yet despised; of rising deference to public opinion in a nation thoroughly united and true to its nationality, Louis the Sixteenth, while not yet twenty years old, entered as king. When, on the tenth of May, 1774, he and the still younger Marie Antoinette were told that his grandfather was no more, they threw themselves on their knees, crying, "We are too young to reign;" and prayed God to direct their inexperience. The city of Paris was delirious with joy at their accession. "It is our paramount wish to make our people happy," was the language of the first edict of the new absolute prince. "He excels in writing prose," said Voltaire, on reading the words of promise; "he seems inspired by Marcus Aurelius; he desires what is good and does it. Happy they, who, like him, are but twenty years old, and will long enjoy the sweets of his reign." Caron de Beaumarchais, the sparkling dramatist and restless plebeian adventurer, made haste to solicit the royal patronage of his genius for intrigue. "Is there," said he through De Sartines, the head of the police, "any thing which the king wishes to know alone and at once, any thing which he wishes done quickly and secretly, here am I, who have at his service a head, a heart, arms, and no tongue." CHAP. I. 1774 May.

The young monarch, with all his zeal for administrative improvements, had no revolutionary tendencies, and held, like his predecessor, that the king alone should reign; yet his state papers were soon to cite reverently the law of nature and the rights of man; and the will of the people, shrouded in majesty, was to walk its rounds in the palace invisible, yet supreme.

The sovereign of Spain, on wishing his kinsman joy of his accession, reminded him, as the head of the Bourbons, of their double relationship by his mother's side, as well as his father's; and expressed the wish for "their closest union and most perfect harmony;" for, said he, "the family compact guarantees the prosperity and glory of our House." At that time, the Catholic king was fully employed in personally regulating his finances, and in preparations to chastise the pirates of Algiers, as well as to extort from Portugal a renunciation of its claims to extend the boundaries of Brazil. The sovereign of France was engrossed by the pressing anxieties attending the dismissal of an odious ministry, and the inauguration of domestic reform; so that neither of the princes seemed at leisure to foment troubles in North America.

Yet, next to Du Barry and her party, there was no such sincere mourner for Louis the Fifteenth as George the Third. The continuance of the cordial understanding between the two crowns would depend upon the persons in whom the young king should

CHAP. I. 1774. May. place his confidence. To conciliate his good will, the London Court Gazette announced him as "king of France," though English official language had heretofore spoken only of "the French king," and the Herald's office still knew no other king of France than the head of the House of Brunswick.

At the same time the British ministers, always jealous of the Bourbons, kept spies to guess at their secrets; to hearken after the significant whispers of their ministers; to bribe workmen in their navy yards for a report of every keel that was laid, every new armament or reinforcement to the usual fleets. Doubting the French assurances of a wish to see the troubles in America quieted, they resolved to force the American struggle to an immediate issue, hoping not only to insulate Massachusetts, but even to confine the contest to its capital.

10. On the day of the accession of Louis the Sixteenth, the act closing the port of Boston, transferring the board of customs to Marblehead, and the seat of government to Salem, reached the devoted town. The king was confident that the slow torture which was to be applied, would constrain its inhabitants to cry out for mercy and promise unconditional obedience. Success in resistance could come only from an American union, which was not to be hoped for, unless Boston should offer herself as a willing sacrifice. The mechanics and merchants and laborers, altogether scarcely so many as thirty-five hundred able-bodied men, knew that they were acting, not for the liberty of a province or of America, but for freedom itself. They were inspired by the thought that the Providence which rules the world demanded of them heroic self-denial,

as the champions of humanity. The country never doubted their perseverance, and they trusted the fellow-feeling of the continent.

As soon as the act was received, the Boston committee of correspondence, by the hand of Joseph Warren, invited eight neighboring towns to a conference "on the critical state of public affairs." On the twelfth, at noon, Metcalf Bowler, the speaker of the assembly of Rhode Island, came before them with the cheering news, that, in answer to a recent circular letter from the body over which he presided, all the thirteen governments were pledged to union. Punctually, at the hour of three in the afternoon of that day, the committees of Dorchester, Roxbury, Brookline, Newton, Cambridge, Charlestown, Lynn, and Lexington, joined them in Faneuil Hall, the cradle of American liberty, where for ten years the freemen of the town had debated the great question of justifiable resistance. The lowly men who now met there were most of them accustomed to feed their own cattle; to fold their own sheep; to guide their own plough; all trained to public life in the little democracies of their towns; some of them captains in the militia and officers of the church according to the discipline of Congregationalists; nearly all of them communicants, under a public covenant with God. They grew in greatness as their sphere enlarged. Their virtues burst the confines of village life. They felt themselves to be citizens not of little municipalities, but of the whole world of mankind. In their dark hour light broke upon them from their own truth and courage. Placing Samuel Adams at their head, and guided by a report prepared by Joseph

CHAP. I. 1774. May.

Warren of Boston, Gardner of Cambridge, and others, they agreed unanimously on the injustice and cruelty of the act, by which parliament, without competent jurisdiction, and contrary as well to natural right as to the laws of all civilized states, had, without a hearing, set apart, accused, tried, and condemned the town of Boston. The delegates from the eight villages were reminded by those of Boston, that that port could recover its trade by paying for the tea which had been thrown overboard; but they held it unworthy even to notice the humiliating offer, promising on their part to join "their suffering brethren in every measure of relief."

To make a general union possible, self-restraint must regulate courage. The meeting knew that a declaration of independence would have alienated their sister colonies, and thus far they had not discovered that independence was really the desire of their own hearts. To suggest nothing till a congress could be convened, would have seemed to them like abandoning the town to bleed away its life without relief or solace. The king had expected to starve its people into submission; in their circular letter to the committees of the other colonies, they proposed as a counter action a general cessation of trade with Britain. "Now," they added, "is the time when all should be united in opposition to this violation of the liberties of all. The single question is, whether you consider Boston as suffering in the common cause, and sensibly feel and resent the injury and affront offered to her? We cannot believe otherwise; assuring you that, not in the least intimidated by this inhuman treatment, we are still determined to maintain to the utmost of our abilities the rights of America." CHAP. I.

The next day, while Gage was sailing into the harbor with the vice-regal powers of commander-in-chief for the continent, as well as the civil authority of governor in the province, Samuel Adams presided over a very numerous town meeting, which was attended by many that had hitherto kept aloof. The thought of republican Rome, in its purest age, animated their consultations. The port-act was read, and in bold debate was pronounced repugnant to law, religion, and common sense. At the same time, those who, from loss of employment, were to be the first to encounter want, were remembered with tender compassion, and measures were put in train for their relief. Then the inhabitants, by the hand of Samuel Adams, made their touching appeal "to all the sister colonies, promising to suffer for America with a becoming fortitude, confessing that singly they might find their trial too severe, and entreating not to be left to struggle alone, when the very being of every colony, considered as a free people, depended upon the event." 1774. May.

On the seventeenth of May, Gage, who had remained four days with Hutchinson at Castle William, landed at Long Wharf amidst salutes from ships and batteries. Received by the council and civil officers, he was escorted by the Boston Cadets, under Hancock, to the State House, where the counsel presented a loyal address, and his commission was proclaimed with three volleys of musketry and as many cheers. He then partook of a public dinner in Faneuil Hall. A hope still lingered that relief might come through

CHAP. I. 1774. May. his intercession. But Gage was neither fit to reconcile nor to subdue. By his mild temper and love of society, he gained the good-will of his boon companions, and escaped personal enmities; but in earnest business he inspired neither confidence nor fear. Though his disposition was far from being malignant, he was so poor in spirit and so weak of will, so dull in his perceptions and so unsettled in his opinions, that he was sure to follow the worst advice, and vacillate between smooth words of concession and merciless severity. He had promised the king that with four regiments he would play the "lion," and troops beyond his requisition were hourly expected. His instructions enjoined upon him the seizure and condign punishment of Samuel Adams, Hancock, Joseph Warren, and other leading patriots; but he stood in such dread of them that he never so much as attempted their arrest.

The people of Massachusetts were almost exclusively of English origin; beyond any other colony, they loved the land of their ancestors; but their fond attachment made them only the more sensitive to its tyranny. To subject them to taxation without their consent, was robbing them of their birthright; they scorned the British parliament as "a junto of the servants of the crown, rather than the representatives of England." Not disguising to themselves their danger, but confident of victory, they were resolved to stand together as brothers for a life of liberty.

The merchants of Newburyport were the first who agreed to suspend all commerce with Britain and Ireland. Salem, also, the place marked out as the new seat of government, in a very full town meeting and after unimpassioned debates, decided almost unanimously to stop trade not with Britain only, but even with the West Indies. If in Boston a few cravens proposed to purchase a relaxation of the blockade by quailing before power, the majority were beset by no temptation so strong as that of routing at once the insignificant number of troops who had come to overawe them. But Samuel Adams, while he compared their spirit to that of Sparta or Rome, was ever inculcating "patience as the characteristic of a patriot," and the people, having sent forth their cry to the continent, waited self-possessed for voices of consolation.

CHAPTER II.

NEW YORK PROPOSES A GENERAL CONGRESS.

May, 1774.

CHAP. II. 1774. May. New York anticipated the prayer of Boston. Its people, who had received the port-act directly from England, felt the wrong to that town, as a wound to themselves, and even the lukewarm kindled with resentment. From the epoch of the stamp-act, their Sons of Liberty, styled by the royalists "the Presbyterian junto," had kept up a committee of correspondence. Yet Sears, MacDougal, and Lamb, still its principal members, represented the sympathies of the mechanics of the city, more than of the merchants; and they never enjoyed the full confidence of the great landed proprietors who, by the tenure of estates throughout New York, formed a recognised aristocracy. To unite the whole province on the side of liberty, a more comprehensive combination was, therefore, required. The old committee advocated the questionable policy of an immediate suspension of commerce with Britain; but they also proposed—and they were the first to propose—"a general congress."

CHAP. II. 1774. May.

These recommendations they forwarded through Connecticut to Boston, with entreaties to that town to stand firm; and in full confidence of approval, they applied not to New England only, but to Philadelphia, and through Philadelphia to every colony at the South.

Such was the inception of the continental congress of 1774. It was the last achievement of the Sons of Liberty of New York. Their words of cheering to Boston, and their summons to the country, had already gone forth, when, on the evening of the sixteenth of May, they convoked the inhabitants of their city. A sense of the impending change pervaded the meeting and tempered passionate rashness. Some who were in a secret understanding with officers of the crown, sought to evade all decisive measures; the merchants were averse to headlong engagements for suspending trade; the gentry feared, lest the men, who on all former occasions had led the multitude, should preserve the control in the day, which was felt to be near at hand, when an independent people would shape the permanent institutions of a continent. Under a conservative influence, the motion prevailed to supersede the old committee of correspondence by a new one of fifty, and its members were selected by open nomination. The choice included men from all classes. Nearly a third part were of those who followed the British standard to the last; others were lukewarm, unsteady, and blind to the nearness of revolution; others again were enthusiastic Sons of Liberty. The friends to government claimed that the majority was inflexibly loyal; the control fell into the hands of men who, like John

CHAP. II. 1774. May. Jay, still aimed at reconciling a continued dependence on England with the just freedom of the colonies.

Meantime, the port-act was circulated with incredible rapidity. In some places it was printed upon mourning paper with a black border, and cried about the streets as a barbarous murder; in others, it was burned with great solemnity in the presence of vast bodies of the people. On the seventeenth the representatives of Connecticut, with clear perceptions and firm courage, made a declaration of rights. "Let us play the man," said they, "for the cause of our country; and trust the event to Him who orders all events for the best good of His people." On the same day, the freemen of the town of Providence, unsolicited from abroad, and after full discussion, voted to promote "a congress of the representatives of all the North American colonies." Declaring "personal liberty an essential part of the natural May 19. rights of mankind," they also expressed the wish to prohibit the importation of negro slaves, and to set free all negroes born in the colony.

Two days after these spontaneous movements, the people of the city and county of New York assembled to inaugurate their new committee with the formality of public approval. Two parties appeared in array; on the one side men of property, on the other tradesmen and mechanics. Foreboding a revolution, they seemed to contend in advance, whether their future government should be formed upon the basis of property, or on purely popular principles. It was plain that knowledge had penetrated the mass of the people, who were growing accustomed to reason for themselves, and were ready to found a new social order in which they would rule. But on that day they chose to follow the wealthier class, if it would but make with them a common cause; and the nomination of the committee was accepted, even with the addition of Isaac Low as its chairman, who was more of a loyalist than a patriot.

The letter from the New York Sons of Liberty had been received in Philadelphia; and when on the nineteenth the messenger from Boston arrived with despatches, he found Charles Thomson, Thomas Mifflin, Joseph Reed and others, ready to call a public meeting on the evening of the next day. May 20.

On the morning of the twentieth, the king gave in person his assent to the act which made the British commander-in-chief in America, his army, and the civil officers, no longer amenable to American courts of justice; and also to that which mutilated the charter of Massachusetts, and destroyed the freedom of its town meetings. "The law," said Garnier, the French minister, "must either lead to the complete reduction of the colonies, or clear the way for their independence." "I wish from the bottom of my heart," said the duke of Richmond, during a debate in the house of lords, "that the Americans may resist, and get the better of the forces sent against them."

While the British parliament was conferring on Gage power to take the lives of Bostonians with impunity, the men of Philadelphia were asking each other, if there remained a hope that the danger would pass by. The Presbyterians, true to their traditions, held it right to war against tyranny; the merchants refused to sacrifice their trade; the Quakers in any event scrupled to use arms; a numerous class, like

CHAP. II. 1774. May. Reed, cherished the most passionate desire for a reconciliation with the mother country. In the chaos of opinion, the cause of liberty needed wise and intrepid counsellors; but during the absence of Franklin, Pennsylvania fell under the influence of Dickinson. His claims to public respect were indisputable. He was honored for spotless morals, eloquence, and good service in the colonial legislature; his writings had endeared him to America as a sincere friend of liberty. Possessed of an ample fortune, it was his pride to call himself a "farmer." Residing at a country seat which overlooked Philadelphia and the Delaware river, he delighted in study and repose, and was wanting in active vigor of will. Free from personal cowardice, his shrinking sensitiveness bordered on pusillanimity. "He had an excellent heart, and the cause of his country lay near it;" "he loved the people of Boston with the tenderness of a brother;" yet he was more jealous of their zeal than touched by their sorrows. "They will have time enough to die," were his words on that morning. "Let them give the other provinces opportunity to think and resolve. If they expect to drag them by their own violence into mad measures, they will be left to perish by themselves, despised by their enemies, and almost detested by their friends." Having matured his scheme in the solitude of his retreat, he received at dinner Thomson, Mifflin, and Reed; who, for the sake of his public coöperation, acquiesced in his delays.

In the evening, about three hundred of the principal citizens of Philadelphia assembled in the Long Room of the City Tavern. The letter from the Sons of Liberty of New York was read aloud, as well as the letters from Boston. Two measures were thus brought under discussion; that of New York for a congress; that of Boston for an immediate cessation of trade. The latter proposition was received with loud and general murmurs. Dickinson conciliated the wavering merchants by expressing himself strongly against it; but he was heard with applause as he spoke for a general congress. He insisted, however, on a preliminary petition to his friend, John Penn, the proprietary governor, to call together the legislature of the colony. This request every one knew would be refused. But then, reasoned Mifflin and the ardent politicians, a committee of correspondence, after the model of Boston, must, in consequence of the refusal, be named for the several counties in the province. Delegates will thus be appointed to a general congress, "and when the colonies are once united in councils, what may they not effect?" At an early hour Dickinson retired from the meeting, of which the spirit far exceeded his own; but even the most zealous acknowledged the necessity of deferring to his advice. Accepting, therefore, moderation and prudence as their watchwords, they did little more than coldly resolve, that Boston was suffering in the general cause, and they appointed a committee of intercolonial correspondence, with Dickinson as its chief.

On the next day, Dickinson, with calculating reserve, embodied in a letter to Boston the system which, for the coming year, was to form the policy of America. It proposed a general congress of deputies from the different colonies, who, in firm but dutiful

CHAP. II. 1774. May. terms, should make to the king a petition of their rights. This, he was confident, would be granted through the influence of the wise and good in the mother country; and the most sanguine of his supporters predicted that the very idea of a general congress would compel a change of policy.

In like manner the fifty-one who now represented the city and county of New York, adopted from their predecessors the plan of a continental congress, and to that body they referred all questions relating to commerce; thus postponing the proposal for an immediate suspension of trade, but committing themselves irrevocably to union and resistance. At the same time they invited every county in the colony to make choice of a committee.

The messenger, on his return with the letters from Philadelphia and New York, found the people of Connecticut anxious for a congress, even if it should not at once embrace the colonies south of the Potomac; and their committee wisely entreated Massachusetts to fix the place and time for its meeting.

At Boston, the agents and supporters of the British ministers strove to bend the firmness of its people by holding up to the tradesmen the grim picture of misery and want, while Hutchinson promised to obtain in England a restoration of trade if the town would but pay the first cost of the tea. Before his departure, one hundred and twenty-three merchants and others of Boston clandestinely addressed him, "lamenting the loss of so good a governor," confessing the propriety of indemnifying the East India company, and appealing to his most benevolent disposition to procure by his representations some speedy relief; but at a full meeting of merchants and traders the address was disclaimed. Thirty-three citizens of Marblehead, who signed a similar paper, brought upon themselves the public reprobation of their townsmen. Hutchinson had merited in civil cases the praise of an impartial judge; twenty-four lawyers, including judges of admiralty and attorneys of the crown, subscribed an extravagant panegyric of his general character and conduct; but those who, for learning and integrity, most adorned their profession, withheld their names.

On the other hand, the necessity of a response to the courage of the people, the hearty adhesion of the town of Providence, and the cheering letter from the old committee of New York, animated a majority of the merchants of Boston, and through their example those of the province, to an engagement to cease all importations from England. Confidence prevailed that their brethren, at least as far south as Philadelphia, would embrace the same mode of peaceful resistance. The letter which soon arrived from that city, and which required the people of Massachusetts to retreat from their advanced position, was therefore received with impatience. But Samuel Adams suppressed all murmurs. "I am fully of the Farmer's sentiments," said he; "violence and submission would at this time be equally fatal;" but he exerted himself the more to promote the immediate suspension of commerce.

The legislature of Massachusetts, on the last Wednesday of May, organised the government for the year by the usual election of councillors; of these, the governor negatived the unparalleled number of

CHAP. II. 1774. May. thirteen, among them James Bowdoin, Samuel Dexter, William Phillips, and John Adams, than whom the province could not show purer or abler men. The desire of the assembly that he would appoint a fast was refused; "for," said he to Dartmouth, "the request was only to give an opportunity for sedition to flow from the pulpit." On Saturday, the twenty-eighth, Samuel Adams was on the point of proposing a general congress, when the assembly was unexpectedly prorogued, to meet after ten days, at Salem.

The people of Boston, then the most flourishing commercial town on the continent, never regretted their being the principal object of ministerial vengeance. "We shall suffer in a good cause," said the thousands who depended on their daily labor for bread; "the righteous Being, who takes care of the ravens that cry unto him, will provide for us and ours."

CHAPTER III.

VOICES FROM THE SOUTH.

MAY, 1774, CONTINUED.

CHAP. III. 1774. May.

HEARTS glowed more warmly on the banks of the Patapsco. That admirable site of commerce, whose river side and hill-tops are now covered with stately warehouses, mansions and monuments, whose bay sparkles round the prows of the swiftest barks, whose wharves receive to their natural resting-place the wealth of the West Indies and South America, and whose happy enterprise sends across the mountains its iron pathway of many arms to reach the valley of the Mississippi, had for a century been tenanted only by straggling cottages. But its convenient proximity to the border counties of Pennsylvania and Virginia had at length been observed by Scotch Irish Presbyterians, and other bold and industrious men; and within a few years they had created the town of Baltimore, which already was the chief emporium within the Chesapeake Bay, and promised to become one of the most opulent and populous cities of the world. When the messages from the old com-

CHAP. III. 1774. May. mittee of New York, from Philadelphia, and from Boston, reached its inhabitants, they could not "see the least grounds for expecting relief from a petition and remonstrance." They called to mind the contempt with which for ten years their petitions had been thrust aside, and were "convinced that something more sensible than supplications would best serve their purpose."

After consultation with the men of Annapolis, to whom the coolness of the Philadelphians seemed like insulting pity, and who promptly resolved to stop all trade with Great Britain, the inhabitants of the city and county of Baltimore advocated suspending commerce with Great Britain and the West Indies, chose deputies to a colonial convention, recommended a continental congress, appointed a numerous committee of correspondence, and sent cheering words to their "friends" at Boston, as sufferers in the common cause. "The Supreme Disposer of all events," said they, "will terminate this severe trial of your patience in a happy confirmation of American freedom." For this spirited conduct Baltimore was applauded as the model; and its example kindled new life in New York.

On the twenty-eighth, the assembly of New Hampshire, though still desiring to promote harmony with the parent land, began its organization for resisting encroachments on American rights.

Three days later the people of New Jersey declared for a suspension of trade and a congress, and claimed "to be fellow-sufferers with Boston in the cause of liberty."

On South Carolina the restrictive laws had never

pressed with severity. They had been beneficially modified in favor of its great staple, rice; and the character of the laborers on its soil forbade all thought of rivalling British skill in manufactures. Its wealthy inhabitants, shunning the occupations of city life, loved to reside in hospitable elegance on their large and productive estates. Its annual exports to the northern provinces were of small account, while to Great Britain they exceeded two millions of dollars in value. Enriched by this commerce, its people cherished a warm affection for the mother country, and delighted in sending their sons "home," as England was called, for their education. The harbor of Charleston was almost unguarded, except by the sand-bar at its entrance. The Creeks and Cherokees on the frontier, against whom the English government had once been solicited by South Carolina herself to send over a body of troops as a protection, were still numerous and warlike. The negro slaves who, in the country near the ocean very far outnumbered all the free, were so many hostages for the allegiance of their masters. The trade of Charleston was in the hands of British factors, some of whom speculated already on the coming confiscation of the rice swamps and indigo fields of "many a bonnie rebel." The upland country was numerously peopled by men who felt no grievances, and were blindly devoted to the king. And yet the planters, loving their civil rights more than security and ease, refused to take counsel of their interests or their danger. "Boston," said they, "is but the first victim at the altar of tyranny." Reduced to the dilemma either to consent to hold their liberties only

CHAP. III. 1774. May.

as tenants at will of the British house of commons, or to prepare for resistance, their choice was never in doubt. "The whole continent," they said, "must be animated with one great soul, and all Americans must resolve to stand by one another even unto death. Should they fail, the constitution of the mother country itself would lose its excellence." They knew the imminent ruin which they risked; but they "remembered that the happiness of many generations and many millions depended on their spirit and constancy."

The burgesses of Virginia sat as usual in May. The extension of the province to the west and northwest was their great ambition, which the governor, greedy of large masses of land, and of fees for conniving at the acquisitions of others, selfishly seconded, in flagrant disregard of his instructions. To Lady Dunmore, who had just arrived, the assembly voted a congratulatory address, and its members joined to give her a ball. The feeling of loyalty was still predominant; the thought of revolution was not harbored; but they none the less held it their duty to resist the systematic plan of parliamentary despotism, and without waiting for an appeal from Boston, they resolved on its deliverance. First among them as an orator stood Patrick Henry, whose words had power to kindle in his hearers passions like his own. But eloquence was his least merit; he was revered as the ideal of a patriot of Rome in its austerest age. The approach of danger quickened his sagacity, and his language gained the boldness of prophecy. He was borne up by the strong support of Richard Henry Lee and Washington. It chanced that George Ma-

CHAP. III. 1774. May.

son also was then at Williamsburg, a man of strong and true affections; learned in constitutional law; a profound reasoner; honest and fearless in council; shunning ambition and public life, from desponding sorrow at the death of his wife, for whom he never ceased to mourn; but earnestly mindful of his country as became one whose chastened spirit looked beyond the interests of the moment. After deliberation with these associates, Jefferson prepared the measure that was to declare irrevocably the policy of Virginia; and its house of burgesses, on the twenty-fourth, on motion of Robert Carter Nicholas, adopted the concerted resolution, which was in itself a solemn invocation of God as the witness of their deliberate purpose to rescue their liberties even at the risk of being compelled to defend them with arms. It recommended to their fellow-citizens that the day on which the Boston port-act was to take effect should be set apart "as a day of fasting and prayer, devoutly to implore the Divine interposition for averting the dreadful calamity which threatened destruction to their civil rights, and the evils of a civil war; and to give to the American people one heart and one mind firmly to oppose by all just and proper means, every injury to American rights." The resolve, which bound only the members themselves, was distributed by express through their respective counties as a general invitation to the people. Especially Washington sent the notice to his constituents; and Mason charged his little household of sons and daughters to keep the day strictly, and attend church clad in mourning.

This was the last regular public act of a colonial

CHAP. III. 1774. May. assembly in the Old Dominion. The morning after its adoption, Dunmore dissolved the House. The burgesses immediately repaired to the Raleigh tavern, about one hundred paces from the capitol, and with Peyton Randolph, their late speaker, in the chair, voted that the attack on Massachusetts was an attack on all the colonies, to be opposed by the united wisdom of all. In conformity with this declaration, they advised for future time an annual continental congress. They named Peyton Randolph, with others, a committee of correspondence to invite a general concurrence in this design. As yet social relations were not embittered. Washington, of whom Dunmore sought information respecting western affairs, continued his visits at the governor's house; the ball in honor of Lady Dunmore was well attended. Not till the offices of courtesy and of patriotism were fulfilled, did most of the burgesses return home, leaving their committee on duty.

On the afternoon of Sunday the twenty-ninth, the letters from Boston reached Williamsburg. So important did they appear, that the next morning, at ten o'clock, the committee having called to their aid Washington and all other burgesses who were still in town, inaugurated a revolution. As they collectively numbered but twenty-five, they refused to assume the responsibility of definite measures of resistance; but as the province was without a legislature, they summoned a convention of delegates to be elected by the several counties, and to meet at the capital on the first day of the ensuing August.

The rescue of freedom even at the cost of a civil war, a domestic convention of the people for their own internal regulation, an annual congress of all the colonies for the perpetual assertion of common rights, were the policy of Virginia. When the report of her measures reached England, the king's ministers were startled by their significance; and called to mind how often she had been the model for other colonies. Her influence continued undiminished; and her system was promptly adopted by the people of North Carolina.

"Lord North had no expectation that we should be thus sustained," said Samuel Adams; "he trusted that Boston would be left to fall alone." But the love of liberty in America did not flash like electricity on the surface; it penetrated the mass with magnetic energy. The port-act had been received on the tenth of May; and in three weeks, less time than was taken by the unanimous British parliament for its enactment, the continent, as "one great commonwealth," made the cause of Boston its own.

CHAPTER IV.

MASSACHUSETTS APPOINTS THE TIME AND PLACE FOR A GENERAL CONGRESS.

June, 1774.

CHAP. IV. 1774. June 1. On the first day of June, Hutchinson embarked for England; and as the clocks in the Boston belfries finished striking twelve, the blockade of the harbor began. The inhabitants of the town were chiefly traders, shipwrights, and sailors; and since no anchor could be weighed, no sail unfurled, no vessel so much as launched from the stocks, their cheerful industry was at an end. No more are they to lay the keel of the fleet merchantman, or shape the rib symmetrically for its frame, or strengthen the graceful hull by knees of oak, or rig the well proportioned masts, or bend the sails to the yards. The king of that country has changed the busy workshops into scenes of compulsory idleness, and the most skilful naval artisans in the world, with the keenest eye for forms of beauty and speed, are forced by act of parliament to fold their hands. Want scowled on the laborer, as he sat with his wife and children at his board. The sailor roamed the streets listlessly without hope of employment. The law was executed with a rigor that went beyond the intentions of its authors. Not a scow could be manned by oars to bring an ox, or a sheep, or a bundle of hay from the islands. All water carriage from wharf to wharf, though but of lumber, or bricks, or lime, was strictly forbidden. The boats between Boston and Charleston could not ferry a parcel of goods across Charles River; the fishermen of Marblehead, when from their hard pursuit, they bestowed quintals of dried fish on the poor of Boston, were obliged to transport their offering in wagons by a circuit of thirty miles. The warehouses of the thrifty merchants were at once made valueless; the costly wharves, which extended far into the channel, and were so lately covered with the produce of the tropics and with English fabrics, were become solitary places; the harbor, which had resounded incessantly with the cheering voices of prosperous commerce, was now disturbed by no sounds but from British vessels of war.

At Philadelphia, the bells of the churches were muffled and tolled; the ships in port hoisted their colors at half mast; and nine-tenths of the houses, except those of the Friends, were shut during the memorable First of June. In Virginia, the population thronged the churches; Washington attended the service, and strictly kept the fast. No firmer or more touching words were addressed to the sufferers than from Norfolk, which was the largest place of trade in that "well-watered and extensive dominion," and which, from its deep channel and nearness to

CHAP. IV. 1774. June. the ocean, lay most exposed to ships of war. "Our hearts are warmed with affection for you," such was its message; "we address the Almighty Ruler to support you in your afflictions. Be assured we consider you as suffering in the common cause, and look upon ourselves as bound by the most sacred ties to support you."

Jefferson, from the foot of the Blue Ridge of the Alleghanies, condemned the act, which in a moment reduced an ancient and wealthy town from opulence to want, and without a hearing and without discrimination, sacrificed property of the value of millions to revenge—not repay—the loss of a few thousands. "If the pulse of the people beat calmly under such an experiment by the new and till now unheard of executive power of a British parliament," said the young statesman, "another and another will be tried, till the measure of despotism be filled up."

At that time the king was so eager to give effect to the law which subverted the charter of Massachusetts, that acting upon information confessedly insufficient, he, with Dartmouth, made out for that province a complete list of councillors, called mandamus councillors from their appointment by the crown. Copies of letters from Franklin and from Arthur Lee had been obtained; Gage was secretly ordered to procure, if possible, the originals, as the means of arraigning their authors for treason. Bernard and Hutchinson had reported that the military power failed to intimidate, because no colonial civil officer would sanction its employment: to meet the exigency, Thurlow and Wedderburn furnished their opinion, that such power belonged to the governor himself as the conservator of the peace in all cases whatsoever. "I am willing to suppose," says Dartmouth, "that the people will quietly submit to the correction their ill conduct has brought upon them;" but in case they should not prove so docile, Gage was required to bid the troops fire upon them at his discretion; and for his encouragement, he was informed that all trials of officers and troops for homicides in America, were, by a recent act of parliament, removed to England.

CHAP. IV.

1774. June.

This system of measures was regarded by its authors as a masterpiece of statesmanship. But where was true greatness really to be found? At the council board of vindictive ministers? In the palace of the king who preferred the loss of a continent to a compromise of absolute power? Or in the humble mansion of the proscribed Samuel Adams, who shared every sorrow of his native town? "She suffers," said he, "with dignity, and rather than submit to the humiliating terms of an edict, barbarous beyond precedent under the most absolute monarchy, she will put the malice of tyranny to the severest trial." "An empire is rising in America; and Britain, by her multiplied oppressions, is accelerating that independency which she dreads. We have a post to maintain, to desert which would entail upon us the curses of posterity. The virtue of our ancestors inspires us; they were contented with clams and muscles. For my own part, I have been wont to converse with poverty; and however disagreeable a companion she may be thought to be by the affluent and luxurious who never were acquainted with her, I can live happily with her the remainder of my

CHAP. IV. 1774. June.

days, if I can thereby contribute to the redemption of my country."

These were his words, with the knowledge that the king's order for his arrest was hanging over his head, to be enforced, whenever troops enough were brought together to make it safe.

The Boston committee looked the danger full in the face. On the second of June, they received and read the two bills, of which the one was to change the charter and subvert the most cherished rights of the province; the other, to grant impunity to the British army for acts of violence in enforcing the new system. "They excited," says their record, "a just indignation in the mind of the committee," whose members saw their option confined to abject submission or an open rupture. They longed to escape the necessity of the choice by devising some measure which might recall their oppressors to moderation and reason. Accordingly, Warren, on the fifth, reported "a solemn league and covenant" to suspend all commercial intercourse with the mother country, and neither to purchase nor consume any merchandise from Great Britain after the last day of the ensuing August. The names of those who should refuse to sign the covenant, were to be published to the world. Copies of this paper were forwarded to every town in the province, with a letter entreating the subscriptions of all the people, "as the last and only method of preserving the land from slavery without drenching it in blood."

The proposition proved the desire for conciliation. Had a country which was without manufactures and munitions of war, been resolved to take up arms, it

CHAP. IV. 1774. June.

would have extended its commerce, in order to accumulate all articles of first necessity. "Nothing," said the patriots, "is more foreign from our hearts than a spirit of rebellion. Would to God they all, even our enemies, knew the warm attachment we have for Great Britain, notwithstanding we have been contending these ten years with them for our rights. What can they gain by the victory, should they subjugate us? What will be the glory of enslaving their children and brothers? Nay, how great will be the danger to their own liberties?" Thus reasoned the people of the country towns in Massachusetts; and they signed "the league and covenant," confident that they would have only to sit still and await the bloodless restoration of their rights. In this expectation they were confirmed by the opinions of Burke and of Franklin.

From the committee room in Faneuil Hall, Samuel Adams hastened to the general assembly, whose first act at Salem was a protest against the arbitrary order for its removal. The council, in making the customary reply to the governor's speech at the opening of the session, laid claim to the rights of Englishmen without diminution or "abridgment." But as they uttered their hope, "that his administration would be a happy contrast to that of his predecessors," Gage interrupted their chairman, and refused to receive the address; because the conduct of those predecessors had been approved, and therefore the expression "was an insult to the king, and an affront to himself." But the right of a legislative body to express an opinion on a subordinate executive officer was undeniable. Even the king in person hears an address

CHAP. IV. 1774. June. from the house of commons, however severely it may reflect on a minister. When Gage treated the censure on Bernard and Hutchinson as a personal conflict with the sovereign, his petulance only the more tended to bring that sovereign himself into disrepute.

The house of representatives was the fullest ever known. The continent expected of them to fix the time and place for the meeting of the general congress. This required the utmost secrecy; for they were watched by officers in the royal service, and any perceptible movement would have been followed by an instant dissolution. In the confusion of nominations, Daniel Leonard, of Taunton, who had won his election by engaging manners and professions of patriotism, which yet were hollow, succeeded in being appointed one of the committee of nine on the state of the province. Restrained by well-founded distrust of his secret relations, that committee was therefore cautious to entertain nothing but vague propositions for conciliation; so that Leonard deceived not himself only, but the governor, into the belief, that the legislature would lead the way to concession, and that on the arrival of more troops, an indemnity to the East India company would be publicly advocated.

The whole continent was looking towards Boston. "Don't pay for an ounce of the damned tea," wrote Gadsden on the fourteenth of June, as he shipped for the poor of Boston the first gifts of rice from the planters of Carolina. On that day, the fourth regiment, known as "the king's own," encamped on Boston Common; the next, it was joined by the forty-

CHAP. IV. 1774. June.

third. Two companies of artillery and eight pieces of ordnance had already reinforced Castle William; and more battalions of infantry were hourly expected. The friends of government increased their activity, exerted every art to win over the tradesmen, and assumed a menacing aspect. "There will be no congress," they said; "New York will never appoint members; Massachusetts must feel that she is deserted." To a meeting of tradesmen, a plausible speaker ventured to recommend for consideration the manner of paying for the tea; and he met with so much success, that after some altercation, they separated without coming to any resolution. But Warren, who exerted as much energy to save his country as others to paralyze its spirit, proved to his friends, that the payment in any form would open the way for every compliance even to a total submission; and he was himself encouraged by the glowing letter from Baltimore. "Vigilance, activity, and patience," he cried, "are necessary at this time; but the mistress we serve is Liberty, and it is better to die than not to obtain her." "We shall be saved," he added; and that no cloud might rest on the "fortitude, honesty, and foresight" of Boston, a town meeting was called for the following Friday.

Samuel Adams received a summons to come and guide its debates; but a higher duty kept him at Salem. The legislative committee of nine appeared so tame, that Leonard returned to Taunton on business as a lawyer. Meantime, Samuel Adams had on one evening secretly consulted four or five of his colleagues; on another a larger number; on the third so many as thirty; and on the morning of Friday,

CHAP. IV. 1774. June.

the seventeenth of June, confident of having the perfect control of the house, one hundred and twenty-nine being present, he locked the door, and proposed the measure he had matured. The time fixed for the congress was the first day of September, the place Philadelphia, where there was no army to interrupt its sessions. Bowdoin, who, however, proved unable to attend, Samuel Adams, John Adams, Cushing, and Robert Treat Paine were chosen delegates. To defray their expenses, a tax of five hundred pounds was apportioned on the province. The towns were charged to afford speedy and constant relief to Boston and Charlestown, whose fortitude was preserving the liberties of their country. Domestic manufactures were encouraged, and it was strongly recommended to discontinue the use of all goods imported from the East Indies and Great Britain, until the public grievances of America should be radically and totally redressed.

In the midst of these proceedings the governor sent his secretary with a message for dissolving the assembly. But he knocked at its door in vain, and could only read the proclamation to the crowd on the stairs. "I could not get a worse council, or a worse assembly," reported Gage; "with exceptions, they appear little more than echoes to the contrivers of all the mischief in the town of Boston, those demagogues now spiriting up the people throughout the province to resistance."

The number which on that same day thronged to the town meeting in Faneuil Hall, was greater than the room would hold. Samuel Adams was not missed, for his kinsman, John Adams, was elected moderator. When he had taken the chair, the friends to the scheme of indemnifying the East India company for their loss, were invited to "speak freely," that a matter of such importance might be fairly discussed in the presence of the general body of the people; but not a man rose in defence of the proposition. The blockade, the fleets, the army, could not bring out a symptom of compliance.

A month before, John Adams had said, "I have very little connection with public affairs, and I hope to have less." For many years he had refused to attend town meetings; he had kept aloof from the committee of correspondence, even in the time when it concerted the destruction of the tea. The morning of that day dawned on him in private life; the evening saw him a representative of Massachusetts to the general congress. That summer he followed the circuit for the last time. "Great Britain," thus Sewall, his friend and associate at the bar, expostulated with him, as they strolled together on the hill that overhangs Casco Bay, with its thousand isles, "Great Britain is determined on her system; and her power is irresistible." "That very determination of Great Britain in her system, determines mine," answered Adams; "swim or sink, live or die, survive or perish with my country, is my unalterable determination." The White Mountains on the one side, and the ocean on the other, were witnesses to the patriot's vow "I see we must part," rejoined Sewall; "but this adieu is the sharpest thorn on which I ever set my foot."

Two days in advance of Massachusetts, the assembly of Rhode Island unanimously chose delegates to

CHAP. IV. the general congress, which they desired to see annually renewed.

1774. June. The promptness of Maryland was still more remarkable; for it could proceed only by a convention of its people. But so universal was their zeal, so rapid their organization, that their provincial convention met at Annapolis on the twenty-second of June, and before any message had been received from Salem, they elected delegates to the congress. With a modesty worthy of their courage, they apologized to Virginia for moving in advance; pleading as their excuse the inferiority of their province in extent and numbers, so that less time was needed to ascertain its sentiments.

CHAPTER V.

BOSTON MINISTERED TO BY THE CONTINENT.

June, July, 1774.

CHAP. V. 1774. June.

The martyr town was borne up in its agony by messages of sympathy. From Marblehead came offers to the Boston merchants of the gratuitous use of its harbor, its wharves, its warehouses, and of all necessary personal attendance in lading and unlading goods. Forty-eight persons were found in Salem, willing to entreat of Gage his "patronage for the trade of that place;" but a hundred and twenty-five of its merchants and freeholders addressed him in a spirit of disinterestedness, repelling the ungenerous thought of turning the course of trade from Boston. "Nature," said they nobly, "in the formation of our harbor, forbids our becoming rivals in commerce to that convenient mart. And were it otherwise, we must be lost to all the feelings of humanity, could we indulge one thought to seize on wealth and raise our fortunes on the ruin of our suffering neighbors."

The governor, in his answer, threw all blame on Boston, for refusing to indemnify the East India

CHAP. V. 1774. June. company, and he employed every device to produce compliance. It was published at the corners of the streets that Pennsylvania would refuse to suspend commerce; that the society of Friends would arrest every step towards war; that New York had not named, and would never name, deputies to congress; that the power of Great Britain could not fail to crush resistance. The exasperation of the selfish at their losses, which they attributed to the committee of correspondence, the innate reverence for order, the habitual feeling of loyalty, the deeply-seated love for England, the terror inspired by regiments, artillery, and ships of war, the allurements of official favor, the confidence that the king must prevail, disposed a considerable body of men to seek the recovery of prosperity by concession. "The act," wrote Gage on the twenty-sixth, "must certainly sooner or later work its own way; a congress of some sort may be obtained; but, after all, Boston may get little more than fair words."

The day after this was written, a town meeting was held. As Faneuil Hall could not contain the thronging inhabitants, they adjourned to the Old South Meeting-house. There the opposition mustered their utmost strength, in the hope of carrying a vote of censure on the committee of correspondence. The question of paying for the tea was artfully evaded, while "the league and covenant," which in truth was questionable both in policy and form, was chosen as the object of cavil. New York had superseded the old committee by a more moderate one; it was proposed that Boston should do the same. The patriot, Samuel Adams, finding himself not only proscribed by the king, but on trial in a Boston town meeting, left the chair, and took his place on the floor. His enemies summoned hardihood to engage with him in debate, in which they were allowed the utmost freedom. Through the midsummer-day they were heard patiently till dark, and at their own request were indulged with an adjournment. On the next day, notwithstanding the utmost exertion of the influence of the government, the motion of censure was negatived by a vast majority. The town then, by a deliberate vote, bore open testimony "to the upright intentions and honest zeal of their committee of correspondence," and desired them "to continue steadfast in the way of well-doing."

After this result, one hundred and twenty-nine, chiefly the addressers to Hutchinson, confident of a speedy triumph through the power of Britain, ostentatiously set their names to a protest which, under the appearance of anxiety for the prosperity of the town, recommended unqualified submission. They would have robbed Boston of its great name, and made it a byword of reproach in the annals of the world.

The governor hurried to the aid of his partisans, and on the following day, without the consent of the council, issued the proclamation, from which British influence never recovered. He called the combination" not to purchase articles imported from Great Britain "unwarrantable, hostile, and traitorous;" its subscribers "open and declared enemies of the king and parliament of Great Britain;" and he "enjoined and commanded all magistrates and other officers within the several counties of the province, to appre-

CHAP. V. 1774. June. hend and secure for trial, all persons who might publish, or sign, or invite others to sign the covenant."

No act could have been more futile or more unwise. The malignity of the imputation of treason was heightened by the pretended rule of law that the persons so accused might be dragged for trial to England. For any purpose of making arrests the proclamation was useless; but as the exponent of the temper of an administration which chose the gallows to avenge the simple agreement not to buy English goods, it was read throughout the continent with uncontrollable indignation. In Boston the report prevailed that as soon as more soldiers should be landed, six or seven of the leading patriots would be seized; and it was in truth the project of Gage to fasten charges of rebellion on individuals as a pretext
July. for sending them to jail. On Friday, the first of July, Admiral Graves arrived in the "Preston," of sixty guns; on Saturday the train of artillery was encamped on the common by the side of two regiments that were there before. On Monday these were reinforced by the fifth and thirty-eighth. Arrests, it was confidently reported, were now to be made. In this moment of greatest danger, the Boston committee of correspondence, Samuel Adams, the two Greenleafs, Molyneux, Warren and others being present, considered the rumor that some of them were to be taken up, and voted unanimously "that they would attend their business as usual, unless prevented by brutal force."

"The attempt to intimidate," said the patriots, "is lost labor." The spirit of defiance gave an impulse to the covenant. At Plymouth the subscribers increased at once to about a hundred. The general who had undertaken to frighten the people, excused himself from executing his threats, by his dread of the edicts of town meetings, which, he complained to the king, controlled the pulpit, the press, and the multitude, overawed the judges, and screened "the guilty." "The usurpation," said he, "has by time acquired a firmness that is not to be annihilated at once, or by ordinary methods."

The arrival of Hutchinson in England lulled the king into momentary security. Tryon from New York had said, that the ministers must put forth the whole power of Great Britain, if they would bring America to their feet; Carleton, the governor of Canada, thought it not safe to undertake a march from the Saint Lawrence to New York with an army of less than ten thousand men; but Hutchinson, who, on reaching London, was hurried by Dartmouth to the royal presence without time to change his clothes, assured the king, that the port-bill was "the only wise and effective method" of bringing the people of Boston to submission; that it had occasioned among them extreme alarm; that no one colony would comply with their request for a general suspension of commerce; that Rhode Island had accompanied its refusal with a sneer at their selfishness. The king listened eagerly. He had been greedy for all kinds of stories respecting Boston; had been told, and had believed that Hutchinson had needed a guard for his personal safety; that the New England ministers, for the sake of promoting liberty, preached a toleration for any immoralities; that Hancock's bills, to a large amount, had been dishonored. He had himself given

CHAP. V. 1774. July. close attention to the appointments to office in Massachusetts. He knew something of the political opinions even of the Boston ministers, not of Chauncy and Cooper only, but also of Pemberton, whom, as a friend to government, he esteemed "a very good man," though a dissenter. The name of John Adams, who had only in June commenced his active public career, had not yet been heard in the palace which he was so soon to enter as the minister of a republic. Of Cushing, he estimated the importance too highly. Aware of the controlling power of Samuel Adams, he asked, "What gives him his influence?" and Hutchinson answered, "A great pretended zeal for liberty, and a most inflexible natural temper. He was the first who asserted the independency of the colonies upon the supreme authority of the kingdom." For nearly two hours, the king continued inquiries respecting Massachusetts and other provinces, and was encouraged in the delusion that Boston would be left unsupported. The author of the pleasing intelligence became at once a favorite, obtained a large pension, was offered the rank of baronet, and was consulted as an oracle by Gibbon, the historian, and other politicians of the court.

"I have just seen the governor of Massachusetts," wrote the king to Lord North, at the end of their interview, "and I am now well convinced the province will soon submit;" and he gloried in the efficacy of his favorite measure, the Boston port-act. But as soon as the true character of that act became known in America, every colony, every city, every village, and, as it were, the inmates of every farm-house, felt it as a wound of their affections. The towns of Massachusetts abounded in kind offices. The colonies vied with each other in liberality. The record kept at Boston shows that "the patriotic and generous people" of South Carolina were the first to minister to the sufferers, sending early in June two hundred barrels of rice, and promising eight hundred more. At Wilmington, North Carolina, the sum of two thousand pounds currency was raised in a few days; the women of the place gave liberally; Parker Quince offered his vessel to carry a load of provisions freight free, and master and mariners volunteered to navigate her without wages. Lord North had called the American union a rope of sand; "it is a rope of sand that will hang him," said the people of Wilmington.

CHAP. V. 1774. July.

Hartford was the first place in Connecticut to pledge its assistance; but the earliest donation received, was of two hundred and fifty-eight sheep from Windham. "The taking away of civil liberty will involve the ruin of religious liberty also," wrote the ministers of Connecticut to the ministers of Boston, cheering them to bear their heavy load "with vigorous Christian fortitude and resolution." "While we complain to Heaven and earth of the cruel oppression we are under, we ascribe righteousness to God," was the answer. "The surprising union of the colonies affords encouragement. It is an inexhaustible source of comfort that the Lord God omnipotent reigneth."

The small parish of Brooklyn, in Connecticut, through their committee, of which Israel Putnam was a member, opened a correspondence with Boston. "Your zeal in favor of liberty," they said, "has gained a name that shall perish but with the glorious constellations of Heaven;" and they made an

CHAP. V. 1774. July.

offering of flocks of sheep and lambs. Throughout all New England the towns sent rye, flour, peas, cattle, sheep, oil, fish; whatever the land or the hook and line could furnish, and sometimes gifts of money. The French inhabitants of Quebec, joining with those of English origin, shipped a thousand and forty bushels of wheat.

Delaware was so much in earnest, that it devised plans for sending relief annually. All Maryland and all Virginia were contributing liberally and cheerfully; being resolved that the men of Boston, who were deprived of their daily labor, should not lose their daily bread, nor be compelled to change their residence for want. In Fairfax county, Washington presided at a spirited meeting and headed a subscription paper with his own gift of fifty pounds. A special chronicle could hardly enumerate all the generous deeds. Beyond the Blue Ridge, the hardy emigrants on the banks of the Shenandoah, many of them Germans, met at Woodstock, and with Muhlenberg, then a clergyman, soon to be a military chief, devoted themselves to the cause of liberty. Higher up the Valley of Virginia, where the plough already vied with the rifle, and the hardy hunters, not always ranging the hills with their dogs for game, had also begun to till the soil, the summer of that year ripened the wheat-fields of the pioneers, not for themselves alone. When the sheaves had been harvested, and the corn threshed and ground in a country as yet poorly provided with barns or mills, the backwoodsmen of Augusta county, without any pass through the mountains that could be called a road, noiselessly and modestly delivered at Frederick, one hundred and thirty-seven barrels of flour as their remittance to the poor of Boston. Cheered by the universal sympathy, the inhabitants of that town "were determined to hold out and appeal to the justice of the colonies and of the world;" trusting in God that "these things should be overruled for the establishment of liberty, virtue, and happiness in America."

CHAP. V. 1774. July.

CHAPTER VI.

AMERICA RESOLVES TO MEET IN GENERAL CONGRESS.

JULY, 1774.

CHAP. VI. 1774. July. GEORGE THE THIRD ranked "New York next to Boston in opposition to government." There was no place where a congress was more desired, and none where the determinations of the congress were more sure to be observed. The numerous emigrants from New England brought with them New England principles; the Dutch, as a body, never loved Britain. Of the two great families which the system of manorial grants had raised up, the Livingstons inclined to republicanism, and uniting activity to wealth and ability, exercised a predominant influence. The Delanceys, who, by taking advantage of temporary prejudices, had, four years before, carried the assembly, no longer retained the public confidence; and outside of the legislature, their power was imperceptible.

After being severed from Holland, its mother country, New York had no attachment to any European State. All agreed in the necessity of resisting the pretensions of England; but differences arose as to the persons to be intrusted with the direction of that resistance; and as to the imminence and extent of the danger. The merchants wished no interruption to commerce; the Dutch Reformed church, as well as the Episcopalians, were not free from jealousy of the Congregationalists, and the large land-holders were alarmed by the levelling spirit and social equality of New England. The people of New York had destroyed consignments of the East India company's tea; but from them the British ministry had borne the insult without rebuke; striving only by bland language to lull them into repose. The executive officers had for several years avoided strife with the assembly, listening patiently to its complaints, and seeking to comply with its importunities; so that no angry feeling existed between the provincial legislature and the royal governors. The city had, moreover, been the centre of British patronage, and friends had been won by the distribution of contracts, and sometimes by commissions in the army. The organs of the ministry were to cajole, to favor, or to corrupt; above all, to give a promise on the part of the crown of a spirit of equity, which its conduct towards the province seemed to warrant as sincere. Besides, the assembly had Edmund Burke for its agent, and still hoped that his influence in public affairs would correspond to their just estimate of his fidelity. The lovers of peace, which is always so dear to a commercial community, revolted at the thought of an early and unavoidable "appeal" to arms, caught eagerly at every chance of an honorable escape from the certain miseries of a desperate conflict, and exerted them-

CHAP. VI. 1774. July.

CHAP. VI. 1774. July. selves strenuously to secure the management of affairs to men of property. For this-end they relied on the ability of John Jay, a young lawyer of New York, whose name now first appears conspicuously in the annals of his country. Descended from Huguenot refugees, educated in the city at its college, of the severest purity of morals, a hard student, an able writer, a ready speaker; recently connected with the family of Livingston by marriage; his superior endowments, his activity and his zeal for liberty, tempered by a love for order, made him for a quarter of a century distinguished in his native state. At that time he joined the dignity of manhood to the energy of youth. He was both shy and proud, and his pride, though it became less visible, suffered no diminution from time. Tenacious of his purposes and his opinions, sensitive to indignities and prone to sudden resentments, not remarkable for self-possession, with a countenance not trained to concealment, neither easy of access, nor quick in his advances, gifted with no deep insight into character, he had neither talents nor inclination for intrigue; and but for his ambition, in which none exceeded him, he would have seemed formed for study and retirement.

On Monday, the fourth day of July, it was carried in the committee of fifty-one, that delegates should be selected to serve in the general congress. Sears, who was still foremost in the confidence of the mechanics, seconded by Peter Van Brugh Livingston, a man of great intelligence, proposed John Morin Scott and Alexander MacDougal. Fitter candidates could not have been found; but they were both passed over by

CHAP. VI.

1774. July.

a great majority, and the committee nominated Philip Livingston, Alsop, Low, Duane, and Jay for the approval of the people. Of these five, Livingston as yet dreaded the thought of independence; Alsop was incompetent; Low was at heart a tory, as at a later day he avowed; Duane, justly eminent as a lawyer, was embarrassed by large speculations in Vermont lands, from which he could derive no profit but through the power of the crown. The mass of the inhabitants resolved to defeat this selection. On Wednesday, the sixth of July, many of them, especially mechanics, assembled in the Fields, and with MacDougal in the chair, they recommended the Boston policy of suspending trade, and approved a general congress, to which, after the example of Virginia, they proposed to elect representatives by a colonial convention.

It has been kept in memory, that on this occasion a young man from abroad, so small and delicate in his organization, that he appeared to be much younger than perhaps he really was, took part in the debate before the crowd. They asked one another the name of the gifted stranger, who shone like a star first seen above a haze, of whose rising no one had taken note. He proved to be Alexander Hamilton, a West Indian. His mother, while he was yet a child, had left him an orphan and poor. A father's care he seems never to have known. The first written trace of his existence is in 1766, when his name appears as witness to a legal paper executed in the Danish island of Santa Cruz. Three years later, when he had become "a youth," he "contemned the grovelling condition of a clerk,"

CHAP. VI. 1774. July.

fretted at the narrow bounds of his island cage, and to a friend of his own years confessed his ambition. "I would willingly risk my life," said he, "though not my character, to exalt my station. I mean to prepare the way for futurity; we have seen such schemes successful when the projector is constant." That way he prepared by integrity of conduct, diligence and study. After an education as a merchant, during which he once at least conducted a voyage, and once had the charge of his employer's business, he found himself able to repair to New York, where he entered the college before the end of 1773. Trained from childhood to take care of himself, he possessed a manly self-reliance. His first sympathies in the contest had been on the British side against the Americans; but he soon changed his opinions; and in July, 1774, cosmopolitan New York, where he had neither father, nor mother, nor sister, nor brother, nor one person in whose veins ran the same blood as his own, adopted the volunteer from the tropics as its son.

The committee of fifty-one, with some of whom Hamilton was to be bound by the closest political ties, keeping steadily in view the hope of conciliation with England, disavowed the meeting in the Fields. A minority of nine, Sears, MacDougal, Van Brugh Livingston being of the number, in their turn disavowed the committee from which they withdrew. The conservative party, on their side, offered resolutions which Jay had drafted, and which seemed to question the conduct of Boston in destroying the tea; but the people, moved by the eloquence of John Morin Scott, rejected the whole series, as wanting in vigor, sense, and integrity, and tending to disunion.

Thus began the conflict of two parties which were to increase in importance and spread throughout the country. The one held to what was established, and made changes only from necessity; the other welcomed reform, and went out to meet it. The one anchored on men of property; the other on the mass of the people; the one, mildly loving liberty, was ever anxious for order; the other, firmly attached to order which it never doubted its power to maintain, was anxious only for freedom; the one distrusted the multitude as capable of rashness; the other suspected the few as at heart the enemies to popular power.

During this strife in New York, the inhabitants of South Carolina held in Charleston a meeting which continued through three days. The merchants, among whom were factors for British houses, agreed with the planters in the necessity of a congress to which both parties, by way of compromise, referred the regulation of commerce. As the election of deputies was to be contested, the name of each voter was registered, and the ballot kept open till midnight on the seventh. It then appeared that the planters had carried Gadsden, Lynch, and John Rutledge, the faithful members of the congress of 1765, with Edward Rutledge and Middleton. The delegates elect were empowered to agree to a suspension of exports as well as imports. In due time the house of assembly, meeting at eight in the morning, just half an hour before the governor could send to prorogue them, confirmed these proceedings and ratified the choice of delegates. "Don't pay for an ounce of the tea," was the reiterated message from South Carolina.

CHAP. VI. 1774. July.

The convention of Pennsylvania, which was but an echo of the opinion of Dickinson, recommended an indemnity to the East India company, dissuaded from suspending trade, and advised the gentler method of a firm and decent claim of redress. The idea of independence they disowned and utterly abhorred. If Britain on her side would repeal the obnoxious acts, they were ready to engage their obedience to the acts of navigation, and also to settle an annual revenue on the king, subject to the control of parliament.

These views, which were intended as instructions from the people to the men who might be chosen to represent them in congress, Dickinson accompanied with a most elaborate argument, in which with chilling erudition the rights of the colonies were confirmed by citations from a long train of lawyers, philosophers, poets, statesmen, and divines, from the times of Sophocles and Aristotle to Beccaria and Blackstone. Tenderly suceptible to the ideas of justice and right, he refused to believe that a British ministry or king could be deaf to his appeals. Willing to sacrifice himself and his own estate, he shrunk only from perilling the fortunes and lives of millions. His success in allaying the impassioned enthusiasm of patriotism went beyond his intentions. The assembly of Pennsylvania, which was suddenly called together on the eighteenth of July, passed him over in electing their delegates to the continental congress, and preferred Galloway their speaker, whose loyalty was unsuspected.

In New Jersey, Witherspoon, a Presbyterian minister, president of Princeton college, and "as high a son of liberty as any man in America," met the committee at New Brunswick; and with William Livingston labored to instruct their delegates that the tea should not be paid for. The matter was left to the general congress, to which William Livingston was chosen.

In New Hampshire the members of its convention brought with them little stocks of money, contributed by the several towns to defray the expenses of a representation in congress. The inhabitants of that province also solemnized their action by keeping a day of fasting and public prayer. Massachusetts did the same; and Gage, who looked with stupid indifference on the spectacle of thirteen colonies organizing themselves as one people, on occasion of the fast, issued a proclamation against "hypocrisy and sedition."

Meantime New York had grown weary of dissensions. The persons nominated for congress gave in writing a satisfactory profession of their zeal for liberty; and on the twenty-seventh of July, the nomination was unanimously ratified by the inhabitants. Yet the delegation was lukewarm and divided, leaving Virginia to give the example of energy and courage.

Dunmore had issued writs for an assembly; but the delegates from the different counties of Virginia none the less assembled in provincial convention. Illness detained Jefferson on the road, but he sent for consideration a paper which expressed his convictions and distinctly foreshadowed the declaration of independence. Enumerating the grievances which affected all the colonies, he made a special complaint of a

CHAP. VI. 1774. July. wrong to Virginia. "For the most trifling reasons," said he, "and sometimes for no conceivable reason at all, his majesty has rejected laws of the most salutary tendency. The abolition of domestic slavery is the great object of desire in those colonies, where it was unhappily introduced in their infant state. But previous to the enfranchisement of the slaves we have, it is necessary to exclude all further importations from Africa; yet our repeated attempts to effect this by prohibitions, and by imposing duties which might amount to a prohibition, have been hitherto defeated by his majesty's negative; thus preferring the immediate advantage of a few British corsairs, to the lasting interests of the American states, and to the rights of human nature, deeply wounded by this infamous practice." The words of Jefferson were universally approved; and the convention to which they were presented by Peyton Randolph came to this resolution: "After the first day of November next, we will neither ourselves import, nor purchase any slave or slaves imported by any other person, either from Africa, the West Indies, or any other place."

On the affairs of Massachusetts the temper of the Virginians ran exceedingly high. "An innate spirit of freedom," such were the words of Washington, "tells me that the measures which the administration are most violently pursuing, are opposed to every principle of natural justice." He was certain that it was neither the wish nor the interest of any government on the continent, separately or collectively, to set up independence, but he rejected indignantly the claim of parliament, and saw no "reason to expect

CHAP. VI. 1774. July.

any thing from their justice." "The crisis," he said, "is arrived when we must assert our rights, or submit to every imposition that can be heaped upon us, till custom and use shall make us tame and abject slaves." From the first he was convinced that there was not "any thing to be expected from petitioning." "Ought we not, then," he exclaimed, "to put our virtue and fortitude to the severest test?" Thus Washington reasoned privately with his friends. In the convention, Richard Henry Lee and Patrick Henry were heard with such delight that the one was compared to Cicero, the other to Demosthenes. But Washington, who never was able to see distress without a desire to assuage it, made the most effective speech when he uttered the wish to "raise one thousand men, subsist them at his own expense, and march at their head for the relief of Boston."

The resolves and instructions of Virginia corresponded to his spirit. They demanded that the restrictions on navigation should themselves be restrained. Especially were they incensed at the threat of Gage to use the deadly weapon of constructive treason against such inhabitants of Massachusetts as should assemble to consider of their grievances, and form associations for their common conduct; and they voted that "the attempt to execute this illegal and odious proclamation, would justify resistance and reprisal."

CHAPTER VII.

THE CABINET OF LOUIS SIXTEENTH.

July–August, 1774.

CHAP. VII. 1774. July. In France, Louis the Sixteenth had selected ministers, of whom a part only were disposed to take advantage of the perplexities of England; but they were the more likely to prevail from the unsteadiness of the administration, which sprung from his own character and made his life a long equipoise between right intentions and executive feebleness. His countenance, seeming to promise probity, betrayed irresolution. In manner he was awkward and embarrassed, and even at his own court ill at ease. His turn of mind was serious, inclining even to sadness; and his appearance in public did not accord with his station or his youth. He had neither military science, nor martial spirit, nor gallant bearing; and in the eyes of a warlike nation, which interpreted his torpid languor as a want of courage, he was sure to fall into contempt.

In the conduct of affairs, his sphere of vision was narrow; and he applied himself chiefly to details or matters of little importance. Conforming to the public wish, he began by dismissing the ministers of the late king, and then felt the need of a guide. Marie Antoinette would have recalled Choiseul, the supporter of an intimate friendship between France and Austria, the passionate adversary of England, the prophet and the favorer of American independence. But filial respect restrained the king, for Choiseul had been his father's enemy. He turned to his aunts for advice; and their choice fell on the Count de Maurepas from their regard to his experience, general good character, and independence of the parties at court.

Not descended from the old nobility, Maurepas belonged to a family which, within a hundred and fifty years had furnished nine secretaries of state. He had himself held office in the last days of Louis the Fourteenth; and had been sent into retirement by Louis the Fifteenth for writing verses that offended the king's mistress. At the age of seventy-three, and after an exile of twenty-five years, he was still as he had been in youth, polite, selfish, jealous, superficial, and frivolous. Despising gravity of manner and airs of mystery as ridiculous, and incapable of serious passion or profound reflection, he charmed by the courtesy and ease of his conversation. He enjoyed the present moment, and was careless of the future which he was not to share; taking all things so easily, that age did not wear him out. Full of petty artifice in attack, of sly dexterity in defence, he could put aside weighty objections by mirth and laugh even at merit, having no faith in virtues that were difficult, and deriding the love of country as a vain boast or a

CHAP. VII. 1774. July. stratagem to gain an end. With all the patronage of France in his gift, he took from the treasury only enough to meet his increased expenses, keeping house with well-ordered simplicity, and at his death leaving neither debts nor savings. Present tranquillity was his object, rather than honor among coming generations. He was naturally liberal, and willing that the public good should prevail; but not at the cost of his repose, above all, not at the risk of his ascendency with the king. A jealousy of superior talents was his only everwakeful passion. He had no malignity, and found no pleasure in revenge; when envy led him to remove a colleague who threatened to become a rival, he never pursued him with bitterness, or dismissed him to exile. To foreign ambassadors he paid the attentions due to their rank; but the professions which he lavished with graceful levity, had such an air of nothingness, that no one ever confided in them enough to gain the right of charging him seriously with duplicity. To men of every condition he never forgot to show due regard, disguising his unfailing deference to rank by freedom of remark and gaiety. He granted a favor without ever showing the despotism of a benefactor; and he softened a refusal by reasons that were soothing to the petitioner's self-love. His administration was sure to be weak, for it was his maxim never to hold out against any one who had power enough to be formidable, and he wished to please alike the courtiers and public opinion; the nobility and the philosophers; those who stickled for the king's absolute sway, and those who clamored for the restoration of parliaments; those who wished a cordial understanding with England and those who favored her insurgent colonies. CHAP. VII.

Louis the Sixteenth was looking for an experienced and firm guide to correct his own indecision; and he fell upon a complacent, well-mannered old gentleman, who had the same fault with himself, and was only fit to give lessons in etiquette, or enliven business by pleasantry. Yet the king retained Maurepas as minister more than seven years without a suspicion of his incompetency. No statesman of his century had a more prosperous old age, or such felicity in the circumstances of his death, which happened at the moment of his king's greatest domestic happiness in the birth of a son, and amidst the shouts of France for the most important victory of the century, achieved during his administration. 1774. July.

Declining a special department, Maurepas, as the head of the cabinet, selected his own associates, choosing men by whom he feared neither to be superseded nor eclipsed. To the Count de Vergennes was assigned the department of foreign affairs. The veteran statesman, then fifty-seven years old, was of plebeian origin, and married to a plebeian; unsupported by the high nobility and without claims on Austria or Marie Antoinette. His father had been president of the parliament at Dijon. His own diplomatic career began in 1740, and had been marked by moderation, vigilance, and success. He had neither the adventurous daring, nor the levity of Choiseul; but he had equal acquaintance with courts, equal sensitiveness to the dignity of France, and greater self-control. He was distinguished among ministers as indefatigably laborious, conducting affairs with method,

CHAP. VII. 1774. July. rectitude, and clearness. He had not the rapid intuitions of genius, but his character was firm, his mode of thinking liberal, and he loved to surround himself with able men. His conversation was reserved; his manner grave and coldly polite. As he served a weak king, he was always on his guard, and to give a categorical answer was his aversion. Like nearly every Frenchman, he was thoroughly a monarchist; and he also loved Louis the Sixteenth, whose good opinion he gained at once and ever retained. Eleven years before, he had predicted that the conquest of Canada would hasten the independence of British America, and he was now from vantage ground to watch his prophecy come true.

The philosophers of the day, like the king, wished the happiness of the people, and public opinion required that they should be represented in the cabinet. Maurepas complied, and in July, 1774, the place of minister of the marine was conferred on Turgot, whose name was as yet little known at Paris, and whose artlessness made him even less dangerous as a rival than Vergennes. "I am told he never goes to mass," said the king, doubtingly, and yet consented to the appointment. In five weeks, Turgot so won upon his sovereign's good will, that he was transferred to the ministry of finance. This was the wish of all the philosophers; of D'Alembert, Condorcet, Bailly, La Harpe, Marmontel, Thomas, Condillac, Morellet, and Voltaire. Nor of them alone. "Turgot," said Malesherbes, "has the heart of L'Hôpital, and the head of Bacon." His purity, moreover, gave him clearsightedness and distinctness of purpose. At a moment when everybody confessed that reform was essential, it seemed a national benediction that a youthful king should intrust the task of amendment to a statesman, who preserved his purity of nature in a libertine age, and joined unquestioned probity to comprehensive intelligence and administrative experience.

The annual public expenses largely exceeded the revenue, and extortions to meet the deficit fell on the humble and the weak. Yet the chief financial officers grew enormously rich, and were adepts in refined luxury, masking their revels by an affectation of philosophy. "We are well off," they would say; "of what use is reform?" The land tax, the poll tax, the best tithes of the produce for the priest, twentieths, military service, taxes on consumption, labor on the highways, crushed the peasantry. The indirect taxes were farmed out to commissioners, who had power to enforce extortionate demands by summarily sending the demurrers to the galleys or the scaffold.

The protective system superintended the use of capital. The right to labor was a privilege sold for the benefit of the finances, and labor itself was so bound in the meshes of innumerable rules, that manufactures grew up timidly under the dangerous favor of arbitrary encouragement. The progress of agriculture was still hindered by the servitudes of the soil. Each little farm was in bondage under a complicated system of irredeemable dues, to roads and canals; to the bakehouse and the brewery of the lord of the manor; to his winepress and his mill; to his tolls at the river, the market, or the fair; to ground rents, and quit rents, and fines on alienation.

CHAP. VII. 1774. July. The game laws let in the wild beasts and birds to fatten on the growth of the poor man's fields; and after his harvest provincial custom-houses blocked domestic commerce; the export of corn, and even its free circulation within the realm, was prohibited; so that one province might waste from famine, and another want a market for its superfluous production.

Out of this sad state Turgot undertook to lift his country. "It is to you personally," said he to Louis the Sixteenth, "to the man, honest, just, and good, rather than to the king, that I give myself up. You have confided to me the happiness of your people, and the care of making you and your authority beloved; but I shall have to combat those who gain by abuses, the prejudices against all reform, the majority of the court, and every solicitor of favors. I shall sacrifice myself for the people; but I may incur even their hatred by the very measures I shall take to prevent their distress." "Have no fear," said the king, pressing the hand of his new comptroller-general; "I shall always support you."

The exigencies of his position made Turgot a partisan of the central unity of power; he was no friend to revolutions; he would have confined the parliaments of France to their simple office as judges; he had no predilection for states general, or a system like that of England. To unobstructed power, enlightened by advice, he looked for good laws, and a vigorous administration. He would have no bankruptcy, whether avowed or disguised; no increase of taxes, no new loans; and the king solemnly accepted his financial system.

The vices of the nobility had demoralized the army; from the navy there was also little promise, for that department was intrusted to Sartines, who had been trained to public life only as an officer of police. The warlike nation had never had so unwarlike an administration. Maurepas had been feeble, even from his youth; the king was neither a soldier, nor capable of becoming one.

Yet in France the traditional policy, which regarded England as a natural enemy, and sought a benefit to the one country by wounding the other, was kept alive by the Bourbon princes; by the nobles who longed to efface the shame of the last treaty of peace; by the farmers of the revenue, who were sure to derive rapid fortunes from the necessities of war; by the ministers who brooded over the perfidious conduct of the British government in 1755 with a distrust that never slumbered. France, therefore, bent its ear to catch the earliest surging of American discontent. This it discerned in the instructions from the congress of Virginia to its delegates in the continental congress. "They are the first," observed the statesmen of France, "which propose to restrain the act of navigation itself, and give pledges to oppose force by force.'

CHAPTER VIII.

HOW THE MANDAMUS COUNCILLORS WERE DEALT WITH.

AUGUST, 1774.

CHAP. VIII. 1774. Aug.

ON Saturday, the sixth day of August, Gage received an authentic copy of the act of parliament "for the better regulating the province of the Massachusetts bay," introduced by Lord North in April, and, as we have seen, assented to by the king on the twentieth of May. Rockingham and his friends have left on the records of the house of lords their protest against the act, "because," said they, "a definitive legal offence, by which a forfeiture of the charter is incurred, has not been clearly stated and fully proved; neither has notice of this adverse proceeding been given to the parties affected; neither have they been heard in their own defence; and because the governor and council are intrusted with powers, with which the British constitution has not trusted his majesty and privy council, so that the lives and properties of the subjects are put into their hands without control."

The principle of the statute was the concentration

CHAP. VIII. 1774. Aug.

of the executive power, including the courts of justice, in the hands of the royal governor. Without previous notice to Massachusetts and without a hearing, it arbitrarily took away rights and liberties which the people had enjoyed from the foundation of the colony, except in the evil days of James the Second, and which had been renewed in the charter from William and Mary. That charter was coeval with the great English revolution, had been the fundamental law of the colonists for more than eighty years, and was associated in their minds with every idea of English liberty and loyalty to the English crown. Under its provisions the councillors, twenty-eight in number, had been annually chosen by a convention of the council for the former year and the assembly, subject only to the negative of the governor; henceforward they were to be not less than twelve and not more than thirty-six, were to receive their appointments from the king, and were removable at his pleasure. The governor received authority, without consulting his council, to appoint and to remove all judges of the inferior courts, justices of the peace, and all officers belonging to the council and the courts of justice. The sheriffs were changeable by the governor and council as often and for such purposes as they should deem expedient. In case of a vacancy, the governor was himself to appoint the chief justice and judges of the superior court, who were to hold their commissions during the pleasure of the king, and depend on his good-will for the amount and the payment of their salaries. That nothing might be wanting to executive power, the right of selecting juries was taken from the inhabit-

CHAP. VIII. 1774. Aug.

ants and freeholders of the towns, and conferred on the sheriffs of the several counties within the province. This regulating act, moreover, uprooted the dearest institution of New England, whose people, from the first settlement of the country, had been accustomed in their town meetings to transact all business that touched them most nearly as fathers, as freemen, and as Christians. There they adopted local taxes to keep up their free-schools; there they regulated all the municipal concerns of the year; there they instructed the representatives of their choice; and as the limits of the parish and the town were usually the same, there most of them took measures for the invitation and support of ministers of the gospel in their congregations; there, whenever they were called together by their selectmen, they were accustomed to express their sentiments on all subjects connected with their various interests, their rights and liberties, and their religion. The regulating act, sweeping away the provincial law which had received the approval of William and Mary, permitted two meetings annually in which town officers and representatives might be chosen, but no other matter be introduced; every other assembling of a town was forbidden except by the written leave of the governor, and then only for business expressed in that leave. A wise ruler respects the feelings, usages, and opinions of the governed. The king trampled under foot the affections, customs, laws, and privileges of the people of Massachusetts. He was willing to spare them an explicit consent to the power of parliament in all cases whatever; but he required proof that Boston had compensated the East India company, that the tax on tea could be safely collected, and that the province would peacefully acquiesce in the change of their charter.

With the regulating act Gage received copies of two other acts which were to facilitate its enforcement. He was surrounded by an army; had been enjoined repeatedly to arrest the leading patriots, even at the risk of producing a riot; and had been instructed that even in time of peace he could of himself order the troops to fire upon the people. By one of the two additional acts, he was authorized to quarter his army in towns; by the other, to transfer to another colony or to Great Britain any persons informed against or indicted for crimes committed in supporting the revenue laws or suppressing riots.

The regulating act complicated the question between America and Great Britain. The country, under the advice of Pennsylvania, might have indemnified the East India company; might have obtained by importunity the repeal of the tax on tea; or might have borne the duty as it had borne that on wine; but parliament, after ten years of premeditation, had exercised the power to abrogate the laws, and to change the charter of a province without its consent; and on this arose the conflict of the American revolution. The act went into effect on the moment of its being received; and of necessity precipitated the choice between submission and resistance. Within a week, eleven of the mandamus councillors took the oath of office, and were followed in a few days by fourteen more. They were persuaded that the province could by no possibility hold out; the promise of assistance from other colonies was scoffed at as a

CHAP. VIII. 1774. Aug.

delusion, intended only to keep up the spirit of the mob. No assembly existed in the province to remonstrate; and Gage might delay or wholly omit to send out writs for a new election. But a people who were trained to read and write; to discuss all political questions, privately and in public; to strive to exhibit in their lives the Christian system of ethics, the beauty of holiness, and the unselfish nature of virtue; to reason on the great ends of God in creation; to believe in their own immortality; and to venerate their ancestry as above all others pure, enlightened, and free, could never forego the civil rights which were their most cherished inheritance.

The committee of Boston, exasperated by a military camp in the heart of their town, acknowledged themselves unable to deliberate "as the perils and exigencies of the times might demand." "Being stationed by Providence in the front rank of the conflict," such was their letter to all the other towns in the province, "we trust we shall not be left by Heaven to do any thing derogatory to our common liberties, unworthy of the fame of our ancestors, or inconsistent with our former professions. Though surrounded with a large body of armed men, who, having the sword, have also our blood in their hands, we are yet undaunted. To you, our brethren and dear companions in the cause of God, we apply. From you we have received that countenance and aid which have strengthened our hands, and that bounty, which hath occasioned smiles on the face of distress. To you, therefore, we look for that advice and example, which, with the blessing of God, shall save us from destruction."

CHAP. VIII. 1774. Aug.

The earnest message was borne to the northern border of the province, where the brooks run to the Nashua, and the upland farms yielded but scanty returns to the hardest toil. The husbandmen in that region had already sent many loads of rye to the poor of Boston. In the coming storm they clustered round William Prescott, of Pepperell, who stood as firm as Monadnoc, that rose in sight of his homestead; and on the day after the first mandamus councillors took their oath of office, they put their soul into his words as he wrote for them to the men of Boston: "Be not dismayed nor disheartened in this day of great trials. We heartily sympathize with you, and are always ready to do all in our power for your support, comfort, and relief; knowing that Providence has placed you where you must stand the first shock. We consider we are all embarked in one bottom, and must sink or swim together. We think if we submit to these regulations, all is gone. Our forefathers passed the vast Atlantic, spent their blood and treasure, that they might enjoy their liberties, both civil and religious, and transmit them to their posterity. Their children have waded through seas of difficulty, to leave us free and happy in the enjoyment of English privileges. Now if we should give them up, can our children rise up and call us blessed? Is a glorious death in defence of our liberties better than a short infamous life, and our memories to be had in detestation to the latest posterity? Let us all be of one heart, and stand fast in the liberties wherewith Christ has made us free; and may he of his infinite mercy grant us deliverance out of all our troubles." Such were the cheering words of

CHAP. VIII. Prescott and his companions, and they never forgot their pledge.

1774. Aug. Everywhere the rural population of Massachusetts were anxiously weighing the issues in which they were involved. One spirit moved through them all. From the hills of Berkshire to the Penobscot, they debated the great question of resistance as though God were hearkening; and they took counsel reverently with their ministers, and the aged, the pious, and the brave in their villages. Adjoining towns held conferences. The shire of Worcester in August set the example of a county congress, which disclaimed the jurisdiction of the British house of commons, asserted the exclusive right of the colonies to originate laws respecting themselves, rested their duty of allegiance on the charter of the province, and declared the violation of that charter a dissolution of their union with Britain.

Thomas Gardner, a Cambridge farmer, promised a similar convention of the county of Middlesex. "Friends and brethren," he wrote to Boston, as if at once to allay anxiety and prophesy his own approaching end, "the time is come that every one that has a tongue and an arm is called upon by their country to stand forth in its behalf. I consider the call as the call of God, and desire to be all obedience. The people will choose rather to fall gloriously in the cause of their country than meanly submit to slavery." The passion for liberty was felt to be so hallowed, that in a land, remarkable for piety, a father of a family in his last hour would call his sons about his death-bed and charge them on his blessing to love freedom more than life.

In June there had been a review of the Boston regiment. The patriots speculated on the total number of the militia. After searching the rolls of the several towns, the population of the province was estimated at four hundred thousand souls, and the number of men between sixteen and sixty years of age, at about one hundred and twenty thousand, most of whom possessed arms, and were expert in their use. There could be no general muster; but during the summer, the drum and fife were heard in every hamlet, and the several companies paraded for discipline. One day in August, Gage revoked Hancock's commission in the Boston cadets; and that company resented the insult by returning the king's standard and disbanding.

Putnam, of Connecticut, famous for service near Lake George and Ticonderoga, before the walls of Havana, and far up the lakes against Pontiac, a pioneer of emigration to the southern banks of the Mississippi, the oracle of all patriot circles in his neighborhood, rode to Boston with one hundred and thirty sheep, as a gift from the parish of Brooklyn. The "old hero" became Warren's guest, and every one's favorite. The officers whom he visited on Boston Common bantered him about coming down to fight. "Twenty ships of the line and twenty regiments," said Major Small, "may be expected from England in case a submission is not speedily made by Boston." "If they come," said the veteran, "I am ready to treat them as enemies."

The growing excitement attracted to New England Charles Lee, the restless officer whom the Five Nations had named the Boiling Water. As aide-de-camp

CHAP. VIII. 1774. Aug.

to the king of Poland, he assumed the rank of a major-general, which on occasion of his visit was universally acknowledged; so that of all who were likely to draw the sword for America, he had the precedence in military rank. He paid court to the patriots of Massachusetts, and left them confident of his aid in the impending struggle. He on his part saw in the New England yeomanry the best materials for an army.

Meantime the delegates of Massachusetts to the general congress were escorted by great numbers as far as Watertown, where many had gathered to bid them a solemn and affectionate farewell. As they reached Connecticut river, they received a letter of advice from the great patriot of Northampton. "We must fight," wrote Hawley, "we must fight, if we cannot otherwise rid ourselves of British taxation. The form of government enacted for us by the British parliament is evil against right, utterly intolerable to every man who has any idea or feeling of right or liberty. There is not heat enough yet for battle; constant and negative resistance will increase it. There is not military skill enough; that is improving and must be encouraged. Fight we must finally, unless Britain retreats. But it is of infinite consequence that victory be the end of hostilities. If we get to fighting before necessary dispositions are made for it, we shall be conquered and all will be lost for ever. A clear plan for an adequate supply of arms and military stores must be devised. This is the main thing. Men, in that case, will not be wanting. Our salvation depends upon a persevering union. Every grievance of any one colony must be held as a grievance to the whole, and some plan be settled for a continuation of congresses, even though congresses will soon be declared by parliament to be high treason." CHAP. VIII. 1774. Aug.

Hawley spoke the genuine sentiments of western Massachusetts. When on Tuesday, the sixteenth of August, the judges of the inferior court of Hampshire met at Great Barrington, it was known that the regulating act had received the royal approval. Before noon the town was filled with people of the county and five hundred men from Connecticut, armed with clubs and staves. Suffering the courts of justice to sit, seemed a recognition of the act of parliament, and the chief judge was forced to plight his honor that he and his associates would do no business. When it became known that a great effort to execute the new statute was designed to be made at Worcester, the uncompromising inhabitants of that town purchased and manufactured arms, cast musket-balls, and provided powder for the occasion; and as Gage meditated employing a part of his army, they threatened openly to fall upon any body of soldiers who should attack them.

The mandamus councillors began to give way. Williams of Hatfield refused to incur certain ruin by accepting his commission; so did Worthington of Springfield. Those who accepted dared not give advice.

Boston held town meetings as before. Gage reminded the selectmen of the act of parliament, restricting town meetings without the governor's leave. "It is only an adjourned one," said the selectmen. "By such means," said Gage, "you may keep your meeting alive these ten years." He brought the sub-

CHAP. VIII. 1774. Aug.

ject before the new council. "It is a point of law," said they, "and should be referred to the crown lawyers." He asked their concurrence in removing a sheriff. "The act of parliament," they replied, "confines the power of removal to the governor alone." Several members gave an account of the frenzy which was sweeping from Berkshire over the province, and might reach them collectively even in the presence of the governor. "If you value your life, I advise you not to return home at present," was the warning received by Ruggles from the town of Hardwicke, whose freemen with those of New Braintree and of Greenwich so resented his accepting a place in the council, that they vowed he should never again pass the great bridge of the town alive.

By nine o'clock on the morning of the twenty-sixth, more than two thousand men marched in companies to the common in Worcester, where they forced Timothy Paine to walk through their ranks with his hat off as far as the centre of their hollow square, and read a written resignation of his seat at the council board. A large detachment then moved to Rutland to deal with Murray. The next day at noon Wilder of Templeton and Holden of Princeton brought up their companies, and by three in the afternoon, about fifteen hundred men had assembled, most of them armed with bludgeons. But Murray had escaped on the previous evening, just before the sentries were set round his house and along the roads; they therefore sent him a letter requiring him to resign. The temper of the people brooked no division; they held every person that would not join them an enemy to his country. "The consequences of your proceedings

CHAP. VIII. 1774. Aug.

will be rebellion, confiscation and death," said the younger Murray; and his words were as oil to the flame. "No consequences," they replied to him, "are so dreadful to a free people as that of being made slaves." "This," wrote he to his brother, "is not the language of the common people only; those that have heretofore sustained the fairest character are the warmest in this matter; and among the many friends you have heretofore had, I can scarcely mention any to you now."

One evening in August the farmers of Union in Connecticut found Willard of Lancaster, Massachusetts, within their precinct. They kept watch over him during the night, and the next morning five hundred men would have taken him to the county jail; but after a march of six miles he begged forgiveness of all honest men for having taken the oath of office, and promised never to sit or act in council.

The people of Plymouth were grieved that George Watson, their respected townsman, was willing to act under his appointment. On the first Lord's day after his purpose was known, as soon as he took his seat in meeting, his neighbors and friends put on their hats before the congregation and walked out of the house. The extreme public indignity was more than he could bear. As they passed his pew, he hid his face by bending his head over his cane, and determined to resign. Of thirty six who received the king's summons as councillors, more than twenty declined to obey them or revoked their acceptance. The rest fled in terror to the army at Boston, and even there could not hide their sense of shame.

CHAPTER IX.

MASSACHUSETTS DEFEATS THE REGULATING ACT.

AUGUST, 1774.

CHAP. IX. 1774. Aug.

THE congressional delegates from Massachusetts, consecrated by their office as her suppliant ambassadors in the day of her distress, were welcomed everywhere on their journey with hospitable feasts and tears of sympathy. No governor in the pride of office was ever attended with more assiduous solicitude; no general returning in triumph with sincerer love. The men of Hartford, after giving pledges to abide by the resolutions of the congress, attended them to Middletown, from which place they were escorted by carriages and a cavalcade. The bells of New Haven were set ringing as they drew near, and those who had not gone out to meet them, thronged the windows and doors to gaze. There they were encouraged by Roger Sherman, whom solid sense and the power of clear analysis were to constitute one of the master builders of our republic. "The parliament of Great Britain," said he, "can rightfully make laws for America in no case whatever." The freeholders of Albemarle county, in Virginia, had a month earlier expressed the same conclusion, and, in the language of Jefferson, claimed to hold the privilege of exemption from the authority of every other legislature than their own as one of the common rights of mankind." CHAP. IX. 1774. Aug.

After resting one night at New Haven, and visiting the grave of the regicide Dixwell, the envoys continued on their way. As they reached the Hudson, they found that the British ministry had failed to allure, to intimidate, or to divide New York. A federative union of all the English colonies, under the sovereignty of the British king, had for a quarter of a century formed the aspiration of its ablest men, who long remained confident of the ultimate consummation of their hopes. The great design had been repeatedly promoted by the legislature of the province. The people wished neither to surrender liberty, nor to dissolve their connection with the crown of England. The possibility of framing an independent republic with one jurisdiction from the far North to the Gulf of Mexico, from the Atlantic indefinitely to the West, was a vision of which nothing in the history of man could promise the realization. Lord Kames, the friend of Franklin, though he was persuaded that the separation of the British colonies was inevitably approaching, affirmed that their political union was impossible. Prudent men long regarded the establishment of a confederacy of widely extended territories, as a doubtful experiment, except under the moderating influence of a permanent executive. That the colonies, if disconnected from England, would fall into bloody dissensions among them-

CHAP. IX. 1774. Aug. selves, had been the anxious fear of Otis of Massachusetts; and was now the apprehension of Philip Livingston of New York. Union, with the security of all constitutional rights, under the auspices of the British king, was still the purpose of Jay and his intimate associates. This policy had brought all classes together, and loyal men who, like William Smith, were its advocates, passed for "consistent, unshaken friends to their country and her liberties." The community did not as yet know with what sullen passion the idea had been trampled under foot by the British ministry, nor how it was hated by the British king; and as yet prudence suppressed every allusion to an "appeal" to arms. But the appeal was nearer at hand than the most sagacious believed.

The last Tuesday in August was the day for holding the supreme court in Boston; Oliver, the impeached chief justice, was to preside; and in the conduct of business to conform for the first time to the new act of parliament. The day was to decide whether Massachusetts would submit to the regulating act; and Gage, who thought it might be necessary for a part of his army to escort the judges in their circuit as far as Worcester, anticipated no opposition to organizing the court in the heart of the garrisoned town. But neither he nor his employers had computed the power of resistance in a community where the great mass is inflamed with love for a sacred cause.

Before Samuel Adams departed, he had concerted the measures by which Suffolk county would be best able to bring the wrongs of the town and the province before the general congress; and he left the direction with Warren, whose impetuous fearlessness was tempered by self-possession, gentleness, and good sense, and who had reluctantly become convinced that all connection with the British parliament must be thrown off. On the sixteenth of August a county congress of the towns of Suffolk, which then embraced Norfolk, met at a tavern in the village of Stoughton. As the aged Samuel Dunbar, the rigid Calvinist minister of its first parish, breathed forth among them his prayer for liberty, the venerable man seemed inspired with "the most divine and prophetical enthusiasm." "We must stand undisguised upon one side or the other," said Thayer, of Braintree. The members were unanimous and firm; but they postponed their decision, till it could be promulgated with greater formality. To this end, and in contempt of Gage and the act of parliament, they directed special meetings in every town and precinct in the county, to elect delegates with full powers to appear at Dedham on the first Monday in September. From such a county congress Warren predicted "very important consequences."

CHAP. IX. 1774. Aug.

Meantime Boston was not left to deliberate alone. On Friday, the twenty-sixth, its committee were joined at Faneuil Hall by delegates from the several towns of the counties of Worcester, Middlesex, and Essex; and on the next day, after calm consultation, they collectively denied the power of parliament to change the minutest tittle of their laws. As a consequence, they found that all appointments to the newly-instituted council, and all authority exercised by the courts of justice, were unconstitutional; and therefore that the officers, should they attempt to act,

CHAP. IX. 1774. Aug. would become "usurpers of power" and enemies to the province, even though they bore the commission of the king. The Boston port-act they found to be a wicked violation of the rights to life, liberty, and the means of sustenance, which all men hold by the grace of Heaven, irrespectively of the king's leave. The act of parliament removing from American courts the trials of officers who should take the lives of Americans, they described as the extreme measure in the system of despotism.

For remedies, the convention proposed a provincial congress with large executive powers. In the mean time the unconstitutional courts were to be forbidden to proceed, and their officers to be detested as "traitors cloaked with a pretext of law." It was known that Gage had orders to make arrests; each individual patriot was therefore placed under the protection of his county and of the province. The practice of the military art was declared to be the duty of the people.

Gage began to show alarm. He looked about him for more troops; he recommended the repair of Crown Point; and a strong garrison at Ticonderoga; a well-guarded line of communication between New York and Canada. He himself came from Salem to support the chief justice in opening the court at Boston.

On the same day began the term of the inferior court at Springfield. But early in the morning, fifteen hundred or two thousand men, with drums and trumpets, marched into that town, set up a black flag at the court-house, and threatened death to any one who should enter. After some treaty, the judges executed a written covenant not to put their commissions in force; Worthington resigned his office of councillor; those of the lawyers who had sent an address to Gage, atoned for their offence by a written confession. Williams, the tory of Hatfield, and others were compelled successively to go round a large circle, and ask forgiveness. Catlin and Warner fell upon their knees; old Captain Mirreck, of Monson, was drawn in a cart and threatened to be tarred and feathered. The people agreed that the troops, if Gage should march them to Worcester, should be resisted by at least twenty thousand men from Hampshire county and Connecticut.

At Boston the judges took their seats, and the usual proclamations were made; when the men who had been returned as jurors, one and all, refused to take the oath. Being asked why they refused, Thomas Chase, who was of the petit jury, gave as his reason, "that the chief justice of the court stood impeached by the late representatives of the province." In a paper offered by the jury, the judges found their authority disputed for the further reasons, that the charter of the province had been changed with no warrant but an act of parliament, and that three of the judges, in violation of the constitution, had accepted seats in the new council.

The chief justice and his colleagues, repairing in a body to the governor, represented the impossibility of exercising their office in Boston or in any other part of the province; the army was too small for their protection; and besides, none would act as jurors. Thus the authority of the new government,

CHAP. IX. 1774. Aug.

as established by act of parliament, perished in the presence of the governor, the judges, and the army.

Gage summoned his council, but only to meet new discomfitures. Its members dared not show themselves at Salem, and he consented to their violating the act of parliament by meeting in Boston. Hutchinson, the son of the former governor, withdrew from the council. The few who retained their places advised unanimously to send no troops into the interior, but so to reinforce the army as to constitute Boston a "place of safe retreat."

Far different was the spirit displayed on that day at Concord by the county convention, in which every town and district of Middlesex was represented. "We must now exert ourselves," said they, "'or all those efforts which for ten years past have brightened the annals of this country, will be totally frustrated. Life and death, or what is more, freedom and slavery, are now before us." In behalf, therefore, of themselves and of future generations, they enumerated the violations of their rights by late acts of parliament, which they avowed their purpose to nullify, and they sent their resolves by an express to the continental congress. "We are grieved," said they, "to find ourselves reduced to the necessity of entering into the discussion of those great and profound questions; but we deprecate a state of slavery. Our fathers left us a fair inheritance, purchased by blood and treasure; this we are resolved to transmit equally fair to our children; no danger shall affright, no difficulties intimidate us; and if, in support of our rights, we are called to encounter even death, we are yet undaunted; sensible that he can never die too soon who lays down his life in support of the laws and liberties of his country."

The convention separated in the evening of the last day of August, to await the decisions of the continental congress; but before the next sun was up the aspect of affairs was changed.

CHAPTER X.

THE SUFFOLK COUNTY CONVENTION.

SEPTEMBER, 1774.

CHAP. X. 1774. Sept.

THE province kept its powder for its militia at Quarry Hill on a point of land between Medford and Cambridge, then within the limits of Charlestown. In August, the towns had been removing their stock, each according to its proportion. On Thursday morning, the first day of September, at half past four, about two hundred and sixty men, commanded by Lieutenant Colonel Madison, embarked on board thirteen boats at Long Wharf, rowed up Mystic river, landed at Temple's farm, took from the public magazine all the powder that was there, amounting to two hundred and fifty half barrels, and transferred it to the castle. A detachment from the corps brought off two field-pieces from Cambridge.

This forcible seizure, secretly planned and suddenly executed, set the country in a flame. Before evening, large bodies of the men of Middlesex began to collect; and on Friday morning, thousands of freeholders, leaving their guns in the rear, advanced to

CHAP. X. 1774. Sept.

Cambridge, armed only with sticks, and led by captains of the towns, representatives, and committee men. Warren, hearing that the roads from Sudbury to Cambridge were lined by men in arms, took with him as many of the Boston committee as came in his way, crossed to Charlestown, and with the committee of that town hastened to meet the committee of Cambridge. On their arrival, they found Danforth, a county judge and mandamus councillor, addressing four thousand people who stood in the open air round the court house steps; and such order prevailed, that the low voice of the feeble old man was heard by the whole multitude. He finished by giving a written promise, never "to be any way concerned as a member of the council." Lee, in like manner, confirmed his former resignation. The turn of Phipps, the high sheriff, came next, and he signed an agreement not to execute any precept under the new act of parliament.

Oliver, the lieutenant governor, who resided at Cambridge, repaired to Boston in the "greatest distress." "It is not a mad mob," said he to the British admiral; and he warned Gage that "sending out troops would be attended with the most fatal consequences." Had they marched only five miles into the country, Warren was of opinion that not a man of them would have been saved. Gage decided to remain inactive; writing, as his justification to the ministry, "the people are numerous, waked up to a fury, and not a Boston rabble, but the freeholders and farmers of the county. A check would be fatal, and the first stroke will decide a great deal. We should, therefore, be strong, and proceed on a good

CHAP. X. foundation, before any thing decisive is urged, which it is to be presumed will prove successful."

1774. Sept. Oliver returned to Cambridge with the assurance that no troops would appear, and to beg the committee's leave to retain his places. But in the afternoon three or four thousand men surrounded his house, and demanded his resignation. "My honor is my first consideration," said Oliver; "the next my life. Put me to death or destroy my property, but I will not submit." Yet, on the first appearance of danger, he yielded to all their demands; then walking into his own court-yard, he reassumed the air of a hero, and comforted himself by repeating, "I will do no more, even though they put me to death."

For three hours, beneath the scorching sun of the hottest day of that summer, the people kept the ranks in which they were marshalled, and their "patience, temperance, and fortitude" were remarked upon as the chief elements "of a good soldier." They allowed the force of the suggestion, that the governor, in removing the stores of the province, had broken no law; and they voted unanimously their abhorrence of mobs and riots, and of the destruction of private property.

Their conduct showed how capable they were of regular movements, and how formidable they might prove in the field; but rumors reached England of their cowardice and defeat. "What a dismal piece of news!" said Charles Fox to Edmund Burke; "and what a melancholy consideration for all thinking men, that no people, animated by what principle soever, can make a successful resistance to military discipline. I was never so affected with any public event, either in history or in life. The introduction of great standing armies into Europe has made all mankind irrecoverably slaves. The particular business I think very far from being decided; but I am dejected at heart from the sad figure that men make against soldiers." Fox was misinformed. In the British camp in Boston, an apprehension at once prevailed of an invasion from armed multitudes. The guards were doubled; cannon were placed at the entrance of the town, and the troops lay on their arms through the night.

CHAP. X. 1774. Sept.

Gage wrote home, that if the "king would insist on reducing New England, a very respectable force should take the field." He already had five regiments at Boston, one more at the Castle, and another at Salem; two more he summoned hastily from Quebec; he sent transports to bring another from New York; he still required reinforcements from England, and he resolved also to raise "irregulars, of one sort or other, in America." The sort of irregulars he had in his mind, he explained in a letter to Carleton, who was just then expected to arrive at Quebec from England. "I ask your opinion," wrote he, "what measures would be most efficacious to raise a body of Canadians and Indians, and for them to form a junction with the king's forces in this province." The threat to employ the wild Indians in war against the colonists, had been thrown out at the time of Tryon's march against the Regulators of North Carolina, and may be traced still further back, at least to the discussions in the time of Shirley on remedies for the weakness of British power. This is

CHAP. X. 1774. Sept. the moment when it was adopted in practice. The commission to Carleton, as governor of the province of Quebec under the act of parliament, conveyed full authority to levy, arm, and employ not the Canadians only, but "all persons whatsoever," including the Indian tribes from the coast of Labrador to the Ohio; and to march them against rebels "into any one of the plantations in America."

It was pretended that there were English precedents for the practice; but it was not so. During the French war, England had formed connections with the Indian tribes, through whose territory lay the march of the hostile armies; and warriors of the Six Nations were enrolled and paid rather to secure neutrality than service. But this system had never been extended beyond the bounds of obvious prudence as a measure of self-defence. No war party of savages was ever hounded at Canadian villages. The French, on the other hand, from their superior skill in gaining the love of the Red Men, and from despair at their own relative inferiority in numbers, had in former wars increased their strength by Indian alliances. These alliances the British king and his ministers now revived; and against their own colonies and kindred, wished to loose from the leash their terrible auxiliaries.

The ruthless policy was hateful to every right-minded Englishman, and as soon as the design roused attention, the protest of the nation was uttered by Chatham and Burke, its great representatives; meantime the execution of the sanguinary scheme fell naturally into the hands of the most unscrupulous and subservient English officers, and the most

CHAP. X. 1774. Sept.

covetous and cruel of the old French partisans. Carleton, from the first, abhorred the measure, which he was yet constrained to promote. "You know," wrote he of the Indians to Gage, "what sort of people they are." It was true: Gage had himself, in the West and in Canada, grown thoroughly familiar with their method of warfare; and his predecessor in the chief command in America had recorded his opinions of their falseness and cruelty in the most impassioned language of reprobation. But partly from the sense of his own impotence for offensive war, partly from a moral feebleness which could not vividly picture to itself the atrocity of his orders, Gage was unsusceptible of the suggestions of mercy; and without much compunction, he gave directions to propitiate and inflame the Indians by gifts, and to subsidize their war parties. Before he left America, his commands to employ them pervaded the wilderness to the utmost bounds of his military authority, even to the south and south-west; so that the councils of the Cherokees and Choctaws and Mohawks were named as currently in the correspondence of the secretary of state as the German courts of Hesse and Hanau and Anspach.

In the hope to subdue by terror, the intention of employing Indians was ostentatiously proclaimed. Simultaneously with the application of Gage to the province of Quebec, the president of Columbia college, an Englishman by birth and education, published to the world, that in case submission to parliament should be withheld, civil war would follow, and the Indians would be let loose upon the back settlements to scalp the inhabitants along the border. In this

CHAP. X. 1774. Sept.

kind of warfare there could be no parity between the English and the Americans. The cannibal Indian was a dangerous incumbrance in the camp of a regular army, and not formidable in the array of battle; he was a deadly foe only as he skulked in ambush; or prowled on the frontier; or burned the defenceless farm-house; or struck the laborer in the field; or smote the mother at her household task; or crashed the infant's head against a rock or a tree; or tortured the prisoner on whose flesh he was to gorge. The women and children of England had an ocean between them and the Indian's tomahawk, and had no share in the terror that went before his path, or the sorrows that he left behind.

While Gage was writing for troops from England, from New York, and from Quebec, for French Canadian regiments, and for war-parties of Indians, the militia of Worcester county, hearing of the removal of the powder belonging to the province, rose in a mass and began the march to Boston. On Friday afternoon and Saturday morning, the volunteers from Hampshire county advanced eastward as far as Shrewsbury. On the smallest computation twenty thousand were in motion. The rumor of the seizure reached Israel Putnam, in Connecticut, with the addition, that the British troops and men-of-war had fired on the people and killed six men at the first shot. Sending forward the report to Norwich, New London, New Haven, New York, and so to Philadelphia, he summoned the neighboring militia to take up arms. Thousands started at his call; but these, like the volunteers of Massachusetts, were stopped by expresses from the patriots of Boston, who sent word

CHAP. X. 1774. Sept.

that at present nothing was to be attempted. In return, assurances were given of most effectual support, whenever it might be required. "Words cannot express," wrote Putnam and his committee in behalf of five hundred men under arms at Pomfret, "the gladness discovered by every one at the appearance of a door being opened to avenge the many abuses and insults which those foes to liberty have offered to our brethren in your town and province. But for counter intelligence, we should have had forty thousand men, well equipped and ready to march this morning. Send a written express to the foreman of this committee, when you have occasion for our martial assistance; we shall attend your summons, and shall glory in having a share in the honor of ridding our country of the yoke of tyranny, which our forefathers have not borne, neither will we; and we much desire you to keep a strict guard over the remainder of your powder, for that must be the great means, under God, of the salvation of our country."

"How soon we may need your most effectual aid," answered the Boston committee, "we cannot determine; but agreeably to your wise proposal, we shall give you authentic intelligence on such contingency. The hour of vengeance comes lowering on; repress your ardor, but let us adjure you not to smother it."

This rising was followed by many advantages. Every man was led to supply any deficiencies in his equipments; the people gained confidence in one another; and a method was concerted for calling them into service. Outside of Boston the king's rule was at an end; no man dared to invoke his protection. The wealthy royalists, who entertained no

CHAP. X. 1774. Sept. doubt that all resistance would be crushed by the massive power of Britain, were silent from fear, or fled to Boston, as their "only asylum." Even there they did not feel safe.

By the fifth of September Gage had ordered ground to be broken for fortifications on the neck which formed the only entrance by land into Boston. In the evening the selectmen remonstrated, but with no effect. The next day the convention of Suffolk county, which it had been agreed between Samuel Adams and Warren should send a memorial to the general congress, met in Dedham. Every town and district was represented; and their grand business was referred to a committee, of which Warren was the chairman.

While their report was preparing, the day came for holding the county assize at Worcester. On that morning the main street of the town was occupied on each side by about five thousand men, arranged under their leaders in companies, six deep, and extending for a quarter of a mile. Through this great multitude the judges and their assistants passed safely to the court house; but there they were compelled to stay proceedings, and promise not to take part in executing the unconstitutional act of parliament.

An approval of the resistance of the people was embodied in the careful and elaborate report which Warren on the ninth presented to the adjourned Suffolk convention. "On the wisdom and on the exertions of this important day," such were its words, "is suspended the fate of the new world and of unborn millions." The resolutions which followed, declared that the sovereign who breaks his compact

CHAP. X. 1774. Sept.

with his people, forfeits their allegiance. By their duty to God, their country, themselves and posterity, they pledged the county to maintain their civil and religious liberties, and to transmit them entire to future generations. They rejected as unconstitutional the regulating act of parliament and all the officers appointed under its authority. They enjoined the mandamus councillors to resign their places within eleven days. Attributing to the British commander-in-chief hostile intentions, they directed the collectors of taxes to pay over no money to the treasurer whom he recognised. The governor and council had formerly appointed all military officers; now that the legal council was no longer consulted, they advised the towns to elect for themselves officers of their militia from such as were inflexible friends to the rights of the people. For purposes of provincial government they advised a provincial congress, while they promised respect and submission to the continental congress. In reference to the present hostile appearances on the part of Great Britain, they expressed their determination "to act upon the defensive so long as such conduct might be vindicated by reason and the principles of self-preservation, but no longer." Should Gage arrest any one for political reasons, they promised to seize every crown officer in the province as hostages; and should it become necessary suddenly to summon assistance from the country, they arranged a system of couriers who were to bear written messages to the selectmen or corresponding committees of the several towns. The resolutions which thus concerted an armed resistance, were unanimously adopted, and forwarded by express

CHAP. X. 1774. Sept.

to the continental congress for their consideration and advice. "In a cause so solemn," they said, "our conduct shall be such as to merit the approbation of the wise and the admiration of the brave and free, of every age and of every country."

The good judgment and daring of Warren singled him out above all others then in the province, as the leader of "rebellion." The intrenchments on the neck placed all within the lines at the mercy of the army; yet fearless of heart, he hastened into the presence of Gage, to protest in the name of Suffolk county against the new fortifications that closed the town.

All the while the sufferings of Boston grew more and more severe; yet in the height of distress for want of employment, its carpenters refused to construct barracks for the army. Its inhabitants, who were all invited to share the hospitality of the interior, themselves desired to abandon the town, and even to see it in flames, rather than "to be totally enslaved" by remaining at home; but not knowing how to decide, they looked to congress for advice. Meantime the colony desired to guard against anarchy, by instituting a government of their own, for which they found historical precedents. In the days of William the Deliverer and Mary, Connecticut and Rhode Island had each resumed the charter of government, which James the Second had superseded; the people of Massachusetts now wished to revive their old charter; and continue allegiance to George the Third on no other terms than those which their ancestors had stipulated with Charles the First; "otherwise," said they, "the laws of God of nature, and of nations oblige us to cast about for safety." "If the four New England governments alone adopt the measure," said Hawley of Hampshire, "I will venture my life to carry it against the whole force of Great Britain." In the congress of Worcester county, a motion was made at once to reassume the old charter and elect a governor. Warren, careful lest the province should be thought to aim at greater advantages than the other colonies might be willing to contend for, sought first the consent of the continental congress; reminding its members that one colony of freemen would be a noble bulwark for all America.

New England had already surmounted its greatest difficulties; its enemies now placed their hopes on the supposed timidity of the general congress.

CHAPTER XI.

THE CONTINENT SUPPORTS MASSACHUSETTS.

SEPTEMBER, 1774.

CHAP. XI. 1774. Sept. AMONG the members elected to the continental congress, Galloway of Philadelphia was so thoroughly royalist that he acted as a volunteer spy for the British government. To the delegates from other colonies, as they arrived, he insinuated that "commissioners with full powers should repair to the British court, after the example of the Roman, Grecian, and Macedonian colonies on occasions of the like nature;" but his colleagues spurned the thought of sending envoys to dangle at the heels of a minister, and undergo the scorn of parliament. Yet there was great diversity of opinions respecting the proper modes of resisting the aggressions of the mother country, and conciliation was the ardent wish of all. The South Carolinians greeted the delegates of Massachusetts as the envoys of freedom herself; and the Virginians equalled or surpassed their colleagues in resoluteness and spirit; but all united in desiring to promote "the union of Great Britain and the colonies on a constitutional foundation."

CHAP. XI.

1774. Sept.

On Monday the fifth day of September, the members of congress, meeting at Smith's tavern, moved in a body to select the place for their deliberations. Galloway, the speaker of Pennsylvania, would have had them use the State House, but the carpenters of Philadelphia offered their plain but spacious hall; and from respect for the mechanics, it was accepted by a great majority. The names of the members were then called over, and Patrick Henry, Washington, Richard Henry Lee, Samuel Adams, John Adams, Jay, Gadsden, John Rutledge of South Carolina, the aged Hopkins of Rhode Island, and others, representing eleven colonies, answered to the call. Peyton Randolph, late speaker of the assembly of Virginia, was nominated president by Lynch of Carolina, and was unanimously chosen. The body then named itself "the congress," and its chairman "the president." Jay and Duane would have selected a secretary from among the members themselves, but they found no support; and on the motion of Lynch, Charles Thomson was appointed without further opposition. The measures that were to have divided America bound them closely together. Colonies differing in religious opinions and in commercial interests, in every thing dependent on climate and labor, in usages and manners, swayed by reciprocal prejudices, and frequently quarrelling with each other respecting boundaries, found themselves united in one representative body, and deriving from that union a power that was to be felt throughout the civilized world.

Then arose the question, as to the method of voting. There were fifty-five members; each colony

CHAP. XI. 1774. Sept.

having sent as many as it pleased. Henry, a representative of the largest state, intimated that it would be unjust for a little colony to weigh as much in the councils of America as a great one. "A little colony," observed Sullivan of New Hampshire, "has its all at stake as well as a great one." John Adams admitted that the vote by colonies was unequal, yet that an opposite course would lead to perplexing controversy, for there were no authentic records of the numbers of the people, or the value of their trade. Reserving the subject for further consideration the congress adjourned.

The discussion led the members to exaggerate the population of their respective colonies; and the aggregate of the estimates was made to exceed three millions. Few of them possessed accurate materials; Virginia and the Carolinas had never enumerated the woodsmen among the mountains and beyond them. From returns which were but in part accessible to the congress, it appears that the whole number of white inhabitants in all the thirteen colonies was, in 1774, about two millions one hundred thousand; of blacks, about five hundred thousand; the total population very nearly two millions six hundred thousand.

At the opening of the next day's session, a long and deep silence prevailed. Every one feared the responsibility of a decision which was to influence permanently the relations of independent states. The voice of Virginia was waited for, and was heard through Patrick Henry.

Making a recital of the wrongs inflicted on the colonies by acts of parliament, he declared that all government was dissolved; that they were reduced to a state of nature; that the congress then assembled was but the first in a never ending succession of congresses; that their present decision would form a precedent. Asserting the necessity of union and his own determination to submit to the opinion of the majority, he discussed the mischiefs of an unequal representation, the advantage of a system that should give each colony its just weight; and he breathed the "hope that future ages would quote their proceedings with applause." The democratical part of the constitution, he insisted, must be preserved in its purity. Without absolutely refusing some regard in the adjustment of representation to the opulence of a colony as marked by its exports and imports, he yet himself spoke for a representation of men. "Slaves," said he, "are to be thrown out of the question; if the freemen can be represented according to their numbers, I am satisfied." To the objection that such a representation would confer an undue preponderance on the more populous states, he replied, "British oppression has effaced the boundaries of the several colonies; the distinctions between Virginians, Pennsylvanians, New Yorkers, and New Englanders are no more. I am not a Virginian, but an American." "A compound of numbers and property," said Lynch, of South Carolina, "should determine the weight of the colonies." But he admitted that such a rule could not then be settled. In the same spirit spoke the elder Rutledge. "We have," said he, "no legal authority; and obedience to the measures we adopt will only follow their reasonableness, apparent utility, and necessity. We have no

CHAP. XI.

1774. Sept.

CHAP. XI. 1774. Sept.

coercive authority. Our constituents are bound only in honor to observe our determinations." "I cannot see any way of voting but by colonies," said Gadsden. "Every colony," insisted Ward, of Rhode Island, "should have an equal vote. The counties of Virginia are unequal in point of wealth and numbers, yet each has a right to send two members to its legislature. We come, if necessary, to make a sacrifice of our all, and by such a sacrifice the weakest will suffer as much as the greatest." Harrison, of Virginia, spoke strongly on the opposite side, and was "very apprehensive, that if such a disrespect should be put upon his countrymen, as that Virginia should have no greater weight than the smallest colony, they would never be seen at another convention." But his menace of disunion showed only how little he understood the heart of the Ancient Dominion; and he was at once rebuked by his colleagues. "Though a representation equal to the importance of each colony, were ever so just," said Richard Henry Lee, "the delegates from the several colonies are unprepared with materials to settle that equality." Bland, of Virginia, saw no safety but in voting by colonies. "The question," he added, "is, whether the rights and liberties of America shall be contended for, or given up to arbitrary power." Pendleton acquiesced, yet wished the subject might be open for reconsideration, when proper materials should have been obtained.

This opinion prevailed, and it was resolved that, in taking questions, each colony should have one voice; but the journal adds as the reason, that "the congress was not then able to procure proper materials for ascertaining the importance of each colony." CHAP. XI. 1774. Sept.

Henry, during the debate, had declared "that an entire new government must be founded." "I cannot yet think that all government is at an end," said Jay in reply, "or that we came to frame an American constitution, instead of endeavoring to correct the faults in an old one. The measure of arbitrary power is not full, and it must run over, before we undertake to frame a new constitution."

It was next voted that "the doors be kept shut during the time of business;" and the members bound themselves by their honor to keep the proceedings secret, until the majority should direct them to be made public. The treacherous Galloway pledged his honor with the rest.

To the proposal that congress the next day should be opened with prayer, Jay and Rutledge objected, on account of the great diversity of religious sentiments. "I am no bigot," said Samuel Adams, the Congregationalist; "I can hear a prayer from a man of piety and virtue, who is at the same time a friend to his country;" and on his nomination, Duché, an Episcopal clergyman, was chosen for the service. Before the adjournment, Putnam's express arrived with the report of a bloody attack on the people by the troops at Boston; of Connecticut as well as Massachusetts rising in arms. The next day muffled bells were tolled. At the opening of congress, Washington was present, standing in prayer, and Henry, and Randolph, and Lee, and Jay, and Rutledge, and Gadsden; and by their side Presbyterians and Congregationalists, the Livingstons,

CHAP. XI. 1774. Sept.

Sherman, Samuel Adams, John Adams, and others of New England, who believed that a rude soldiery were then infesting the dwellings and taking the lives of their friends. When the psalm for the day was read, it seemed as if Heaven itself was uttering its oracle. "Oh Lord, fight thou against them that fight against me. Let them that imagine mischief for me be as dust before the wind. Lord, who is like unto thee who deliverest the poor from him that is too strong for him? Lord! how long wilt thou look on? Awake, and stand up to judge my quarrel; avenge thou my cause, my God and my Lord. And as for my tongue, it shall be talking of thy righteousness and of thy praise all the day long." After this the minister unexpectedly burst into an extempore prayer for America, for the congress, for Massachusetts, and especially for Boston, with the earnestness of the best divines of New England.

The congress that day appointed one committee on the rights of the colonies, and another on the British statutes affecting their manufactures and trade. They also received by a second express the same confused account of bloodshed near Boston. Proofs both of the sympathy and the resolution of the continent met the delegates of Massachusetts on every hand; and the cry of "war" was pronounced with firmness.

The next day brought more exact information, and the committee of congress on the rights of the colonies began their deliberations. The first inquiry related to the foundation of those rights. Lee of Virginia rested them on nature. "Our ancestors," he said, "found here no government; and as a consequence had a right to make their own. Charters are an unsafe reliance, for the king's right to grant them has itself been denied. Besides, the right to life, and the right to liberty are inalienable." Jay of New York likewise recurred to the laws of nature. He would not admit the pretension to dominion founded on discovery, and he enumerated among natural rights, the right to emigrate, and the right of the emigrants to erect what government they pleased. John Rutledge, on the contrary, held that allegiance is inalienable; that the first emigrants had not had the right to elect their king; that American claims were derived from the British constitution rather than from the law of nature. But Sherman of Connecticut deduced allegiance from consent, without which the colonies were not bound by the act of settlement. Duane, like Rutledge, shrunk back from the appeal to the law of nature, and founded the power of government on property in land.

Behind all these views lay the question of the power of parliament over the colonies. Dickinson, not yet a member of congress, was fully of opinion that no officer under the new establishment in Massachusetts ought to be acknowledged, but advocated "allowing to parliament the regulation of trade upon principles of necessity, and the mutual interest of both countries." "A right of regulating trade," said Gadsden, true to the principle of 1765, "is a right of legislation, and a right of legislation in one case is a right in all;" and he denied the claim with peremptory energy.

Amidst such varying opinions and theories, the congress, increased by delegates from North Carolina, and intent upon securing absolute unanimity, was

CHAP. XI. moving with great deliberation, and Galloway hoped "the two parties would remain on an equal balance."
1774. Sept. But in that body there was a man who knew how to bring the enthusiasm of the people into connection with its representatives. "Samuel Adams," wrote Galloway, "though by no means remarkable for brilliant abilities, is equal to most men in popular intrigue, and the management of a faction. He eats little, drinks little, sleeps little, and thinks much, and is most decisive and indefatigable in the pursuit of his objects. He was the man who, by his superior application managed at once the faction in congress at Philadelphia, and the factions in New England."

One express had brought from Massachusetts the proceedings of Middlesex; another having now arrived, on Saturday, the seventeenth of September, the delegates of Massachusetts laid before congress the address of the Suffolk county convention to Gage, on his seizure of the provincial stock of powder and his hostile occupation of the only approach to Boston by land; and the resolutions of the same convention which declared that no obedience was due to the acts of parliament affecting their colony.

As the papers were read, expressions of esteem, love and admiration broke forth in generous and manly eloquence. In language which but faintly expressed their spirit, members from all the colonies declared their sympathy with their suffering countrymen in Massachusetts, most thoroughly approved the wisdom and fortitude with which opposition to ministerial measures had hitherto been conducted, and earnestly recommended perseverance according to the resolutions of the county of Suffolk. Knowing that a new parliament must soon be chosen, they expressed their trust "that the united efforts of North America would carry such conviction to the British nation of the unjust and ruinous policy of the present administration, as quickly to introduce better men and wiser measures."

To this end they ordered their own resolutions with the communications from Suffolk county to be printed. But their appeal to the electors of Britain was anticipated. The inflexible king, weighing in advance the possible influence of the American congress, overruled Lord North, and on the last day of September suddenly dissolving parliament, he brought on the new election, before proposals for conciliation could be received.

CHAPTER XII.

THE CONTINENTAL CONGRESS SEEKS TO AVERT INDEPENDENCE.

SEPTEMBER—OCTOBER, 1774.

CHAP. XII. 1774. Sept. GAGE, who came flushed with confidence in an easy victory, at the end of four months was care-worn, disheartened and appalled. With the forces under his command, he hoped for no more than to pass the winter unmolested. At one moment, a suspension of the penal acts was his favorite advice, which the king ridiculed as senseless; at the next he demanded an army of twenty thousand men, to be composed of Canadian recruits, Indians, and hirelings from the continent of Europe; again, he would bring the Americans to terms, by casting them off as fellow-subjects, and not suffering even a boat to go in or out of their harbors. All the while he was exerting himself to obtain payment for the tea as a prelude to reconciliation. His agents wrote to their friends in congress, urging concessions. Such was the advice of Church, in language affecting the highest patriotism; and an officer who had served with Washington sought to persuade his old companion in

CHAP. XII. 1774. Sept.

arms, that New England was conspiring for independence. It was, moreover, insinuated, that if Massachusetts should once resume its old charter, and elect its governor, all New England would unite with her, and become strong enough to absorb the lands of other governments; that New Hampshire would occupy both slopes of the Green Mountains; that Massachusetts would seize the western territory of New York; while Connecticut would appropriate northern Pennsylvania, and compete with Virginia for the West.

Out of Boston the power of Gage was at an end. In the county of Worcester, the male inhabitants from the age of sixteen to seventy, formed themselves into companies and regiments, chose their own officers, and agreed that one-third part of the enrolled should hold themselves ready to march "at a minute's warning." "In time of peace, prepare for war," was the cry of the country. The frugal New England people increased their frugality. "As for me," wrote the wife of a member of congress, "I will seek wool and flax, and work willingly with my hands." Yet the poorest man in his distress would not accept employment from the British army; and the twelve nearest towns agreed to withhold from the troops every supply beyond what humanity required. But all the province, even to Falmouth, and beyond it, shared the sorrows of Boston, and cheered its inhabitants in their sufferings. "This much injured town," said the wife of John Adams, "like the body of a departed friend, has only put off its present glory, to rise finally to a more happy state." Nor did its citizens despair. Its newly elected representatives

CHAP. XII. 1774. Sept.

were instructed never to acknowledge the regulating act; and in case of a dissolution, to join the other members in forming a provincial congress.

The assembly was summoned for the fifth of October, at which time the councillors who had been legally commissioned in May, intended to take their seats; their period of office was a year, and the king's good will was not the condition of their tenure. Against so clear a title the mandamus councillors would not dare to claim their places without a larger escort than they could receive. Gage was in a dilemma. On the twenty-eighth of September, by an anomalous proclamation, he neither dissolved nor prorogued the assembly which he himself had called, but declined to meet it at Salem, and discharged the representatives elect from their duty of attendance.

Meantime, the continental committee on the rights of the colonies having been increased by one member from each of the three provinces, Virginia, Massachusetts, and Pennsylvania, extended their searches to the statutes affecting industry and trade. But in a body whose members were collected from remote parts of the country, accustomed to no uniform rules, differing in their ideas and their forms of expression, distrust could be allayed only by the most patient discussions; and for the sake of unanimity, tedious delay was inevitable.

In the first place, it was silently agreed to rest the demands of America not on considerations of natural rights, but on a historical basis. In this manner, even the appearance of a revolution was avoided; and ideal freedom was claimed only as embodied in facts.

How far the retrospect for grievances should be carried, was the next inquiry. South Carolina would have included all laws restrictive of manufactures and navigation; in a word, all the statutes of which Great Britain had been so prodigal towards her infant colonies, for the purpose of confining their trade, and crippling their domestic industry. But the Virginians, conforming to their instructions, narrowed the issue to the innovations during the reign of George the Third; and as Maryland and North Carolina would not separate from Virginia, the acts of navigation, though condemned by Lee as a capital violation of American rights, were not included in the list of grievances.

The Virginians had never meant to own the binding force of the acts of navigation; the proposal to recognise them came from Duane, of New York; and encountered the strongest opposition. Some wished to deny altogether the authority of parliament; others, its power of taxation; others, its power of internal taxation only. These discussions were drawn into great length, and seemed to promise no agreement; till, at last, John Adams was persuaded to shape a compromise in the spirit and very nearly in the words of Duane. His resolution ran thus: "From the necessity of the case, and a regard to the mutual interest of the countries, we cheerfully consent to the operation of such acts of the British parliament, as are bonâ fide, restrained to the regulation of our external commerce, for the purpose of securing the commercial advantages of the whole empire to the mother country, and the commercial benefits of its respective members; excluding every

CHAP. XII. 1774. Sept.

idea of taxation, internal or external, for raising a revenue on the subjects in America without their consent."

This article was contrary to the principles of Otis at the commencement of the contest; to the repeated declarations of Samuel Adams; to the example of the congress of 1765, which had put aside a similar proposition, when offered by Livingston, of New York. Not one of the committee was fully satisfied with it; yet, as the ablest speaker from Massachusetts was its advocate, the concession was irrevocable. It stands as a monument that the congress harbored no desire but of reconciliation. "I would have given every thing I possessed for a restoration to the state of things before the contest began;" said John Adams at a later day. His resolution accepted that badge of servitude, the British colonial system.

During these discussions, Galloway, of Pennsylvania, in secret concert with the governor of New Jersey and with Colden of New York, proposed for the government of the colonies a president-general, to be appointed by the king, and a grand council to be chosen once in three years by the several assemblies. The British parliament was to have the power of revising the acts of this body; which in its turn was to have a negative on British statutes relating to the colonies. "I am as much a friend to liberty as exists," blustered Galloway, as he presented his insidious proposition, "and no man shall go further in point of fortune or in point of blood, than the man who now addresses you." His scheme held out a hope of a continental union, which was the long cherished policy of New York; it was seconded by

Duane, and advocated by Jay; but opposed by Lee of Virginia. Patrick Henry objected to entrusting the power of taxation to a council to be chosen not directly by the people, but indirectly by its representatives; and he condemned the proposal in all its aspects. "The original constitution of the colonies," said he, "was founded on the broadest and most generous base. The regulation of our trade compensates all the protection we ever experienced. We shall liberate our constituents from a corrupt house of commons, but throw them into the arms of an American legislature, that may be bribed by a nation which in the face of the world avows bribery as a part of her system of government. Before we are obliged to pay taxes as they do, let us be as free as they; let us have our trade open with all the world." "I think the plan almost perfect," said Edward Rutledge. But not one colony, unless it may have been New York, voted in its favor; and no more than a bare majority would consent that it should even lie on the table. Its mover boasted of this small courtesy as of a triumph, though at a later day the congress struck the proposal from its record.

1774. Sept.

With this defeat, Galloway lost his mischievous importance. At the provincial elections in Pennsylvania, on the first day of October, Dickinson, his old opponent, was chosen almost unanimously a representative of the county. Mifflin, though opposed by some of the Quakers as too warm, was elected a burgess of Philadelphia by eleven hundred votes out of thirteen hundred, with Charles Thomson as his colleague. The assembly, on the very day of its organi-

Oct. 1.

CHAP. XII. 1774. Oct.

zation, added Dickinson to its delegation in congress, and he took his seat in season to draft the address of that body to the king.

During the debates on the proper basis of that address, letters from Boston announced that the government continued seizing private military stores, suffering the soldiery "to treat both town and country as declared enemies," fortifying the place, and mounting cannon at its entrance, as though he would hold its inhabitants as hostages, in order to compel a compliance with the new laws. As he had eluded the meeting of the general court, they applied to congress for advice; if the congress should instruct them to quit the town, they would obey. The citizens, who, as a body, had been more affluent than those of any other place of equal numbers in the world, made a formal offer, to abandon their homes, and throw themselves, with their wives and children, their aged and infirm, on the charity of the country people, or build huts in the woods, and never revisit their native walls until re-established in their rights and liberties. The courage of Gadsden blazed up at the thought, and he proposed that Gage should be attacked and routed before reinforcements could arrive; but the congress was resolved to exhaust every means of redress, before sanctioning an appeal to arms.

The spirit of the people was more impetuous; confident in their strength they scorned the thought of obedience, except on conditions that should be satisfactory to themselves. About the middle of October the brig Peggy Stewart, from London, arrived at Annapolis, with two thousand three hun-

CHAP. XII. 1774. Oct.

dred and twenty pounds of tea, on which the owner of the vessel made haste to pay the duty. The people of Maryland resented this voluntary submission to the British claim which their delegates to the general congress were engaged in contesting. The fidelity and honor of the province seemed in question. A committee therefore kept watch, to prevent the landing of the tea; successive public meetings drew throngs even from distant counties; till the two importers and the ship owner jointly expressed their contrition, asked forgiveness in the most humiliating language, and offered to expiate their offence by burning the "detestable article" which had been the cause of their misconduct. When it appeared that this offer did not wholly satisfy the crowd, the owner of the brig, after a little consultation with Charles Carroll, himself proposed to devote that also to the flames. The offer was accepted. The penitent importers and owner went on board the vessel, and with her sails and colors flying, in the presence of a large multitude of gazers, they themselves set fire to the packages of tea, all which, together with the Peggy Stewart, her canvas, cordage, and every appurtenance, was consumed.

CHAPTER XIII.

CONGRESS WILL MAKE THE LAST APPEAL IF NECESSARY.

October, 1774.

CHAP. XIII. 1774. Oct.

Washington was convinced that not one thinking man in all North America desired independence. He ardently wished to end the horrors of civil discord, and restore tranquillity upon constitutional grounds, but his indignation at the wrongs of Boston could be appeased only by their redress; and his purpose to resist the execution of the regulating act was unalterable. "Permit me," said he, addressing a British officer, then serving under Gage, "with the freedom of a friend, to express my sorrow that fortune should place you in a service, that must fix curses to the latest posterity upon the contrivers, and if success (which by the by is impossible) accompanies it, execrations upon all those who have been instrumental in the execution. The Massachusetts people are every day receiving fresh proofs of a systematic assertion of an arbitrary power, deeply planned to overturn the laws and constitution of their country, and to violate the most essential and valuable rights of mankind. It is not the wish of that government, or any other upon this continent, separately or collectively, to set up for independence; but none of them will ever submit to the loss of those rights and privileges without which life, liberty, and property are rendered totally insecure. Is it to be wondered at, that men attempt to avert the impending blow in its progress, or prepare for their defence if it cannot be averted? Give me leave to add as my opinion, that if the ministry are determined to push matters to extremity, more blood will be spilled on this occasion, than history has ever yet furnished instances of in the annals of North America."

Ross, a Pennsylvanian, moved that Massachusetts should be left to her own discretion with respect to government and the administration of justice as well as defence. The motion was seconded by Galloway, in the hope of obstructing the interference of congress. Had it been adopted, under the Pine Tree flag of her forefathers she would have revived her first charter, elected her governor, and established a popular government. But the desire of conciliation forbade a policy so revolutionary. The province was therefore left to its anarchy; but on the eighth of October it was resolved, though not unanimously, "that this congress approve the opposition of the inhabitants of the Massachusetts Bay to the execution of the late acts of parliament; and if the same shall be attempted to be carried into execution by force, in such case, all America ought to support them in their opposition." This is the measure which hardened George the Third to listen to no terms. He was inexorably bent on enforcing the new system of govern-

CHAP. XIII. 1774. Oct. ment in Massachusetts, and extending it to Connecticut and Rhode Island. The congress, when it adopted this resolve, did not know the extent of the aggressions which the king designed. Henceforth conciliation became impossible. Galloway and Duane desired leave to enter their protests against the measure; and as this was refused, they gave to each other privately certificates that they had opposed it as treasonable. But the decision of congress was made deliberately. Two days later, they further "declared that every person who should accept or act under any commission or authority derived from the regulating act of parliament, changing the form of government and violating the charter of Massachusetts, ought to be held in detestation;" and in their letter to Gage, they censured his conduct, as tending "to involve a free people in the horrors of war."

In adopting a declaration of rights, the division which had shown itself in the committee was renewed. "Here," said Ward of Rhode Island, "no acts of parliament can bind. Giving up this point is yielding all." Against him spoke John Adams and Duane. "A right," said Lynch of Carolina, "to bind us in one case may imply a right to bind us in all; but we are bound in none." The resolution of concession was at first arrested by the vote of five colonies against five, with Massachusetts and Rhode Island divided, but at last was carried by the influence of John Adams. Duane desired next to strike the Quebec act from the list of grievances; but of all the bad acts of parliament Richard Henry Lee pronounced it the worst. His opinion prevailed upon a vote which Duane's adhesion made unanimous.

CHAP. XIII. 1774. Oct.

Thus eleven acts of parliament or parts of acts, including the Quebec act and the acts specially affecting Massachusetts, were declared to be such infringements and violations of the rights of the colonies, that the repeal of them was essentially necessary, in order to restore harmony between the colonies and Great Britain.

The congress had unanimously resolved, from the first day of the coming December, not to import any merchandise from Great Britain and Ireland. If the redress of American grievances should be delayed beyond the tenth day of September of the following year, a resolution to export no merchandise to Great Britain, Ireland and the West Indies after that date was carried, but against the voice of South Carolina. When the members proceeded to bind themselves to these measures by an association, three of the delegates of that colony refused their names. "The agreement to stop exports to Great Britain is unequal," reasoned Rutledge; "New England ships little or nothing there, but sends fish, its great staple, to Portugal or Spain; South Carolina annually ships rice to England to the value of a million and a half of dollars. New England would be affected but little by the prohibition; Carolina would be ruined;" and he and two of his colleagues withdrew from the congress. Gadsden, who never counted the cost of patriotism, remained in his place, and trusting to the generosity of his constituents, declared himself ready to sign the association. All business was interrupted for several days; but in the end congress recalled the seceders by allowing the unconditional export of rice.

The association further contained this memorable

CHAP. XIII. 1774. Oct.

covenant, which was adopted without opposition, and inaugurated the abolition of the slave-trade: "We will neither import, nor purchase any slave imported after the first day of December next; after which time we will wholly discontinue the slave-trade, and will neither be concerned in it ourselves, nor will we hire our vessels, nor sell our commodities or manufactures to those who are concerned in it."

This first American congress also adopted another measure, which was without an example. It recognised the political existence and power of the people. While it refused to petition parliament, it addressed the people of the provinces from Nova Scotia to Florida, the people of Canada, the people of Great Britain; making the printing press its great ambassador to the rising power.

Of the British people, congress entreated a return to the system of 1763: "Prior to this era," said they in the language of Jay, "you were content with wealth produced by our commerce. You restrained our trade in every way that could conduce to your emolument. You exercised unbounded sovereignty over the sea." Still assenting to these restrictions, they pleaded earnestly for the enjoyment of equal freedom, and demonstrated that a victory over the rights of America, would not only be barren of advantage to the English nation, but increase their public debt with its attendant pensioners and placemen, diminish their commerce, and lead to the overthrow of their liberties by violence and corruption. "To your justice," they said, "we appeal. You have been told that we are impatient of government and desirous of independency. These are calumnies. Permit us to be as free as yourselves, and we shall ever esteem a union with you to be our greatest glory and our greatest happiness. But if you are determined that your ministers shall wantonly sport with the rights of mankind; if neither the voice of justice, the dictates of law, the principles of the constitution, or the suggestions of humanity, can restrain your hands from shedding human blood in such an impious cause, we must then tell you that we will never submit to any ministry or nation in the world."

CHAP. XIII. 1774. Oct.

A second congress was appointed for May, at which all the colonies of North America, including Nova Scotia and Canada, were invited to appear by their deputies. The ultimate decision of America was then embodied in a petition to the king, written by Dickinson, and imbued in every line with a desire for conciliation. In the list of grievances, congress enumerated the acts, and those only which had been enacted since the year 1763, for the very purpose of changing the constitution or the administration of the colonies. They justified their discontent by fact and right; by historic tradition, and by the ideas of reason. "So far from promoting innovations," said they truly, "we have only opposed them; and can be charged with no offence, unless it be one to receive injuries and be sensible of them." Acquiescing in the restrictions on their ships and industry, they professed a readiness on the part of the colonial legislatures to make suitable provision for the administration of justice, the support of civil government, and for defence, protection, and security in time of peace; in case of war, they pledged the colonies to "most strenuous efforts in granting supplies and rais-

CHAP. XIII. 1774. Oct.

ing forces." But the privilege of thus expressing their affectionate attachment they would "never resign to any body of men upon earth." "We ask," they continued, "but for peace, liberty, and safety. We wish not a diminution of the prerogative, nor the grant of any new right. Your royal authority over us, and our connection with Great Britain, we shall always support and maintain;" and they besought of the king "as the loving father of his whole people, his interposition for their relief, and a gracious answer to their petition."

No more was asked by congress for their constituents than security in their ancient condition. From complacency towards Rockingham, they passed over the declaratory act in silence; and they expressed their cheerful assent to that power of regulating commerce, for which the elder Pitt had always been strenuous. But the best evidence of their sincerity is found in the measure which they recommended. Had independence been their object, they would have strained every nerve to increase their exports, and fill the country in return with the manufactures and munitions which they required. The suspension of trade was the most disinterested manner of expressing to the mother country how deeply they felt their wrongs, and how earnestly they desired a peaceful restoration of reciprocal confidence. While Britain would have only to seek another market for her surplus manufactures and India goods, the American merchant sacrificed nearly his whole business. The exchequer might perhaps suffer some diminution in the revenue from tobacco, but the planters of Maryland and Virginia gave up the entire exchangeable produce of their estates. The cessation of the export of provisions to the West Indies, of flax-seed to Ireland, injured the Northern provinces very deeply; and yet it would touch only the British merchants who had debts to collect in the West Indies or Ireland, or the English owners of West Indian or Irish estates. Every refusal to import was made by the colonist at the cost of personal comfort; every omission to export was a waste of the resources of his family. Moreover, no means existed of enforcing the agreement; so that the truest patriots would suffer most. And yet the people so yearned for a bloodless restoration of the old relations with Britain, that they cheerfully entered on the experiment, in the hope that the extreme self-denial of the country would at least distress British commerce enough to bring the government to reflection.

CHAP. XIII. 1774. Oct.

But since their efforts to avert civil war might fail, John Adams expressed his anxiety to see New England provided with money and military stores. Ward, of Rhode Island, regarded America as the rising power that was to light all the nations of the earth to freedom. Samuel Adams urged his friends incessantly to study the art of war, and organize resistance; for he would never admit that the danger of a rupture with Britain was a sufficient plea for giving way. "I would advise," said he, "persisting in our struggle for liberty, though it were revealed from heaven that nine hundred and ninety-nine were to perish, and only one of a thousand to survive and retain his liberty. One such freeman must possess more virtue, and enjoy more happiness, than a thousand slaves; and let him propagate his like, and

CHAP. XIII. 1774. Oct.

transmit to them what he hath so nobly preserved." "Delightful as peace is," said Dickinson, "it will come more grateful, by being unexpected." Washington, while he promoted the measures of congress, dared not hope that they would prove effectual. When Patrick Henry read the prophetic words of Hawley, "after all we must fight," he raised his hand, and with the entire energy of his nature, called God to witness as he cried out, "I am of that man's mind."

CHAPTER XIV.

HOW CATHOLIC EMANCIPATION BEGAN.

OCTOBER, 1774.

THE congress of 1774 contained statesmen of the highest order of wisdom. For eloquence Patrick Henry was unrivalled; next to him, the elder Rutledge of South Carolina was the ablest in debate; "but if you speak of solid information and sound judgment," said Patrick Henry, "Washington is unquestionably the greatest man of them all." CHAP. XIV. 1774. Oct.

While the delegates of the twelve colonies were in session in Philadelphia, ninety of the members just elected to the Massachusetts assembly appeared on Wednesday the fifth of October at the court house in Salem. After waiting two days for the governor, they passed judgment on his unconstitutional proclamation against their meeting, and resolving themselves into a provincial congress, they adjourned to Concord. There, on Tuesday the eleventh, about two hundred and sixty members took their seats, and elected John Hancock their president. On the fourteenth they sent a message to the governor, that for

CHAP. XIV. 1774. Oct.

want of a general assembly they had convened in congress; and they remonstrated against his hostile preparations. A committee from Worcester county made similar representations. "It is in your power to prevent civil war, and to establish your character as a wise and humane man," said the chairman. "For God's sake," replied Gage, in great trepidation, "what would you have me do?" for he vacillated between a hope that the king would give way, and a willingness to be the instrument of his obstinacy. To the president of the continental congress, he expressed the wish that the disputes between the mother country and the colonies might terminate like lovers' quarrels; but he did not conceal his belief that its proceedings would heighten the anger of the king.

To the provincial congress, which had again adjourned from Concord to Cambridge, Gage made answer by recriminations. They on their part were surrounded by difficulties. They wished to remove the people of Boston into the country, but found it impracticable. A committee appointed on the twenty-fourth of October to consider the proper time to provide a stock of powder, ordnance, and ordnance stores, reported on the same day, that the proper time was now. Upon the debate for raising money to prepare for the crisis, one member proposed to appropriate a thousand pounds, another two thousand; a committee reported a sum of less than ninety thousand dollars, as a preparation against a warlike empire, flushed with victory, and able to spend twenty million pounds sterling a year in the conduct of a war. They elected three general officers by ballot. A committee of safety, Hancock and Warren being of the number, was invested with power to alarm and muster the militia of the province, of whom one-fourth were to hold themselves ready to march at a minute's notice. CHAP. XIV. 1774. Oct.

In Connecticut, which, from its compactness, numbers, and wealth, was second only to Massachusetts in military resources, the legislature of 1774 provided for effectively organizing the militia, prohibited the importation of slaves, and ordered the several towns to provide double the usual quantity of powder, balls, and flints. They also directed the issue of fifteen thousand pounds in bills of credit of the colony, and made a small increase of the taxes. This was the first issue of paper money in the colonies preparatory to war.

The congress of Massachusetts, in like manner, directed the people of the province to perfect themselves in military skill, and each town to provide a full stock of arms and ammunition. Having voted to pay no more money to the royal collector, they chose a receiver-general of their own, and instituted a system of provincial taxation. They appointed executive committees of safety, of correspondence, and of supplies. As the continental congress would not sanction their resuming the charter from Charles the First, they adhered as nearly as possible to that granted by William and Mary; and summoned the councillors duly elected under that charter, to give attendance on the fourth Wednesday of November, to which time they adjourned. To their next meeting they referred the consideration of the propriety of sending agents to Canada.

The American revolution was destined on every

CHAP. XIV. 1774. Oct.

side to lead to the solution of the highest questions of state. Principles of eternal truth, which in their universality are superior to sects and separate creeds, were rapidly effacing the prejudices of the past. The troubles of the thirteen colonies led the court of Great Britain to its first step in the emancipation of Catholics; and with no higher object in view than to strengthen the authority of the king in America, the Quebec act of 1774 began that series of concessions, which did not cease till the British parliament itself, and the high offices of administration have become accessible to "papists."

In the belief that the loyalty of its possessions had been promoted by a dread of the French settlements on their northern and western frontier, Britain sought to create under its own auspices a distinct empire, suited to coerce her original colonies, and restrain them from aspiring to independence. For this end it united into one province the territory of Canada, together with all the country northwest of the Ohio to the head of Lake Superior and the Mississippi, and consolidated all authority over this boundless region in the hands of the executive power. The Catholics were not displeased that the promise of a representative assembly was not kept. In 1763 they had all been disfranchised in a land where there were few Protestants, except attendants on the army and government officials. A representative assembly, to which none but Protestants could be chosen, would have subjected almost the whole body of resident inhabitants to an oligarchy, hateful by their race and religion; their supremacy as conquerors, and their selfishness. The Quebec act authorized the crown to confer posts of honor and of business upon Catholics; and they chose rather to depend on the clemency of the king, than to have an exclusively Protestant parliament, like that of Ireland. This limited political toleration left no room for the sentiment of patriotism. The French Canadians of that day could not persuade themselves that they had a country. They would have desired an assembly, to which they should be eligible; but since that was not to be obtained, they accepted their partial enfranchisement by the king, as a boon to a conquered people.

CHAP. XIV.

1774. Oct.

The owners of estates were further gratified by the restoration of the French system of law. The English emigrants might complain of the want of jury trials in civil processes; but the French Canadians were grateful for relief from statutes which they did not comprehend, and from the chicanery of unfamiliar courts. The nobility of New France, who were accustomed to arms, were still further conciliated by the proposal to enroll Canadian battalions, in which they could hold commissions on equal terms with English officers. Here also the inspiration of nationality was wanting; and the whole population could never crowd to the British flag, as they had rallied to the lilies of France. There would remain always the sentiment, that they were waging battle not for themselves, and defending a government which was not their own.

The great dependence of the crown was on the clergy. The capitulation of New France had guaranteed to them freedom of public worship; but the laws for their support were held to be no longer valid. By the Quebec act they were confirmed in the posses-

CHAP. XIV. 1774. Oct.

sion of their ancient churches and their revenues; so that the Roman Catholic worship was as effectually established in Canada, as the Presbyterian Church in Scotland. When Carleton returned to his government, bearing this great measure of conciliation, of which he was known to have been the adviser, he was welcomed by the Catholic bishop and priests of Quebec with professions of loyalty; and the memory of Thurlow and Wedderburn, who carried the act through parliament, is gratefully embalmed in Canadian history. And yet the clergy were conscious that the concession of the great privileges which they now obtained, was but an act of worldly policy, mainly due to the disturbed state of the Protestant colonies. Their joy at relief was sincere, but still, for the cause of Great Britain, Catholic Canada could not uplift the banner of the King of Heaven, or seek the perils of martyrdom. The tendency to revolution on the part of its Roman Catholic hierarchy was restrained, but England never acquired the impassioned support of its religious zeal.

Such was the frame of mind of the French Canadians when the American congress sent among them its appeal. The time was come for applying the new principle of the power of the people to the old divisions in Christendom between the Catholic and the Protestant world. Protestantism, in the sphere of politics, had hitherto been the representative of that increase of popular liberty which had grown out of free inquiry; while the Catholic Church, under the early influence of Roman law, had inclined to monarchical power. These relations were now to be modified.

The Catholic church asserted the unity, the universality, and the unchangeableness of truth; and this principle, however it may have been made subservient to ecclesiastical organization, tyranny, or superstition, rather demanded than opposed universal emancipation and brotherhood. Yet the thirteen colonies were all Protestant; even in Maryland the Catholics formed but an eighth, or perhaps not more than a twelfth, part of the population; their presence in other provinces was hardly perceptible, except in Pennsylvania. The members of congress had not wholly purged themselves of Protestant bigotry. Something of this appeared in their resolutions of rights, and in their address to the people of British America. In the address to the people of Great Britain, it was even said that the Roman Catholic religion had "dispersed impiety, bigotry, persecution, murder, and rebellion through every part of the world." But the desire of including Canada in the confederacy compelled the Protestants of America to adopt and promulgate the principle of religious equality and freedom. In the masterly address to the inhabitants of the province of Quebec, drawn by Dickinson, all old religious jealousies were condemned as low-minded infirmities; and the Swiss cantons were cited as examples of a union composed of Catholic and Protestant states.

Appeals were also made to the vanity and the pride of the French population. After a clear and precise analysis of the Quebec act, and the contrast of its provisions with English liberties, the shade of Montesquieu was evoked, as himself saying to the Canadians: "Seize the opportunity presented to you

CHAP. XIV. 1774. Oct.

by Providence itself. You have been conquered into liberty, if you act as you ought. This work is not of man. You are a small people, compared to those who with open arms invite you into a fellowship. The injuries of Boston have roused and associated every colony from Nova Scotia to Georgia. Your province is the only link wanting to complete the bright and strong chain of union. Nature has joined your country to theirs; do you join your political interests; for their own sakes they never will desert or betray you. The happiness of a people inevitably depends on their liberty, and their spirit to assert it. The value and extent of the advantages tendered to you are immense. Heaven grant you may not discover them to be blessings after they have bid you an eternal adieu."

With such persuasions, the congress unanimously invited the Canadians to "accede to their confederation." Whether the invitation should be accepted or repelled, the old feud between the nations which adhered to the Roman Catholic church, and the free governments which had sprung from Protestantism, was fast coming to an end.

CHAPTER XV.

THE GOVERNOR OF VIRGINIA NULLIFIES THE QUEBEC ACT.

OCTOBER—NOVEMBER, 1774.

CHAP. XV. 1774.

THE attempt to extend the jurisdiction of Quebec to the Ohio river had no sanction in English history, and was resisted by the older colonies, especially by Virginia. The interest of the crown offices in the adjacent provinces was also at variance with the policy of parliament.

No royal governor showed more rapacity in the use of official power than Lord Dunmore. He had reluctantly left New York, where, during his short career, he had acquired fifty thousand acres of land, and himself acting as chancellor, was preparing to decide in his own court in his own favor, a large and unfounded claim which he had preferred against the lieutenant governor. Upon entering on the government of Virginia, his passion for land and fees, outweighing the proclamation of the king and reiterated and most positive instructions from the secretary of state, he advocated the claims of the colony to the West; and was himself a partner in two immense purchases of

CHAP. XV. 1774. land from the Indians in southern Illinois. In 1773, his agents, the Bullets, made surveys at the falls of the Ohio; and a part of Louisville, and of the towns opsite Cincinnati, are now held under his warrant. The area of the Ancient Dominion expanded with his cupidity.

Pittsburg, and the country as far up the Monongahela as Redstone Old Fort, formed the rallying point for western emigration and Indian trade. It was a part of the county of Westmoreland, in Pennsylvania. Suddenly and without proper notice to the council of that province, Dunmore extended his own jurisdiction over the tempting and well-peopled region. He found a willing instrument in one John Conolly, a native of Pennsylvania, a physician, land-jobber, and subservient political intriguer, who had travelled much in the Ohio valley, both by water and land. Commissioned by Dunmore as captain-commandant for Pittsburg and its dependencies, that is to say of all the western country, Conolly opened the year 1774 with a proclamation of his authority; and he directed a muster of the militia. The western people, especially the emigrants from Maryland and Virginia, spurned the meek tenets of the Quakers, and inclined to the usurpation. The governor and council of Pennsylvania took measures to support their indisputable right. This Dunmore passionately resented as a personal insult, and would neither listen to irrefragable arguments, nor to candid offers of settlement by joint commissioners, nor to the personal application of two of the council of Pennsylvania. Jurisdiction was opposed to jurisdiction; arrests were followed by counter arrests; the country on the Monongahela, then the great avenue to the West, became a scene of confusion. CHAP. XV.

The territory north and west of the Ohio, belonged by act of parliament to the province of Quebec; yet Dunmore professed to conduct the government and grant the lands on the Scioto, the Wabash and the Illinois. South of the Ohio river Franklin's inchoate province of Vandalia stretched from the Alleghanies to Kentucky river; the treaty at Fort Stanwix bounded Virginia by the Tennessee; the treaty at Lochaber carried its limit only to the mouth of the Great Kanawha. The king's instructions confined settlements to the east of the mountains. There was no one, therefore, having authority to give an undisputed title to any land west of the Alleghanies, or to restrain the restlessness of the American emigrants. With the love of wandering that formed a part of their nature, the hardy backwoodsman, clad in a hunting shirt and deerskin leggins, armed with a rifle, a powder horn, and a pouch for shot and bullets, a hatchet and a hunter's knife, descended the mountains in quest of more distant lands which he forever imagined to be richer and lovelier than those which he knew. Wherever he fixed his halt, the hatchet hewed logs for his cabin, and blazed trees of the forest kept the record of his title deeds; nor did he conceive that a British government had any right to forbid the occupation of lands, which were either uninhabited or only broken by a few scattered villages of savages, whom he looked upon as but little removed above the brute creation. 1774.

The Indians themselves were regardless of treaties. Notwithstanding the agreement with Bouquet

CHAP. XV. 1774. they still held young men and women of Virginia in captivity; and the annals of the wilderness never ceased to record their barbarous murders. The wanderer in search of a new home on the banks of the Mississippi, risked his life at every step; so that a system of independent defence and private war became the custom of the backwoods. The settler had every motive to preserve peace; yet he could not be turned from his purpose by fear, and trusted for security in the forest to his perpetual readiness for self-defence. Not a year passed away without a massacre of pioneers. Near the end of 1773, Daniel Boone would have taken his wife and children to Kentucky. At Powell's valley, he was joined by five families and forty men. On or near the tenth of October, as they approached Cumberland Gap, the young men who had charge of the pack-horses and cattle in the rear, were suddenly attacked by Indians; one only escaped; the remaining six, among whom was Boone's eldest son, were killed on the spot; so that the survivors of the party were forced to turn back to the settlements on Clinch river. When the Cherokees were summoned from Virginia to give up the offenders, they shifted the accusation from one tribe to another, and the application for redress had
Oct. 1. no effect; but one of those who had escaped, murdered an Indian at a horse race on the frontier, notwithstanding the interposition of all around. This was the first Indian blood shed by a white man from the time of the treaty of Bouquet.

In the beginning of February, 1774, the Indians killed six white men and two negroes; and near the end of the same month, they seized a trading canoe on the Ohio, killed the men on board, and carried their goods to the Shawanese towns. In March, Michael Cresap, after a skirmish, and the loss of one man on each side, took from a party of Indians five loaded canoes. It became known that messages were passing between the tribes of the Ohio, the western Indians, and the Cherokees. In this state of affairs, Conolly, from Pittsburg, on the twenty-first of April, wrote to the inhabitants of Wheeling to be on the alert.

Incensed by the succession of murders, the backwoodsmen, who were hunters like the Indians and equally ungovernable, were forming war parties along the frontier from the Cherokee country to Pennsylvania. When the letter of Conolly fell into Cresap's hands, he and his party esteemed themselves authorized to engage in private war, and on the twenty-sixth of April, they fired upon two Indians who were with a white man in a canoe on the Ohio, and killed them both. Just before the end of April, five Delawares and Shawanese, with their women, among whom was one at least of the same blood with Logan, happening to encamp near Yellow Creek, on the site of the present town of Wellsville, were enticed across the river by a trader; and when they had become intoxicated, were murdered in cold blood. Two others, crossing the Ohio to look after their friends, were shot down as soon as they came ashore. At this five more, who were following, turned their course; but being immediately fired at, two were killed and two wounded. The day following, a Shawanese was killed, and another man wounded. The whole number of Indians killed between the

CHAP. XV. twenty-first of April and the end of the month, was about thirteen.

1774. At the tidings of this bloodshed, fleet messengers of the Red Men ran with the wail of war to the Muskingum, and to the Shawanese villages in Ohio. The alarm of the emigrants increased along the frontier from the Watauga to the lower Monongahela; and frequent expresses reached Williamsburg, entreating assistance. The governor, following an intimation from the assembly in May, ordered the militia of the frontier counties to be embodied for defence. Meantime Logan's soul called within him for revenge. In his early life he had dwelt near the beautiful plain of Shamokin, which overhangs the Susquehanna and the vale of Sunbury. There Zinzendorf introduced the Cayuga chief, his father, to the Moravians; and there, three years later, Brainerd wore away life as a missionary among the fifty cabins of the village. Logan had grown up as the friend of white men; but the spirits of his kindred clamored for blood. With chosen companions, he went out upon the war path, and added scalp to scalp, till the number was also thirteen. "Now," said the chief, "I am satisfied for the loss of my relations, and will sit still."

But the Shawanese, the most warlike of the tribes, prowled from the Alleghany river to what is now Sullivan county in Tennessee. One of them returned with the scalps of forty men, women, and children. On the other hand, a party of white men, with Dunmore's permission, destroyed an Indian village on the Muskingum.

To restrain the backwoodsmen and end the mise-

CHAP. XV. 1774. Sept.

ries which distracted the frontier, and to look after his own interests and his agents, Dunmore, with the hearty approbation of the colony, called out the militia of the southwest, and himself repaired to Pittsburg. In September he renewed peace with the Delawares and the Six Nations. Then, with about twelve hundred men from the counties around him, he descended the Ohio; and without waiting, as he had promised, at the mouth of the little Kanawha, for the men from the southwestern counties of Virginia, he crossed the river and proceeded to the Shawanese towns, which he found deserted.

The summons from Dunmore, borne beyond the Blue Ridge, roused the settlers on the Green Briar, the New River, and the Holston. The Watauga republicans also, who never owned English rule, and never required English protection, heard the cry of their brethren in distress; and a company of nearly fifty of them, under the command of Evan Shelby, with James Robertson and Valentine Sevier as sergeants, marched as volunteers. The name of every one of them is preserved and cherished. Leaving home in August, they crossed the New river, and joined the army of western Virginia at Camp Union, on the Great Levels of Green Briar. From that place, now called Lewisburg, to the mouth of the Great Kanawha, the distance is about one hundred and sixty miles. At that time there was not even a trace over the rugged mountains; but the gallant young woodsmen who formed the advance party, moved expeditiously with their packhorses and droves of cattle through the old home of the wolf, the deer, and the panther. After a fortnight's strug-

CHAP. XV. gle, they left behind them the last rocky masses of the hill-tops; and passing between the gigantic
1774. Sept. growth of primeval forests where, in that autumnal season, the golden hue of the linden, the sugar tree, and the hickory, contrasted with the glistening green of the laurel, the crimson of the sumach, and the shadows of the sombre hemlock, they descended to where the valley of Elk river widens into a plain.
Oct. There they paused only to build canoes; having been joined by a second party, so that they made a force of nearly eleven hundred men, they descended the Kanawha, and on the sixth of October encamped on Point Pleasant, near its junction with the Ohio. But no message reached them from Dunmore.

Of all the Western Indians, the Shawanese were the fiercest. They despised other warriors, red or white; and made a boast of having killed ten times as many of the English as any other tribe. They stole through the forest with Mingoes and Delawares, to attack the army of southwestern Virginia.

At daybreak on Monday, the tenth of October, two young men, rambling up the Ohio in search of deer, fell on the camp of the Indians, who had crossed the river the evening before, and were just preparing for battle. One of the two was instantly shot down; the other fled with the intelligence to the camp. In two or three minutes after, Robertson and Sevier of Shelby's company came in and confirmed the account. Colonel Andrew Lewis, who had the command, instantly ordered out two divisions, each of one hundred and fifty men; the Augusta troops, under his brother Charles Lewis, the Botetourt troops under Fleming. Just as the sun was rising, the Indians opened a heavy fire on both parties; wounding Charles Lewis mortally. Fleming was wounded thrice; and the Virginians must have given way, but for successive reinforcements from the camp. "Be strong," cried Cornstalk, the chief of the Red Men; and he animated them by his example. Till the hour of noon, the combatants fought from behind trees, never above twenty yards apart, often within six, and sometimes close enough to strike with the tomahawk. At length the Indians, under the protection of the close underwood and fallen trees, retreated, till they gained an advantageous line extending from the Ohio to the Kanawha. A desultory fire was kept up on both sides till after sunset, when under the favor of night, the savages fled across the river. The victory cost the Virginians three colonels of militia, forty-six men killed and about eighty wounded.

This battle was the most bloody and best contested in the annals of forest warfare. The number of the Red Men who were engaged, was probably not less than eight hundred; how many of them fell was never ascertained.

The heroes of that day proved themselves worthy to found states. Among them were Isaac Shelby, the first governor of Kentucky; William Campbell; the brave George Matthews; Fleming; Andrew Moore, afterwards a senator of the United States; Evan Shelby, James Robertson, and Valentine Sevier. Their praise resounded not in the backwoods only, but through all Virginia.

Soon after the battle a reinforcement of three hundred troops arrived from Fincastle. Following

CHAP. XV. 1774. Oct.

orders tardily received from Dunmore, the little army, leaving a garrison at Point Pleasant, dashed across the Ohio to defy new battles. After a march of eighty miles through an untrodden wilderness, on the twenty-fourth of October they encamped on the banks of Congo Creek in Pickaway, near old Chillicothe. The Indians, disheartened at the junction, threw themselves on the mercy of the English; and at Camp Charlotte, which stood on the left bank of Sippo Creek, about seven miles southeast of Circleville, Dunmore admitted them to a conference. Logan did not appear; but through an Indian interpreter he sent this message:

"I appeal to any white man to say if he ever entered Logan's cabin, and I gave him not meat; if he ever came naked, and I clothed him not. In the course of the last war Logan remained in his cabin, an advocate for peace. Such was my love for the whites that the rest of my nation pointed at me, and said, 'Logan is the friend of white men.' I should have ever lived with them, had it not been for one man, who, last spring, cut off, unprovoked, all the relations of Logan, not sparing women and children. There runs not a drop of my blood in the veins of any living creature. This called upon me for revenge. I have sought it; I have killed many, and fully glutted my revenge. For my nation, I rejoice in the beams of peace; but nothing I have said proceeds from fear! Logan disdains the thought! He will not turn on his heel to save his life! Who is there to mourn for Logan? Not one."

Before the council was brought to a close, all differences were adjusted. The Shawanese agreed to deliver up their prisoners without reserve; to restore all horses and other property which they had carried off; to hunt no more on the Kentucky side of the Ohio; to molest no boats passing on the river; to regulate their trade by the king's instructions, and to deliver up hostages. Virginia has left on record her judgment, that Dunmore's conduct in this campaign was "truly noble, wise, and spirited." The results inured exclusively to the benefit of America. The Indians desired peace; the rancor of the white people changed to confidence, and the Virginian army, appearing as umpire in the valley of the Scioto, nullified the statute which extended the jurisdiction of Quebec to the Ohio.

CHAP. XV. 1774. Oct.

The western Virginians, moreover, halting at Fort Gower on the north of the Ohio, on the fifth of November, took their part in considering the grievances of their country. They were "blessed with the talents" to bear all hardships of the woods; to pass weeks comfortably without bread or salt; for dress, to be satisfied with a blanket, or a hunting shirt and skins; to sleep with no covering but heaven; to march further in a day than any men in the world, and to use the rifle with a precision that to all but themselves was a miracle. For three months they had heard nothing from the east, where some jealousy might arise of so large a body of armed men under a leader like Dunmore. They, therefore, held themselves bound to publish their sentiments. Professing zeal for the honor of America and especially Virginia, they promised continued allegiance to the king, if he would but reign over them as "a brave and free people." "But," said they, "as attachment to the

Nov. 5.

CHAP. XV. 1774. real interests and just rights of America outweigh every other consideration, we resolve that we will exert every power within us for the defence of American liberty, when regularly called forth by the unanimous voice of our countrymen."

America contrasted the regiments of regulars at Boston, ingloriously idle and having no purpose but to enslave a self-protected province, with the noble Virginians braving danger at the call of a royal governor, and pouring out their blood to win the victory for western civilization."

CHAPTER XVI.

THE FOURTEENTH PARLIAMENT OF GREAT BRITAIN.

October—December, 1774.

"It is the united voice of America to preserve their freedom, or lose their lives in defence of it. Their resolutions are not the effect of inconsiderate rashness, but the sound result of sober inquiry and deliberation. The true spirit of liberty was never so universally diffused through all ranks and orders of people in any country on the face of the earth, as it now is through all North America. If the late acts of parliament are not to be repealed, the wisest step for both countries is to separate, and not to spend their blood and treasure in destroying each other. It is barely possible that Great Britain may depopulate North America; she never can conquer the inhabitants." So wrote Joseph Warren, and his words were the mirror of the passions of his countrymen. They were addressed to the younger Quincy, who as a private man had crossed the Atlantic to watch the disposition of the ministry; they were intended to be made known in England, in the hope of awaken-

CHAP. XVI. ing the king and his ministers from the delusion that America could be intimidated into submission.

1774. Oct. Nov. The eyes of the world were riveted on Franklin and George the Third. The former was environed by dangers; Gage was his willing accuser from Boston; the hatred which Hutchinson bore him never slumbered; the ministry affected to consider him as the cause of all the troubles; he knew himself to be in daily peril of arrest; but "the great friends of the colonies" entreated him to stay, and some glimmering of hope remained, that the manufacturers and merchants of England would successfully interpose their mediating influence. The king on his part never once harbored the thought of concession; and "left the choice of war or peace" to depend on the obedience of Massachusetts.

The new elections to parliament came on, while the people of England were still swayed by pride; and the question was artfully misrepresented, as though it were only that Massachusetts refused to pay a just and very moderate indemnity for property destroyed by a mob, and resisted an evident improvement in its administrative system, from a deliberate conspiracy with other colonies to dissolve the connection with the mother country. During the progress of the canvass, bribery came to the aid of the ministry, for many of the members who were purchasing seats, expected to reimburse themselves by selling their votes to the government.

The shrewd French minister at London, witnessing the briskness of the traffic, bethought himself that where elections depended on the purse, the king of France might buy a borough as rightfully at least as the king of England, who, by law and the constitution, was bound to guard the franchises of his people against corruption. "You will learn with interest," thus Garnier, in November, announced his bargain to Vergennes, "that you will have in the house of commons, a member who will belong to you. His vote will not help us much; but the copies of even the most secret papers, and the clear and exact report which he can daily furnish us, will contribute essentially to the king's service."

Excess had impoverished many even of the heirs to the largest estates, and lords as well as commoners offered themselves at market; so that "if America," said Franklin, "would save for three or four years the money she spends in the fashions and fineries and fopperies of this country, she might buy the whole parliament, ministry and all."

In the general venality, Edmund Burke was displaced. Lord Varney, who had hitherto gratuitously brought him into parliament, had fallen into debt, and instead of carrying along his investment in the chance of Rockingham's return to the ministry, he turned his back on deferred hopes and friendship, and pocketed for his borough the most cash he could get.

Burke next coquetted with Wilkes for support at Westminster; but "the great patriot" preferred Lord Mahon. "Wilkes has touched Lord Mahon's money, and desires to extort more by stirring up a multitude of candidates," said Burke, in the fretful hallucinations of his chagrin; while, in fact, the influence of Wilkes was of no avail; Westminster shared the prevalent excitement against America and elected to-

CHAP. XVI. 1774. Oct. Nov. ries. Sometimes, when alone, Burke fell into an inexpressible melancholy, and thought of renouncing public life, for which he owned himself unfit. There seemed for him no way to St. Stephen's chapel, except through a rotten borough belonging to Rockingham; and what influence would the first man in England for speculative intelligence exert in the house of commons, if he should appear there as the paid agent of an American colony and the nominee of an English patron?

Such seemed his best hope, when, on the eleventh of October, he was invited to become a candidate at Bristol against Viscount Clare, the statesman who in the debates on repealing the stamp act, had stickled for "the peppercorn" from America. He hastened to the contest with alacrity, avowing for his principle British superiority, which was yet to be reconciled with American liberty; and after a struggle of three weeks, he, with Cruger of New York as his colleague, was elected one of the representatives of the great trading city of western England.

Bristol was almost the only place which changed its representation to the advantage of America; Wilkes was successful in the county of Middlesex, and after a ten years' struggle, the king, from zeal to concentrate opinion against America, made no further opposition to his admittance; but in the aggregate the ministry increased its majorities.

It was noticeable that Sir William Howe was returned for Nottingham. To the questions of that liberal constituency he freely answered, that the ministry had pushed matters too far; that the whole British army would not be sufficient to conquer

America; that if offered a command there, he would refuse it; that he would vote for the repeal of the four penal acts of parliament; and he turned to his advantage the affectionate respect still cherished for his brother who fell near Lake George. 1774. Oct. Nov.

The elections were over, and it was evident that the government might have every thing its own way, when, on the eighteenth of November, letters of the preceding September, received from Gage, announced that the act of parliament for regulating the government of Massachusetts could be carried into effect only after the conquest of all the New England colonies; that the province had warm friends throughout the North American continent; that people in Carolina were "as mad" as in Boston; that the country people in Massachusetts, Connecticut, and Rhode Island were exercising in arms and forming magazines of ammunition and such artillery, good and bad, as they could procure; that the civil officers of the British government had no asylum but Boston. In a private letter Gage proposed that the obnoxious acts should be suspended. In an official paper he hinted that it would be well to cut the colonies adrift, and leave them to anarchy and repentance; they had grown opulent through Britain, and were they cast off and declared aliens, they must become a poor and needy people. But the king heard these suggestions with scorn. "The New England governments," said he to North, "are now in a state of rebellion. Blows must decide whether they are to be subject to this country or to be independent." This was his instant determination, to which he obstinately adhered. On the other hand, Franklin, who was confident of the Nov.

CHAP. XVI. 1774. Nov. 30. triumph of liberty, explicitly avowed to his nearest friends, that there was now no safety for his native country but in total emancipation. In this condition of affairs the fourteenth parliament was opened on the last day of November.

British influence during the summer had assisted in establishing between the Czar and the Ottoman Porte the peace which was so glorious and eventful for Russia. The speech from the throne could offer congratulations on the tranquillity of Europe, and fix attention on the disobedience in Massachusetts. In the house of lords, Hillsborough moved an address, expressing abhorrence of the principles which that province maintained; and when the duke of Richmond attempted to postpone adopting opinions which might lead to measures fatal to the lives, property, and liberties of a very great part of their fellow-subjects, it was replied, that the sooner and the more spiritedly the new parliament spoke out upon the subject, the better. "I advised the dissolution," said one of the ministers, "lest popular dissatisfaction arising from untoward events, should break the chain of those public measures, necessary to reduce the colonies to obedience." "There are now men walking in the streets of London, who ought to be in Newgate, or at Tyburn," said Hillsborough; referring to Quincy and to Franklin. After a long and vehement debate, his motion prevailed by a vote of about five to one. But Rockingham, Shelburne, Camden, Stanhope, and five other peers made a written protest against "the inconsiderate temerity which might precipitate the country into a civil war." "The king's speech," wrote Garnier to Vergennes, "will complete the work of alienating the colonies. Every day makes a conciliation more difficult, and every day will make it more necessary."

On the fifth of December, the new house of commons debated the same subject. Fox, Burke, and others, spoke warmly. The results of the congress had not yet arrived, for the vessel which bore them had, after ten days, put back to New York in distress. Lord North could therefore say that America had as yet offered no terms; at the same time he avoided the irrevocable word rebellion. Some called the Americans cowards; some questioned their being in earnest; and though Barrē declared the scheme of subduing them "wild and impracticable," the minister was sustained by a very great majority.

The victory brought no peace of mind to Lord North. He had neither originated nor fully approved the American measures, which he had himself brought forward. Constantly thwarted in the cabinet by his colleagues, he vainly struggled to emancipate himself from a system which he abhorred, and for which the real authors were neither legally nor ostensibly answerable, and he sought an escape from his dilemma by proposing to send out commissioners of inquiry. But the king promptly overruled the suggestion.

Friends of Franklin were next employed to ascertain the extent of his demands for America; and without waiting for the proceedings of congress, he wrote "hints on the terms that might produce a durable union between Great Britain and the colonies." Assuming that the tea duty act would be repealed, he offered payment for the tea that had been

CHAP. XVI. 1774. Dec.

destroyed, support of the peace establishment and government, liberal aids in time of war on requisition by the king and parliament, a continuance of the same aids in time of peace, if Britain would give up its monopoly of American commerce. On the other hand, among various propositions, he asked the repeal of the Quebec act, and insisted on the repeal of the acts regulating the government and changing the laws of Massachusetts. "The old colonies," it was objected, "have nothing to do with the affairs of Canada." "We assisted in its conquest," said Franklin; "loving liberty ourselves, we wish to have no foundation for future slavery laid in America." "The Massachusetts act," it was urged, "is an improvement of that government." "The pretended amendments are real mischiefs," answered Franklin; "but were it not so, charters are compacts between two parties, the king and the people, not to be altered even for the better but by the consent of both. The parliament's claim and exercise of a power to alter charters, which had been always held inviolable, and to alter laws which, having received the royal approbation, had been deemed fixed and unchangeable but by the powers that made them, have rendered all our constitutions uncertain. As by claiming a right to tax at will, you deprive us of all property, so by this claim of altering our laws at will, you deprive us of all privilege and right whatever but what we hold at your pleasure. We must risk life and every thing, rather than submit to this."

The words of Franklin offered no relief to Lord North; but they spoke the sense of his countrymen; and were in harmony with the true voice of England. "Were I an American," said Camden in the house of lords, "I would resist to the last drop of my blood." Still the annual estimates indicated no fear of the interruption of peace. The land tax was continued at but three shillings in the pound; no vote of credit was required; the army was neither increased nor reformed; and the naval force was reduced by four thousand seamen. "How is it possible," asked the partisans of authority, "that a people without arms, ammunition, money, or navy, should dare to brave the foremost among all the powers on earth?" Had they been told that the farmers who formed the majority of the congress of Massachusetts, after a proposition to stop at a thousand pounds, then at two thousand, at last authorized an expenditure of but fifteen thousand pounds for military purposes; that the committee of safety of the province was, at that time, instructing the committee of supplies to provide two hundred spades, a hundred and fifty pickaxes, a thousand wooden mess bowls, and other small articles, as well as stores of peas and flour in proportion, their contemptuous confidence might not have been diminished. "I know," said Sandwich, then at the head of the admiralty, "the low establishment proposed will be fully sufficient for reducing the colonies to obedience. Americans are neither disciplined, nor capable of discipline; their numbers will only add to the facility of their defeat;" and he made the lords merry with jests at their cowardice.

This arrogance of men who had on their side the block and the gallows, demonstrated the purpose of reducing the colonies by force. "Prepare for the

CHAP. XVI. 1774. Dec.

worst," wrote Quincy; "forbearance, delays, indecision, will bring greater evils." But the advice had not been waited for. The congress of Massachusetts, on hearing of the sudden dissolution of parliament, foresaw that the new house of commons would be chosen under the influence of the ministry. Though in November, denounced by Gage in a proclamation as "an unlawful assembly, whose proceedings tended to ensnare the inhabitants of the province, and draw them into perjuries, riots, sedition, treason and rebellion," though destitute of disciplined troops, munitions of war, armed vessels, military stores, and money, they had confidence that a small people, resolute in its convictions, outweighs an empire. Encouraged by the presence of Samuel Adams, after his return from Philadelphia, they adopted all the recommendations of the continental congress. While Gage delayed to strengthen Crown Point and Ticonderoga, the keys of the North, they established a secret correspondence with Canada. They entreated the ministers of the gospel in the colony, "to assist in avoiding that dreadful slavery, with which all were now threatened." "You," said they to the collective inhabitants of Massachusetts, "are placed by Providence in the post of honor, because it is the post of danger; and while struggling for the noblest objects, the eyes not only of North America and the whole British empire, but of all Europe are upon you. Let nothing unbecoming our character as Americans, as citizens and Christians, be justly chargeable to us. Whoever considers the number of brave men inhabiting North America, will know, that a general attention to military discipline, must so establish their rights and liberties, as under God, to render it impossible to destroy them. But we apprise you of your danger, which appears to us imminently great. The minute men, not already provided, should be immediately equipped, and disciplined three times a week, or oftener. With the utmost cheerfulness we assure you of our determination to stand or fall with the liberties of America." With such words they adjourned, to keep the annual Thanksgiving which they themselves had appointed; finding occasion in the midst of all their distress to rejoice at "the smiles of Divine Providence" on "the union of their own province and throughout the continent."

As ships of the line successively arrived, they brought for the land service no more than six hundred recruits, which only made good the losses by sickness and desertion; so that altogether Gage had scarcely three thousand effective men. Before the middle of December, it became known that the king in council had forbidden the export of arms to America; at once men from Providence removed more than forty pieces of cannon from the colony's fort near Newport; and the assembly of Rhode Island and its merchants took measures to import military stores.

At Portsmouth, New Hampshire, on Wednesday, the fourteenth of December, just after letters were received from Boston, members of the town committee, with other Sons of Liberty, preceded by a drum and fife, paraded the streets till their number grew to four hundred, when they made their way in scows and "gondolas" to the fort at the entrance of the harbor, overpowered the few invalids who formed its

CHAP. XVI. 1774. Dec.

garrison, and carried off upwards of one hundred barrels of powder, that belonged to the province. The next day, without waiting for a large body on the way from Exeter, John Sullivan, who had been a member of the continental congress, led a party to dismantle the fort completely; and they brought away all the small arms, a quantity of shot, and sixteen small pieces of artillery.

The condition of Massachusetts was anomalous; three hundred thousand people continued their usual avocations, and enjoyed life and property in undisturbed tranquillity without a legislature or executive officers; without sheriffs, judges, or justices of the peace. As the supervision of government disappeared, each man seemed more and more a law to himself; and as if to show that the world had been governed too much, order prevailed in a province where in fact there existed no regular government; no administration but by committees; no military officers but those chosen by the militia. Yet never were legal magistrates obeyed with more alacrity. The selectmen continued their usual functions; the service in the churches increased in fervor. From the sermons of memorable divines, who were gone to a heavenly country, leaving their names precious among the people of God on earth, a brief collection of faithful testimonies to the cause of God and his New England people was circulated by the press, that the hearts of the rising generation might know what had been the great end of the plantations, and count it their duty and their glory to continue in those right ways of the Lord wherein their fathers walked before them. Their successors in the ministry, all pupils of Harvard college, lorded over by no prelate, with the people, and of the people, and true ministers to the people, unsurpassed by the clergy of an equal population in any part of the globe for learning, ability, and virtue, for metaphysical acuteness, familiarity with the principles of political freedom, devotedness, and practical good sense, were heard as of old with reverence by their congregations in their meeting-houses on every Lord's day, and on special occasions of fasts, thanksgivings, lectures, and military musters. Elijah's mantle being caught up, was a happy token that the Lord would be with this generation as he had been with their fathers. Their exhaustless armory was the Bible, whose scriptures were stored with weapons for every occasion; furnishing sharp words to point their appeals, apt examples of resistance, prophetic denunciations of the enemies of God's people, and promises of the divine blessing on the defenders of his law.

But what most animated the country was the magnanimity of Boston; "suffering amazing loss, but determined to endure poverty and death, rather than betray America and posterity." Its people, under the eyes of the general, disregarding alike his army, his proclamations against a provincial congress, and the British statute against town-meetings, came together according to their ancient forms; and with Samuel Adams as moderator, elected delegates to the next provincial congress of Massachusetts.

CHAPTER XVII.

THE KING REJECTS THE OFFERS OF CONGRESS.

DECEMBER, 1774—JANUARY, 1775.

CHAP. XVII. 1774. Dec.

"IT will be easy to sow division among the delegates to the congress," said Rochford to Garnier, "they will do nothing but bring ridicule upon themselves by exposing their weakness." Their firmness, moderation, and unanimity took the ministry by surprise, when just before the adjournment of parliament their proceedings reached England. "It is not at all for the interests of France that our colonies should become independent," repeated Rochford. "The English minister," reasoned Garnier, "thinks, that after all they may set up for themselves."

Franklin invited the colonial agents to unite in presenting the petition of congress, but he was joined only by those who were employed by Massachusetts. Dartmouth received it courteously, and laid it before the king, who promised that after the recess it should be communicated to parliament. Barrington, the military secretary, was the first to confess the weakness of his department and to remonstrate against war. British industry made every able-bodied man of so much value, that considerable enlistments at home were out of the question; rank in the army was bestowed by favor, or sold for money, so that even boys at school sometimes held commissions; and under the corrupt system, not one general officer of that day had gained a great name. Aristocratic selfishness had unfitted England for war, unless under a minister who could inspirit the nation. Barrington, therefore, who had in advance advised, "that the seven regiments in Boston should be directed to leave a place where they could do no good, and without intention might do harm," and who was persuaded that the navy by itself was able to worry Massachusetts into "submission without shedding a drop of blood," once more pressed his opinions upon the government. "The contest," said he, "will cost more than we can gain by success. We have not strength to levy internal taxes on America; many amongst ourselves doubt their equity; all the troops in North America are not enough to subdue the Massachusetts; the most successful conquest must produce the horrors of civil war. Till the factious chiefs can be secured, judicial proceedings would confer the palm of martyrdom without the pain;" and he urged an immediate withdrawal of the troops, the "abandonment of all ideas of internal taxation," and such "concessions" as could be made "with dignity."

Lord North was disquieted. He rejected the propositions of congress, which included the repeal of the act regulating Massachusetts, but he was ready to negotiate with the Americans for the right to tax

CHAP. XVII. 1774. Dec. themselves. Franklin appeared as the great agent of the continent; and it was believed that his secret instructions authorized him to modify the conditions proposed for conciliation. Lord Howe undertook to ascertain the extent of his powers.

The name was dear to Americans. The elder Lord Howe had fallen on their soil, as their companion in arms, and Massachusetts raised to him a monument in Westminster Abbey. His brother, Sir William Howe, who had served with Americans in America, was selected as the new colonial commander-in-chief; and his oldest surviving brother, now Lord Howe, also honored in America as a gallant and upright naval officer, was to be commissioned as a pacificator.

"No man," said Lord Howe to Franklin at their first interview on Christmas-day evening, "can do more towards reconciling our differences than you. That you have been very ill-treated by the ministry, I hope will not be considered by you. I have a particular regard for New England, which has shown an endearing respect for my family. If you will indulge me with your ideas, I may be a means of bringing on a good understanding." At the unexpected prospect of restoring harmony, tears of joy wet Franklin's cheeks. He had remained in London at the peril of his liberty, perhaps of his life, to promote reconciliation, and the only moment for securing it was now come. With firmness, candor, and strict fidelity to congress, he explained the measures by which alone tranquillity could be restored; and they included the repeal of the regulating act for Massachusetts.

Lord Howe reported the result of the interview

to Dartmouth and North; but as they had no hope of inducing their colleagues, or the king, or parliament to concede so much, they trusted to the plan of commissioners who should repair to America and endeavor to agree with its leading people upon some means of composing all differences. Every prospect of preferment was opened to Franklin, if he would take part in such a commission. With exact truth and frankness, he pointed out, as the basis for a cordial union, the repeal of the acts complained of; the removal of the fleet and the troops from Boston; and a voluntary recall of some oppressive measures which the colonists had passed over in silence; leaving the questions, which related to aids, general commerce, and reparation to the India company, to be arranged with the next general congress.

The assembly of Jamaica at their session in December endeavored to interpose. They affirmed the rights of the colonies, enumerated their grievances, enforced their claims to redress, and entreated the king as a common parent to become the mediator between his European and American subjects, and to recognise the title of the Americans to the benefits of the English constitution as the bond of union between the colonists and Britain. At the same time they disclaimed the intention of joining the American confederacy; "for," said they, "weak and feeble as this colony is, from its very small number of white inhabitants, and its peculiar situation from the incumbrance of more than two hundred thousand slaves, it cannot be supposed that we now intend, or ever could have intended, resistance to Great Britain." The vast commercial importance of

CHAP. XVII. 1774. Dec. the island gave them a claim to be heard; but their petition, though in due time received by the king and communicated to the house of commons, had no effect whatever.

"It is plain enough," said Vergennes at Paris, "the king of England is puzzled between his desire of reducing the colonies, and his dread of driving them to a separation; so that nothing could be more interesting than the affairs of America." As the king of France might be called upon to render assistance to the insurgent colonies, the conduct of the English in their support of the Corsicans was cited as a precedent to the French embassy at London, and brought before the cabinet at Versailles. To Louis the Sixteenth Vergennes explained, that the proceedings of the continental congress contained the germ of a rebellion; that while the Americans really desired a reconciliation with the mother country, the ministry from their indifference would prevent its taking place; that Lord North, no longer confident of having America at his feet, was disconcerted by the unanimity and vigor of the colonies; and that France had nothing to fear but the return of Chatham to power.

The interests of Britain required Chatham's return; for he thoroughly understood the policy of the French as well as the disposition of the colonies. In his interview with Americans he said without reserve: "America under all her oppressions and provocations, holds out to us the most fair and just opening for restoring harmony and affectionate intercourse." No public body ever gained so full and unanimous a recognition of its integrity and its wisdom, as the general congress of 1774. The policy which its members proposed sprung so necessarily out of the relations of free countries to their colonies, that within a few years it was adopted even by their most malignant enemies among the British statesmen, for three quarters of a century regulated the colonial administration of every successive ministry, and finally gave way to a system of navigation, yet more liberal than the American congress had proposed.

The day after Franklin's first conversation with Lord Howe, Chatham received him at Hayes. "The congress," said he, "is the most honorable assembly of statesmen since those of the ancient Greeks and Romans in the most virtuous times." He thought the petition to the king "decent, manly, and properly expressed." He questioned the assertion, that the keeping up an army in the colonies in time of peace, required their consent; with that exception he admired and honored the whole of the proceedings. "The army at Boston," said Franklin, who saw the imminent hazard of bloodshed, "cannot possibly answer any good purpose, and may be infinitely mischievous. No accommodation can be properly entered into by the Americans, while the bayonet is at their breasts. To have an agreement binding, all force should be withdrawn." The words sank deeply into the mind of Chatham, and he promised his utmost efforts to the American cause, as the last hope of liberty for England. "I shall be well prepared," said he, "to meet the ministry on the subject, for I think of nothing else both night and day."

Like Chatham, Camden desired the settlement

CHAP. XVII. 1774. Dec. of the dispute upon the conditions proposed by congress; and from the temper, coolness, and wisdom of most of the American assemblies, he augured the establishment of their rights on a durable agreement with the mother country.

To unite every branch of the opposition in one line of policy, Chatham desired a cordial junction with the Rockingham whigs. That party had only two friends who spoke in the house of lords, and in the house of commons was mouldering away. And yet Rockingham was impracticable. "I look back," he said, "with very real satisfaction and content, on the line which I, indeed, emphatically I, took in the year 1766; the stamp-act was repealed, and the doubt of the right of this country was fairly faced and resisted." Burke, like his patron, pursued Chatham implacably, and refused to come to an understanding with him on general politics. Neither did he perceive the imminence of the crisis; but believed that the Americans would not preserve their unanimity, so that the controversy would draw into great length, and derive its chief importance from its aspect on parties in England. At the very moment when Burke was still fondly supporting his theory of the omnipotence of parliament over the colonies, he blindly insisted, that Chatham himself was the best bower anchor of the ministry.

With far truer instincts, Chatham divined that peril was near, and that it could be averted only by a circumscription of the absolute power of parliament. To further that end, the aged statesman paid a visit to Rockingham. At its opening, Chatham's countenance beamed with cordiality; but Rockingham had

1774. Dec.

learned as little as the ministers, and with a perverseness equal to theirs, insisted on maintaining the declaratory act. "The Americans have not called for its repeal," was his reply to all objections; and he never could be made to comprehend the forbearance of congress. So nothing remained for Chatham but to rely on himself. The opposition, thus divided, excited no alarm.

The king was inflexible; and the majority of the cabinet, instead of respecting Lord North's scruples, were intriguing to get him turned out, and his place supplied by a thorough assertor of British supremacy. 1775. Jan.
A cabinet council was held on the twelfth of January, and the current of its opinions drifted the minister into the war, which he wished to avoid. His colleagues refused to find in the proceedings of congress any honorable basis for conciliation. It was therefore resolved to interdict all commerce with the Americans; to protect the loyal, and to declare all others traitors and rebels. The vote was designed only to create division in the colonies, but it involved a civil war.

12.

CHAPTER XVIII.

CHATHAM LAYS THE FOUNDATION OF PEACE.

January 20, 1775.

CHAP. XVIII. 1775. Jan. At the meeting of parliament after the holidays, Lord North, who had no plan of his own, presented papers relating to America. Burke complained of them as partial. Chatham, who alone among the public men of England had the sagacity and courage to propose what was necessary for conciliation, was reminded of the statesman who said to his son: "See with how little wisdom this world of ours is governed;" and he pictured to himself Ximenes and Cortes discussing their merits in the shades.

Jan. 20. The twentieth of January was the first day of the session in the house of lords. It is not probable that even one of the peers had heard of the settlements beyond the Alleghanies, where the Watauga and the Forks of Holston flow to the Tennessee. Yet on the same day, the lords of that region, most of them Presbyterians of Scottish Irish descent, met in council near Abingdon. Their united congregations, having suffered from sabbaths too much profaned, or

CHAP XVIII

1775. Jan. 20.

wasted in melancholy silence at home, had called Charles Cummings to the pastoral charge of their precious and immortal souls. The men never went to public worship without being armed, or without their families. Their minister, on Sabbath morning, would ride to the service, armed with shot pouch and rifle. Their meeting-house, which was always filled, was a large cabin of unhewn logs; and when about twice in the year the bread and cup were distributed, the table was spread outside of the church in the neighboring grove. The news from congress reached them slowly; but on receiving an account of what had been done, they assembled in convention, and the spirit of freedom swept through their minds as naturally as the ceaseless forest wind sighs through the firs down the sides of the Black Mountains. They adhered unanimously to the association of congress, and named as their committee, Charles Cummings, their minister; Preston, Christian, Arthur Campbell, John Campbell, Evan Shelby, and others. They felt that they had a country; and adopting the delegates of Virginia as their representatives, they addressed them as men whose conduct would immortalize them in its annals. "We explored," said they, "our uncultivated wilderness, bordering on many nations of savages, and surrounded by mountains almost inaccessible to any but these savages. But even to these remote regions the hand of power hath pursued us, to strip us of that liberty and property, with which God, nature, and the rights of humanity have vested us. We are willing to contribute all in our power, if applied to constitutionally, but cannot think of submitting our liberty or prop-

CHAP. XVIII. 1775. Jan. 20. erty to a venal British parliament, or a corrupt ministry. We are deliberately and resolutely determined never to surrender any of our inestimable privileges to any power upon earth, but at the expense of our lives. These are our real though unpolished sentiments of liberty and loyalty, and in them we are resolved to live and die."

While they were publishing in the western forests this declaration of a purpose, which they were sure to make good, Chatham was attempting to rouse the ministry from its indifference. "Your presence at this day's debate," said he to Franklin, whom he met by appointment in the lobby of the house of lords, "will be of more service to America than mine;" and walking with him arm in arm, he would have introduced him near the throne among the sons and brothers of peers; but being reminded of the rule of the house, placed him below the bar, where he was still more conspicuous.

So soon as Dartmouth had laid the papers before the house, Chatham rose, and after inveighing bitterly against the dilatoriness of the communication, moved to address the king for "immediate orders to remove the forces from the town of Boston as soon as possible."

"My lords!" he continued, with a crowd of Americans as his breathless listeners, "the way must be immediately opened for reconciliation; it will soon be too late; an hour now lost may produce years of calamity. This measure of recalling the troops from Boston, is preparatory to the restoration of your peace, and the establishment of your prosperity.

"Resistance to your acts was necessary as it was

just; and your imperious doctrine of the omnipotence of parliament and the necessity of submission, will be found equally impotent to convince or to enslave.

CHAP. XVIII.

1775. Jan. 20.

"The means of enforcing thraldom are as weak in practice, as they are unjust in principle. General Gage and the troops under his command are penned up, pining in inglorious inactivity. You may call them an army of safety and of guard; but they are in truth an army of impotence; and to make the folly equal to the disgrace, they are an army of irritation. But this tameness, however contemptible, cannot be censured; for the first drop of blood, shed in civil and unnatural war, will make a wound that years, perhaps ages, may not heal. Their force would be most disproportionately exerted against a brave, generous, and united people, with arms in their hands, and courage in their hearts: three millions of people, the genuine descendants of a valiant and pious ancestry, driven to those deserts by the narrow maxims of a superstitious tyranny. And is the spirit of persecution never to be appeased? Are the brave sons of those brave forefathers to inherit their sufferings, as they have inherited their virtues? Are they to sustain the infliction of the most oppressive and unexampled severity? They have been condemned unheard. The indiscriminate hand of vengeance has lumped together innocent and guilty; with all the formalities of hostility, has blocked up the town of Boston, and reduced to beggary and famine thirty thousand inhabitants.

"But his Majesty is advised that the union in America cannot last! I pronounce it a union, solid,

CHAP. XVIII. permanent, and effectual. Its real stamina are to be looked for among the cultivators of the land; in 1775. Jan. 20. their simplicity of life is found the integrity and courage of freedom. These true sons of the earth are invincible.

"This spirit of independence, animating the nation of America, is not new among them; it is, and has ever been, their confirmed persuasion. When the repeal of the stamp act was in agitation, a person of undoubted respect and authenticity on that subject, assured me that these were the prevalent and steady principles of America; that you might destroy their towns, and cut them off from the superfluities, perhaps the conveniences of life; but that they were prepared to despise your power, and would not lament their loss, whilst they have—what, my lords?—their woods and their liberty.

"If illegal violences have been committed in America, prepare the way for acknowledgment and satisfaction; but cease your indiscriminate inflictions; amerce not thirty thousand; oppress not three millions for the fault of forty or fifty individuals. Such severity of injustice must irritate your colonies to unappeasable rancor. What though you march from town to town, and from province to province? How shall you be able to secure the obedience of the country you leave behind you in your progress, to grasp the dominion of eighteen hundred miles of continent?

"This resistance to your arbitrary system of taxation might have been foreseen from the nature of things and of mankind; above all from the whiggish spirit flourishing in that country. The spirit which now resists your taxation in America, is the same which formerly opposed loans, benevolences and ship money in England; the same which, by the bill of rights, vindicated the English constitution; the same which established the essential maxim of your liberties, that no subject of England shall be taxed but by his own consent.

CHAP. XVIII. 1775. Jan. 20.

"This glorious spirit of whiggism animates three millions in America, aided by every whig in England, to the amount, I hope, of double the American numbers. Ireland they have to a man. Let this distinction then remain forever ascertained; taxation is theirs, commercial regulation is ours. They say you have no right to tax them without their consent; they say truly. I recognise to the Americans their supreme, unalienable right in their property; a right which they are justified in the defence of to the last extremity. To maintain this principle is the great common cause of the whigs on the other side of the Atlantic, and on this.

'Tis liberty to liberty engaged;

the alliance of God and nature; immutable and eternal.

"To such united force, what force shall be opposed? What, my lords? A few regiments in America, and seventeen or eighteen thousand men at home! The idea is too ridiculous to take up a moment of your lordships' time. Unless the fatal acts are done away, the hour of danger must arrive in all its horrors, and then these boastful ministers, spite of all their confidence, shall be forced to abandon principles which they avow, but cannot defend; measures

CHAP. XVIII. which they presume to attempt, but cannot hope to effectuate.

1775. Jan. 20. "It is not repealing a piece of parchment, that can restore America to our bosom: you must repeal her fears and her resentments; and you may then hope for her love and gratitude. Insulted with an armed force posted at Boston, irritated with a hostile array before her eyes, her concessions, if you could force them, would be insecure. But it is more than evident, that united as they are, you cannot force them to your unworthy terms of submission.

"When your lordships look at the papers transmitted us from America, when you consider their decency, firmness, and wisdom, you cannot but respect their cause, and wish to make it your own. For myself, I must avow, that in all my reading,—and I have read Thucydides and have studied and admired the master-states of the world,—for solidity of reason, force of sagacity, and wisdom of conclusion under a complication of difficult circumstances, no nation or body of men can stand in preference to the general congress at Philadelphia. The histories of Greece and Rome give us nothing equal to it, and all attempts to impose servitude upon such a mighty continental nation, must be vain. We shall be forced ultimately to retract; let us retract while we can, not when we must. These violent acts must be repealed; you will repeal them; I pledge myself for it, I stake my reputation on it, that you will in the end repeal them. Avoid, then, this humiliating necessity. With a dignity becoming your exalted situation, make the first advances to concord, peace, and happiness, for that is your true dignity. Concession comes with better grace from superior power; and establishes solid confidence on the foundations of affection and gratitude. Be the first to spare; throw down the weapons in your hand.

CHAP. XVIII.

1775. Jan. 20.

"Every motive of justice and policy, of dignity and of prudence, urges you to allay the ferment in America by a removal of your troops from Boston, by a repeal of your acts of parliament, and by demonstrating amicable dispositions towards your colonies. On the other hand, to deter you from perseverance in your present ruinous measures, every danger and every hazard impend; foreign war hanging over you by a thread; France and Spain watching your conduct, and waiting for the maturity of your errors.

"If the ministers persevere in thus misadvising and misleading the king, I will not say that the king is betrayed, but I will pronounce that the kingdom is undone; I will not say, that they can alienate the affections of his subjects from his crown, but I will affirm, that, the American jewel out of it, they will make the crown not worth his wearing."

The words of Chatham, when reported to the king, recalled his last interview with George Grenville, and stung him to the heart. He raved at the wise counsels of the greatest statesman of his dominions, as the words of an abandoned politician; classed him with Temple and Grenville as "void of gratitude;" and months afterwards was still looking for the time, "when decrepitude or age should put an end to him as the trumpet of sedition."

With a whining delivery, of which the bad effect was heightened by its vehemence, Suffolk assured

CHAP. XVIII. 1775. Jan. 20. the house, that in spite of Lord Chatham's prophecy, the government was resolved to repeal not one of the acts, but to use all possible means to bring the Americans to obedience. After declaiming against their conduct with a violence that was almost madness, he boasted of "having been one of the first to advise coercive measures."

Shelburne gave his adhesion to the sentiments of Chatham, not from personal engagements, but solely on account of his conviction of their wisdom, justice, and propriety. Camden, who in the discussion surpassed every one but Chatham, returned to his old ground. "This," he declared, "I will say, not only as a statesman, politician, and philosopher, but as a common lawyer; my lords, you have no right to tax America; the natural rights of man, and the immutable laws of nature, are all with that people. King, lords, and commons, are fine sounding names; but king, lords, and commons may become tyrants as well as others; it is as lawful to resist the tyranny of many as of one. Somebody once asked the great Selden in what book you might find the law for resisting tyranny. 'It has always been the custom of England,' answered Selden, 'and the custom of England is the law of the land.'"

"My lords," said Lord Gower with contemptuous sneers, "let the Americans talk about their natural and divine rights! their rights as men and citizens! their rights from God and nature! I am for enforcing these measures." Rochford held Lord Chatham, jointly with the Americans, responsible in his own person for disagreeable consequences. Lyttelton reproached Chatham with spreading the fire of sedition, and the Americans with designing to emancipate themselves from the act of navigation. CHAP. XVIII.

Chatham closed the debate as he had opened it, by insisting on the right of Great Britain to regulate the commerce of the whole empire; but as to the right of the Americans to exemption from taxation, except by their implied or express assent, they derived it from God, nature, and the British constitution. Franklin with rapt admiration listened to the man, who on that day had united the highest wisdom and eloquence. "His speech," said the young William Pitt, "was the most forcible that can be imagined; in matter and manner far beyond what I can express; it must have an infinite effect without doors, the bar being crowded with Americans." 1775. Jan. 20.

The statesmanship of Chatham and the close reasoning of Camden, "availed no more than the whistling of the winds;" the motion was rejected by a vote of sixty-eight against eighteen; but the duke of Cumberland, one of the king's own brothers, was found in the minority. The king, triumphing in "the very handsome majority," was sure "nothing could be more calculated to bring the Americans to submission;" but the debate of that day, notwithstanding that Rockingham had expressed his adherence to his old opinion of the propriety of the declaratory act, went forth to the colonies as an assurance that the inevitable war would be a war with a ministry, not with the British people. It took from the contest the character of internecine hatred, to be transmitted from generation to generation, and showed that the true spirit of England, which had grown great by freedom, was on the side of America. Its

CHAP. XVIII. 1775. Jan. 20.

independence was foreshadowed, and three of Chatham's hearers on that day, Franklin, Shelburne, and his own son, William Pitt, never ceased in exertions, till their joint efforts established peace and international good will.

CHAPTER XIX.

THE PEOPLE OF NEW YORK TRUE TO UNION.

JANUARY—FEBRUARY, 1775

WHILE Gage was waiting for England to undertake in earnest the subjugation of America, the king expected every moment to hear that the small but well-disciplined force at Boston had struck a decisive blow at a disorderly "rabble." Neither he nor his ministers believed the hearty union of so vast a region as America possible. But at the one extreme, New Hampshire in convention unanimously adhered to the recent congress, and elected delegates to the next. At the other, South Carolina on the eleventh of January held a general meeting, which was soon resolved into a provincial congress, with Charles Pinckney for president. They then called upon their deputies to explain, why they had not included in the list of grievances the entire series of monopolies and restrictions; and they murmured at the moderation of Virginia which had refused to look further back than 1763. Gadsden proposed to strike out the exceptional privilege in

CHAP. XIX. 1775. Jan.

Jan. 11.

CHAP. XIX. 1775. Jan. 11. the association in favor of exporting rice. The torrent of enthusiasm was able to have broken down the plea of interest; and after a debate of a whole day, in which John Rutledge pointed out the practical inequality and general impolicy of extending the restriction, nearly half the body, seventy-five members against eighty-seven, were still ready to sacrifice the whole rice crop. Had the minority prevailed, they would have impoverished the province without benefit to the union; South Carolina wisely adopted the measures of the general congress without change, completed her internal organization, and re-elected delegates to the continental congress. If blood should be spilt in Massachusetts, her sons were to rise in arms.

The congress called at Savannah, failed of its end, since five only out of twelve parishes in the province were represented. But on the southern border, the inhabitants of the parish of St. John, chiefly descendants of New England people, mocked by the royalists as Puritans, Independents, republicans, or at least Oliverians, conformed to the resolutions of the continental congress, appointed Lyman Hall to represent them in Philadelphia, and set apart two hundred barrels of rice for their brethren in Boston.

In Virginia all eyes turned to Washington as the adviser in military affairs. On the seventeenth
Jan. 17. of January he presided over a meeting of the men of Fairfax county between sixteen and fifty years of age, who voted to enroll themselves in companies of sixty-eight men, under officers of their own choice. They also formed an association to defend their re-

ligion, laws, and rights. The committee of Northampton county offered a premium for the manufacture of gunpowder. Dunmore's excursion to the frontiers had justified a prorogation of the assembly until the second of February; but when, near the end of January, the colony was surprised by a further prorogation to May, Peyton Randolph, as the organ of the people against the representative of the crown, called upon the several counties to choose deputies to a colony convention to be held on the twentieth of March.

CHAP. XIX. 1775. Jan.

Maryland was encouraged by Thomas Johnson, a patriot venerated and loved for his private virtues; in public life looking always to the general good; neither hasty nor backward; quick to perceive what was possible, and effectively assisting to do it; joining modesty and practical wisdom to zeal and courage. The Presbyterians of Baltimore resolutely supported "the good old cause." Near Annapolis, the volunteers whom Charles Lee began to muster, melted away before his overbearing manner and incapacity; but the people would hear of no opposition to the recommendations of congress. They invited a voluntary offering to the amount of ten thousand pounds, for the purchase of arms and ammunition; and taking the sword out of the hands of the governor, they elected their own officers to defend Massachusetts and themselves. In the lower counties on Delaware, a little army that stood in the same relation to the people, sprung up from the general enthusiasm.

The trust of the ministry was in the central provinces. To divide the colonies they were urged

CHAP. XIX. 1775. Jan. to petition the king separately, in the hope that some one of them would offer acceptable terms. Especially crown officers and royalists, practised every art to separate New York from the general union. The city of New York, unlike Boston, was a corporation with a mayor of the king's appointment. There the president of the chartered college taught, that "Christians are required to be subject to the higher powers; that an apostle enjoined submission to Nero;" that the friends of the American congress were as certainly guilty of "an unpardonable crime, as that St. Paul and St. Peter were inspired men." There the Episcopal clergy fomented a distrust of the New England people, as "rebellious republicans, hairbrained fanatics; intolerant towards the church of England, Quakers, and Baptists; doubly intolerant towards the Germans and Dutch." There a corrupt influence grew out of contracts for the army. There the timid were incessantly alarmed by stories that "the undisciplined men of America could not withstand a disciplined army;" that "Canadians and unnumbered tribes of savages might be let loose upon them;" and that in case of war, "the Americans must be treated as vanquished rebels." The assembly of New York, which had been chosen six years before during a momentary prejudice against lawyers and Presbyterians, had been carefully continued. New York, too, was the seat of a royal government, which dispensed commissions, offices, and grants of land, gathered round its little court a social circle to which loyalty gave the tone, and had for more than eight years craftily conducted the administration with the design to lull discontent.

CHAP. XIX. 1775 Jan.

It permitted the assembly to employ, as its own agent, Edmund Burke, whose genius might inspire hope to the last. In the name of the ministry, it lavished promises of favor and indulgence; extended the boundaries of the province at the north to the Connecticut river; and contrary to the sense of right of Lord Dartmouth, supported the claims of New York speculators to Vermont lands against the New Hampshire grants, under which populous villages had grown up. Both Tryon and Colden professed, moreover, a sincere desire to take part with the colony in obtaining a redress of all grievances, and an improvement of its constitution; and Dartmouth himself was made to express the hope "of a happy accommodation upon some general constitutional plan." Such a union with the parent state, the New York committee declared to be the object of their earnest solicitude; even Jay "held nothing in greater abhorrence than the malignant charge of aspiring after independence." "If you find the complaints of your constituents to be well grounded," said Colden to the New York assembly in January, "pursue the means of redress which the constitution has pointed out. Supplicate the throne, and our most gracious sovereign will hear and relieve you with paternal tenderness."

In this manner the chain of union was to be broken, and the ministry to win over at least one colony to a separate negotiation. The royalists were so persuaded of the success of their scheme, that Gage, who had a little before written for at least twenty thousand men, sent word to the secretary in January, that "if a respectable force is seen in the field, the

CHAP. XIX. 1775. Jan. most obnoxious of the leaders seized, and a pardon proclaimed for all others, government will come off victorious, and with less opposition than was expected a few months ago."

Jan. 26. On the twenty-sixth of January the patriot Abraham Ten Broeck, of the New York assembly, moved to take into consideration the proceedings of the continental congress; but though he was ably seconded by Philip Schuyler, by George Clinton, and by the larger number of the members who were of Dutch descent, the vote was lost by a majority of one. Of the eleven who composed the majority, eight had been of that committee of correspondence, who in their circular letter to the other colonies, had advised a congress; and Jauncey, a member of the committee of fifty-one, had been present when their letter of May in favor of a congress, was unanimously approved.

The assembly, now in its seventh year, had long since ceased to represent the people; yet the friends to government plumed themselves on this victory, saying openly, "No one among gentlemen dares to support the proceedings of congress;" and Colden exclaimed, "Lord, now lettest thou thy servant depart in peace." "That one vote was worth a million sterling," said Garnier to Rochford with an air of patronage, on hearing the news, while he explained to Vergennes that the vote was to the ministry worth nothing at all, that New York was sure to act with the rest of the continent.

The royalists hoped for a combined expression of opinion in the central states. In January, the Quakers of Pennsylvania published an epistle, declaring that the kingdom of Jesus Christ is not of this world, and that they would religiously observe the rule not to fight; and the meeting of the Friends of Pennsylvania and New Jersey gave their "testimony against every usurpation of power and authority in opposition to the laws of government." But the legislature of Pennsylvania had, in December, unreservedly approved the proceedings of the continental congress, and elected seven delegates to the next congress in May. The popular convention of that colony, supported by the inflexibility of Thomson, and the vivacity and address of Mifflin, now pledged their constituents at every hazard to defend the rights and liberties of America, and, if necessary, to resist force by force. Unanimously adhering to the resolves of the congress, they also recommended domestic manufactures, and led the way to a law "prohibiting the future importation of slaves."

"Do not give up," wrote the town of Monmouth in New Jersey to the Bostonians; "and if you should want any further supply of bread, let us know." On the twenty-fourth of January, the assembly of that colony, without a dissenting voice, adopted the measures of the last general congress, and elected delegates to the next. Three weeks later, it was persuaded, like New York, to transmit a separate petition to the king; but its petition presented the American grievances without abatement.

The assembly of New York would neither print letters of the committee of correspondence; nor vote thanks to the New York delegates to the congress; nor express satisfaction that the merchants and inhabitants of the province adhered to the continental

CHAP. XIX. 1775. Feb. 23. association. On the twenty-third of February, it was moved to send delegates to the general congress in May. Strenuous debates arose; Schuyler and Clinton speaking several times on the one side, Brush and Wilkins very earnestly on the other; but the motion was defeated by a vote of nine to seventeen.

The vote proved nothing but how far prejudice, corruption, pride, and attachment to party could make a legislative body false to its constituents. The people of New York were thrown back upon themselves, under circumstances of difficulty that had no parallel in other colonies. They had no legally constituted body to form their rallying point; and at a time when the continental congress refused to sanction any revolutionary act even in Massachusetts, they were compelled to proceed exclusively by the methods of revolution. Massachusetts was sustained by its elective council and its annually elected assembly; New York had a council holding office at the king's will, and an assembly continued in existence from year to year by the king's prerogative. Yet the patriotism of the colony was sure to emerge from all these obstacles; and its first legitimate organ was the press.

Charles Lee denied the military capacity of England, as she could with difficulty enlist recruits enough to keep her regiments full; and he insisted that in a few months efficient infantry might be formed of Americans.

A pamphlet from the pen of Alexander Hamilton, had been in circulation since December; in February, when the necessity of the appeal to the people was become more and more urgent, the genial pilgrim from the south again put forth all his ability, with a determined interest in the coming struggle, as if he had sprung from the soil whose rights he defended. Strong in the sincerity of his convictions, he addressed the judgment, not the passions, aiming not at brilliancy of expression, but justness of thought, severe in youthful earnestness. "I lament," wrote Hamilton, "the unnatural quarrel between the parent state and the colonies; and most ardently wish for a speedy reconciliation, a perpetual and mutually beneficial union. I am a warm advocate for limited monarchy, and an unfeigned well-wisher to the present royal family; but, on the other hand, I am inviolably attached to the essential rights of mankind, to the true interests of society, to civil liberty as the greatest of terrestrial blessings."

CHAP. XIX.

1775. Feb.

"You are quarrelling for threepence a pound on tea, an atom on the shoulders of a giant," said the tories; and he answered: "The parliament claims a right to tax us in all cases whatever; its late acts are in virtue of that claim; it is the principle against which we contend."

"You should have had recourse to remonstrance and petition," said the time-servers. "In the infancy of the present dispute," rejoined Hamilton, "we addressed the throne; our address was treated with contempt and neglect. The first American congress in 1765 did the same, and met with similar treatment. The exigency of the times requires vigorous remedies; we have no resource but in a restriction of our trade, or in a resistance by arms."

"But Great Britain," it was said, "will enforce her claims by fire and sword. The Americans are with-

CHAP. XIX. 1775. Feb. out fortresses, without discipline, without military stores, without money, and cannot keep an army in the field; nor can troops be disciplined without regular pay and government by an unquestioned legal authority. A large number of armed men might be got together near Boston, but in a week they would be obliged to disperse to avoid starving." "The courage of Americans," replied Hamilton, "has been proved. The troops Great Britain could send against us, would be but few; our superiority in number would balance our inferiority in discipline. It would be hard, if not impracticable, to subjugate us by force. An armament sufficient to enslave America, will put her to an insupportable expense. She would be laid open to foreign enemies. Ruin like a deluge would pour in from every quarter."

"Great Britain," it was said, "will seek to bring us to a compliance by putting a stop to our whole trade." "We can live without trade," answered Hamilton; "food and clothing we have within ourselves. With due cultivation, the southern colonies, in a couple of years, would afford cotton enough to clothe the whole continent. Our climate produces wool, flax, and hemp. The silkworm answers as well here as in any part of the world. If manufactures should once be established, they will pave the way still more to the future grandeur and glory of America; and will render it still securer against encroachments of tyranny."

"You will raise the resentment of the united inhabitants of Great Britain and Ireland," objected his adversaries. "They are our friends," said he; "they know how dangerous to their liberties the loss of ours must be. The Irish will sympathize with us and commend our conduct." CHAP. XIX.

The tories built confidently upon disunion among the colonies. "A little time," replied Hamilton, "will awaken them from their slumbers. I please myself with the flattering prospect, that they will, ere long, unite in one indissoluble chain." 1775. Feb.

It was a common argument among the royalists of those days, that there were no immutable principles of political science; that government was the creature of civil society, and therefore that an established government was not to be resisted. To this the young philosopher answered rightly: "The supreme intelligence, who rules the world, has constituted an eternal law, which is obligatory upon all mankind, prior to any human institution whatever. He gave existence to man, together with the means of preserving and beautifying that existence; and invested him with an inviolable right to pursue liberty and personal safety. Natural liberty is a gift of the Creator to the whole human race. Civil liberty is only natural liberty, modified and secured by the sanctions of civil society. It is not dependent on human caprice; but it is conformable to the constitution of man, as well as necessary to the well being of society."

"The colony of New York," continued his antagonists, "is subject to the supreme legislative authority of Great Britain." "I deny that we are dependent on the legislature of Great Britain," he answered; and he fortified his denial by an elaborate discussion of colonial history and charters.

It was retorted, that New York had no charter. 'The sacred rights of mankind," he rejoined, "are

CHAP. XIX. 1775. Feb.

not to be rummaged for among old parchments or musty records. They are written, as with a sunbeam, in the whole volume of human nature by the hand of the divinity itself; and can never be erased or obscured by mortal power. Civil liberty cannot be wrested from any people without the most manifold violation of justice, and the most aggravated guilt. The nations Turkey, Russia, France, Spain, and all other despotic kingdoms in the world, have an inherent right, whenever they please, to shake off the yoke of servitude, though sanctioned by immemorial usage, and to model their government upon the principles of civil liberty."

So reasoned the gifted West Indian, as though the voices of the Puritans had blended with the soft tropical breezes that rocked his cradle; or rather as one who had caught glimpses of the divine archetype of freedom. The waves of turbulent opinion dashed against the obstacles to their free course; New York still desired a constitutional union, embracing Great Britain and America, but was resolved, at all events, to make common cause with the continent.

CHAPTER XX.

PARLIAMENT DECLARES MASSACHUSETTS IN REBLLION.

JANUARY 23—FEBRUARY 9, 1775.

CHAP. XX. 1775. Jan.

THE confidence of the ministry reposed more and more on the central provinces, and Dartmouth took for granted the peaceful settlement of every question; yet six sloops of war and two frigates were under orders for America, and it was ostentatiously heralded that seven hundred marines from England, and three regiments of infantry with one of light horse from Ireland, making a reinforcement of two thousand four hundred and eighteen men, were to be prepared for embarkation; "less to act hostilely against the Americans, than to encourage the friends of government."

In the house of commons, the various petitions in behalf of America, including those from London and Bristol, were consigned to a committee of oblivion, and ridiculed as already "dead in law." Hayley, of London, rebuked the levity of the house. "The rejection of the petitions of the trading interests," said he, on the twenty-sixth of January, "must drive on a

CHAP. XX. 1775. Jan. civil war with America." "The Americans," argued Jenkinson, "ought to submit to every act of the English legislature." "England," said Burke, "is like the archer that saw his own child in the hands of the adversary, against whom he was going to draw his bow." Fox charged upon North, that the country was on the point of being involved in a civil war by his incapacity." North complained: "The gentleman blames all my administration; yet he defended and supported much of it; nor do I know how I have deserved his reproaches." "I can tell the noble lord how," cried Fox; "by every species of falsehood and treachery." Sir George Savile asked that Franklin might be heard at the bar in support of the address of the American continental congress to the king; and after a violent debate, the house, by the usual majority, refused even to receive Franklin's petition.

The ministry were self-willed and strangely confident. The demand of Gage for twenty thousand men was put aside with scorn. "The violences committed by those who have taken up arms in Massachusetts Bay," wrote Dartmouth, in the king's name, "have appeared to me as the acts of a rude rabble, without plan, without concert, and without conduct; and therefore I think that a smaller force now, if put to the test, would be able to encounter them. The first and essential step to be taken towards re-establishing government, would be to arrest and imprison the principal actors and abettors in the provincial congress, whose proceedings appear in every light to be treason and rebellion. If means be devised to keep the measure secret until the moment of execution, it can hardly fail of success, Even if it cannot be accomplished without bloodshed, and should be a signal for hostilities, I must again repeat, that any efforts of the people, unprepared to encounter with a regular force, cannot be very formidable. The imprisonment of those who shall be made prisoners will prevent their doing any further mischief. The charter for the province of Massachusetts Bay empowers the governor to use and exercise the law martial in time of rebellion. The attorney and solicitor-general report that the facts stated in the papers you have transmitted, are the history of an actual and open rebellion in that province, and therefore the exercise of that power upon your own discretion is strictly justifiable."

"The minister must recede," wrote Garnier to Vergennes, "or lose America forever." "Your chief dependence," such were Franklin's words to Massachusetts, "must be on your own virtue and unanimity, which, under God, will bring you through all difficulties."

There was no hope in England but from Chatham, who lost not a moment in his endeavor to prevent a civil war before it should be inevitably fixed; saying, "God's will be done, and let the old and new world be my judge." On the first day of February, he presented his plan for "true reconcilement and national accord." It was founded substantially on the proposal of the American congress; parliament was to repeal the statutes complained of, and to renounce the power of taxation; America in turn was to recognise its right of regulating the commerce of the whole empire, and by the free grants of her own assemblies, was to defray the expenses of

CHAP. XX. 1775. Feb. her governments. This was the true meaning of his motion, though clauses were added to make it less unpalatable to the pride of the British legislature. Franklin was persuaded that he sincerely wished to satisfy the Americans; Jefferson, on reading the bill, hoped that it might bring on a reconciliation; but Samuel Adams saw danger lurking under even a conditional recognition of the supremacy of parliament. "Let us take care," said he, "lest, instead of a thorn in the foot, we have a dagger in the heart."

No sooner had Chatham concisely invited the assistance of the house in adapting his crude materials to the great end of an honorable and permanent adjustment, than Dartmouth spoke of the magnitude of the subject, and asked his consent that the bill should lie on the table for consideration. "I expect nothing more," was the ready answer. At this concession Sandwich, speaking for the majority in the cabinet, grew petulant. "The proposed measure," he said, "deserves only contempt, and ought to be immediately rejected. I can never believe it to be the production of any British peer. It appears to me rather the work of some American;" and turning his face towards Franklin, who stood leaning on the bar, "I fancy," he continued, "I have in my eye the person who drew it up, one of the bitterest and most mischievous enemies this country has ever known."

The peers turned towards the American, when Chatham retorted: "The plan is entirely my own; but if I were the first minister, and had the care of settling this momentous business, I should not be ashamed of publicly calling to my assistance a person so perfectly acquainted with the whole of American affairs, one whom all Europe ranks with our Boyles and Newtons, as an honor not to the English nation only, but to human nature."

Overawed by the temper of the house, Dartmouth, with his wonted weakness, which made him execute the worst measures even when he seemed inclined to the best, turned round against his own candor, and declared for rejecting the plan immediately. This even Grafton advised; and Gower demanded.

Perceiving the fixed purpose of the ministry, Chatham poured upon them a torrent of invective. "This bill," said he, "though rejected here, will make its way to the public, to the nation, to the remotest wilds of America; and however faulty or defective, it will at least manifest how zealous I have been to avert those storms which seem ready to burst on my country. Yet I am not surprised, that men who hate liberty, should detest those that prize it; or that those who want virtue themselves should persecute those who possess it. The whole of your political conduct has been one continued series of weakness and temerity, despotism and the most notorious servility, incapacity and corruption. I must allow you one merit, a strict attention to your own interests: in that view, who can wonder that you should put a negative on any measure which must deprive you of your places, and reduce you to that insignificance, for which God and nature designed you."

Lord Chatham's bill, though on so important a subject, offered by so great a statesman, and supported by most able and learned speakers, was re-

CHAP. XX. 1775. Feb.

sisted by ignorance, prejudice and passion, by misconceptions and wilful perversion of plain truth, and was rejected on the first reading by a vote of sixty-one to thirty-two.

"Hereditary legislators!" thought Franklin. "There would be more propriety, in having hereditary professors of mathematics! But the elected house of commons is no better, nor ever will be while the electors receive money for their votes, and pay money wherewith ministers may bribe their representatives when chosen." Yet the wilfulness of the lords was happy for America; for Chatham's proposition contained clauses, to which it never could safely have assented, and yet breathed a spirit which must have calmed its resentment, distracted its councils, and palsied its will. It had now no choice left but between submission and independence.

The number and weight of the minority should have led the ministers to pause; but they rushed on with headlong indiscretion, thinking not to involve the empire in civil war, but to subdue the Americans by fear. The first step towards inspiring terror was, to declare Massachusetts in a state of rebellion, and to pledge the parliament and the whole force of Great Britain to its reduction; the next, by prohibiting the American fisheries, to starve New England; the next, to call out the savages on the rear of the colonies; the next, to excite a servile insurrection. Accordingly, Lord North on the day after Chatham's defeat, proposed to the commons a joint address to the king to declare that a rebellion existed in Massachusetts, and to pledge their lives and properties to its suppression.

CHAP. XX. 1775. Feb.

"The colonies are not in a state of rebellion," said Dunning; "but resisting the attempt to establish despotism in America, as a prelude to the same system in the mother country. Opposition to arbitrary measures is warranted by the constitution, and established by precedent." "Nothing but the display of vigor," said Thurlow, "will prevent the American colonies becoming independent states."

Grant, the same officer, who had been scandalously beaten at Pittsburg, and had made himself so offensive in South Carolina, asserted amidst the loudest cheering, that he knew the Americans very well, and was certain they would not fight; "that they were not soldiers and never could be made so, being naturally pusillanimous and incapable of discipline; that a very slight force would be more than sufficient for their complete reduction;" and he fortified his statement by repeating their peculiar expressions, and ridiculing their religous enthusiasm, manners, and ways of living, greatly to the entertainment of the house.

At this stage of the debate, Fox, displaying for the first time the full extent of his abilities, which made him for more than a quarter of a century the leading debater on the side of the liberal party in England, in a speech of an hour and twenty minutes, entered into the history of the dispute with great force and temper, and stated truly, that "the reason why the colonies objected to taxes for revenue was, that such revenue in the hands of government took out of the hands of the people that were to be governed, that control which every Englishman thinks he ought to have over the government to which his

CHAP. XX. 1775. Feb.

rights and interests are intrusted." The defence of the ministry rested chiefly on Wedderburn. Gibbon had prepared himself to speak, but neither he nor Lord George Germaine could find room for a single word.

Lord North again shrunk from measures against which his nature revolted; and Franklin, whose mediation was once more solicited, received a paper containing the results of ministerial conferences on "the hints" which he had written. "We desire nothing but what is necessary to our security and well-being," said Franklin to the friendly agents who came to him. In reply they declared with authority, that the repeal of the tea-act and the Boston port-act would be conceded; the Quebec act might be amended by reducing the province to its ancient limits; but the Massachusetts acts must be continued, both "as real amendments" of the constitution of that province, and "as a standing example of the power of parliament." Franklin's reply was brief: "While parliament claims the right of altering American constitutions at pleasure, there can be no agreement, for we are rendered unsafe in every privilege." "An agreement is necessary for America," it was answered; "it is so easy for Britain to burn all your seaport towns." "My little property," rejoined Franklin, "consists of houses in those towns; you may make bonfires of them whenever you please; the fear of losing them will never alter my resolution to resist to the last the claim of parliament."

The plan of intimidation proceeded. When on the sixth of February the address was reported to the house, Lord John Cavendish earnestly "deprecated civil war, necessarily involving a foreign one also." "A fit and proper resistance," said Wilkes, "is a revolution, not a rebellion. Who can tell, whether in consequence of this day's violent and mad address, the scabbard may not be thrown away by the Americans as well as by us, and should success attend them, whether, in a few years, the Americans may not celebrate the glorious era of the revolution of 1775 as we do that of 1688? Success crowned the generous effort of our forefathers for freedom; else they had died on the scaffold as traitors and rebels, and the period of our history which does us the most honor, would have been deemed a rebellion against lawful authority, not the expulsion of a tyrant."

During the debate, which lasted till half past two in the morning, Lord North threw off the responsibility of the tax on tea, in order to prepare the way for offering the repeal of that tax as the basis for conciliation. It was too late, for a new question of the power of parliament over charters and laws had intervened. The disavowal offended his colleagues, and in itself was not honest; his vote had decided the measure in the cabinet, and it was unworthy of a minister of the crown to intimate that he had obsequiously followed a chief like Grafton, or yielded his judgment to the king.

Lord George Germaine was fitly selected to deliver the message of the commons at the bar of the lords. "There is in the address one paragraph which I totally disclaim;" said Rockingham; "I openly declare, I will risk neither life nor fortune in support of the measures recommended. Four-fifths of the

CHAP. XX. 1775. Feb. 7. nation are opposed to this address; for myself, I shall not tread in the steps of my noble but ill-fated ancestor, Lord Strafford, who first courted popular favor, and then deserted the cause he had embarked in; as I have set out by supporting the cause of the people, so I shall never, for any temptation whatsoever, desert or betray them."

Mansfield, as if in concert with North, took the occasion to deny having advised the tea tax; which he condemned as the most absurd measure that could be imagined. "The original cause of the dispute," said Camden, "is the duty on tea," and he too disclaimed having had the least hand in that measure. "It is mean," said Grafton, "for him at this time to screen himself, and shift the blame off his own shoulders, to lay it on those of others. The measure was consented to in the cabinet. He acquiesced in it; he presided in the house of lords when it passed through its several stages; and he should equally share its censure or its merit."

A passionate debate ensued, during which Mansfield, in reply to Richmond, praised the Boston port act and its attendant measures, including the regulating act for Massachusetts, as worthy to be gloried in for their wisdom, policy, and equity; but he denied that they were in any degree the fruit of his influence. Now they were founded on the legal opinions and speeches of Mansfield, and he had often in the house of lords been the mouth-piece of Hutchinson, whose opinions reached him through Mauduit. Shelburne insinuated that Mansfield's disclaimer was in substance not correct. Mansfield retorted by charging Shelburne with uttering gross falsehoods;

and Shelburne in a rejoinder gave the illustrious jurist the lie. CHAP. XX.

On Thursday, the ninth day of February, the lord chancellor, the speaker, and a majority of the lords and commons went in state to the palace, and in the presence of the representatives of the great powers of Europe, presented to George the Third the sanguinary address which the two houses of parliament had jointly adopted, and which, in the judgment of Rockingham and his friends, "amounted to a declaration of war." The king, in his reply, pledged himself speedily and effectually to enforce "obedience to the laws and the authority of the supreme legislature." His heart was hardened. Having just heard of the seizure of ammunition at the fort in New Hampshire, he intended that his language should "open the eyes of the deluded Americans." "If it does not," said he to his faltering minister, "it must set every delicate man at liberty to avow the propriety of the most coercive measures." 1775. Feb. 9.

CHAPTER XXI.

THE SPIRIT OF NEW ENGLAND.

February, 1775.

CHAP. XXI. 1775. Feb. On the day on which the king received the address of parliament, the members of the second provincial congress of Massachusetts, about two hundred and fourteen in number, appointed eleven men as their committee of safety, charged to resist every attempt at executing the acts of parliament. For this purpose they were empowered to take possession of the warlike stores of the province, to make returns of the militia and minute men, and to muster so many of the militia as they should judge necessary. General officers were appointed to command the force that should be so assembled. First of those who accepted the trust was Artemas Ward, a soldier of some experience in the French war. Next him as brigadier, stood Seth Pomeroy, the still older veteran, who had served at the siege of Louisburg.

"Resistance to tyranny," thus the congress addressed the inhabitants of the Massachusetts Bay, "becomes the Christian and social duty of each individual. Fleets, troops, and every implement of war are sent into the province, to wrest from you that freedom which it is your duty, even at the risk of your lives, to hand inviolate to posterity. Continue steadfast, and with a proper sense of your dependence on God, nobly defend those rights which Heaven gave, and no man ought to take from us."

CHAP. XXI. 1775. Feb.

These rustic statesmen, in their sincere simplicity, were the true representatives of the inhabitants of Massachusetts. They came together tremulous with emotion, yet resolved from duty never to yield. They were frugal even to parsimony, making the most sparing appropriations ever thought of by a nation preparing for war; yet they held their property and their blood of less account than liberty. They were startled at the lightest rustling of impending danger, but they were no more moved from their deep seated purpose than the granite rock which seems to quiver with the flickering shadow of the overhanging cloud, as the wind drives it by. "Life and liberty shall go together," was their language. "Our existence as a free people absolutely depends on our acting with spirit and vigor," said Joseph Warren; and he wished England to know that the Americans had courage enough to fight for their freedom. "The people," said Samuel Adams, "will defend their liberties with dignity. One regular attempt to subdue this or any other colony, whatever may be the first issue of the attempt, will open a quarrel which will never be closed, till what some of them affect to apprehend, and we truly deprecate, shall take effect."

The second provincial congress before its adjournment appointed a committee to prepare in the recess

CHAP. XXI. 1775. Feb. rules and regulations for the constitutional army. They declined to levy taxes in form; but they recommended the inhabitants to pay all their province tax to a treasurer of their appointment. They re-elected their old delegates to congress. They forbade work or supplies for the English tròops, "for," said they, "we may be driven to the hard necessity of taking up arms in our own defence." They urged one of their committees to prepare military stores; and directed reviews of every company of minute men. Aware of the design of the ministry to secure the Canadians and Indians, they authorized communications with the province of Quebec through the committee of correspondence of Boston. A delegation from Connecticut was received, and measures ere concerted for corresponding with that and all the other colonies. After appointing a day of fasting, enjoining the colony to beware of a surprise, and recommending military discipline, they closed a session of sixteen days.

The spies of Gage found everywhere the people intent on military exercises; or listening to confident speeches from their officers; or learning from the clergy to esteem themselves as of the tribe of Judah. "Behold," said one of the ministers at a very full review of the militia, "God himself is with us for our captain, and his priests with sounding trumpets to cry alarm. O children of Israel," thus he rebuked the English; "fight ye not against the Lord God of your fathers; for ye shall not prosper."

On these bustling preparations of men, who had no artillery, very few muskets with bayonets, and no treasury, the loyalists looked with derision;

never for a moment doubting that the power of Great Britain would trample down, repress, and overwhelm every movement of insurrection. To crush the spirit of resistance by terror, and to diffuse a cowardly panic, Daniel Leonard, of Taunton, speaking for them all, held up the spectres of "high treason," "actual rebellion," and "anarchy." He ran through the history of the strife; argued that it was reasonable for America to share in the national burden as in the national benefit; that there was no oppressive exercise of the power of parliament; that the tax of threepence on tea was no tyranny, since a duty of a shilling, imposed as a regulation of trade, had just been taken off; that the bounties paid in England on American produce exceeded the American revenue more than fourfold; that no grievance was felt or seen; that in the universal prosperity, the merchants in the colonies were rich, the yeomanry affluent, the humblest able to gain an estate; that the population doubled in twenty-five years, building cities in the wilderness, and interspersing schools and colleges through the continent; that the country abounded with infallible marks of opulence and freedom; that even James Otis had admitted the authority of parliament over the colonies, and had proved the necessity and duty of obedience to its acts; that resistance to parliament by force would be treason; that rebels would deservedly be cut down like grass before the scythe of the mower, while the gibbet and the scaffold would make away with those whom the sword should spare; that Great Britain was resolved to maintain the power of parliament, and was able to do so; that the colonies south of Pennsylvania had

CHAP. XXI. 1775. Feb. barely men enough to govern their numerous slaves, and defend themselves against the Indians; that the northern colonies had no military stores, nor money to procure them, nor discipline, nor subordination, nor generals capable of opposing officers bred to arms; that five thousand British troops would prevail against fifty thousand Americans; that the British navy on the first day of war would be master of their trade, fisheries, navigation, and maritime towns; that the Canadians and savages would prey upon the back settlements, so that a regular army could devastate the land like a whirlwind; that the colonies never would unite, and New England, perhaps even Massachusetts, would be left to fall alone; that even in Massachusetts thousands among the men of property and others, would flock to the royal standard, while the province would be drenched in the blood of rebels.

The appeal of Leonard was read with triumph by the tories. But John Adams, kindling with indignation at his dastardly menaces and mode of reasoning, entered the lists as the champion of American freedom; employing the fruits of his long study of the British law, the constitution, and of natural right, and expressing the true sentiments of New England.

"My friends: Human nature itself is evermore an advocate for liberty. The people can understand and feel the difference between true and false, right and wrong, virtue and vice. To the sense of this difference the friends of mankind appeal.

"That all men by nature are equal; that kings have but a delegated authority which the people may resume, are the revolution principles of 1688, are the principles of Aristotle and Plato, of Livy and

Cicero, of Sydney, Harrington, and Locke, of nature and eternal reason. CHAP. XXI.

"The people are in their nature so gentle, that there never was a government in which thousands of mistakes were not overlooked. Not ingratitude to their rulers, but much love is their constant fault. Popular leaders never could for any length of time persuade a large people that they were wronged, unless they really were so. They have acted on the defensive from first to last; are still struggling at the expense of their ease, health, peace, wealth, and preferment, and, like the Prince of Orange, resolve never to see their country in entire subjection to arbitrary power, but rather to die fighting against it in the last ditch. 1775. Feb.

"Nor can the people be losers in the end. Should they be unsuccessful, they can but be slaves, as they would have been had they not resisted; if they die, death is better than slavery; if they succeed, their gains are immense, for they preserve their liberties. Without the resistance of the Romans to Tarquin, would the Roman orators, poets, and historians, the great teachers of humanity, the delight and glory of mankind, ever have existed? Did not the Swiss cantons gain by resistance to Albert and Gessler? Did not the Seven United Provinces gain by resistance to Philip, Alva, and Granvelle? Did not the English gain by resistance to John when Magna Charta was obtained? by resistance to Charles the First? to James the Second?

"To the scheme of having a revenue in America by authority of parliament, the active, sagacious, and very able Franklin, the eminent philosopher, the dis-

CHAP. XXI. 1775. Feb. tinguished patriot, in the administration of the busy, intriguing, enterprising Shirley, sent an answer in writing, which exhausted the subject.

"If the parliament of Great Britain had all the natural foundations of authority, wisdom, goodness, justice, power, would not an unlimited subjection of three millions of people to that parliament at three thousand miles distance, be real slavery? But when both electors and elected are become corrupt, you would be the most abject of slaves to the worst of masters. The minister and his advocates call resistance to acts of parliament treason and rebellion. But the people are not to be intimidated by hard words; they know, that in the opinion of all the colonies parliament has no authority over them excepting to regulate their trade, and this merely by consent.

"All America is united in sentiment. When a masterly statesman, to whom America has erected a statue in her heart for his integrity, fortitude, and perseverance in her cause, invented a committee of correspondence in Boston, did not every colony, nay every county, city, hundred, and town upon the whole continent, adopt the measure, as if it had been a revelation from above? Look over the resolves of the colonies for the past year; you will see, that one understanding governs, one heart animates the whole.

"The congress at Philadelphia have assured us, that if force attempts to carry the late innovating measures against us, all America ought to support us. Maryland and Delaware have taken the powers of the militia into the hands of the people, and established it by their own authority for the defence of Massachusetts. Virginia and the Carolinas are preparing. The unanimity in congress can hardly be paralleled. The mighty questions of the revolution of 1688 were determined in the convention of parliament by small majorities of two or three, and four or five only; the almost unanimity in your assemblies and especially in the continental congress, are providential dispensations in our favor, the clearest demonstration of the cordial, firm, radical, and indissoluble union of the colonies.

CHAP. XXI.

1775. Feb.

"If Great Britain were united, she could not subdue a country a thousand leagues off. How many years, how many millions, did it take to conquer the poor province of Canada, which yet would never have submitted but on a capitulation, securing religion and property? But Great Britain is not united against us. Millions in England and Scotland think it unrighteous, impolitic, and ruinous to make war upon us; and a minister, though he may have a marble heart, will proceed with a desponding spirit. London has bound her members under their hands to assist us; Bristol has chosen two known friends of America; many of the most virtuous of the nobility and gentry are for us, and among them a St. Asaph, a Camden, and a Chatham; the best bishop that adorns the bench, as great a judge as the nation can boast, and the greatest statesman it ever saw.

"I would ask, by what law the parliament has authority over America? By the law in the Old and New Testament it has none; by the law of nature and nations it has none; by the common law of England it has none; by statute law it has none; for

CHAP. XXI. 1775. Feb.

no statute for this purpose was made before the settlement of the colonies, and the declaratory act of 1766 was made without our consent by a parliament which had no authority beyond the four seas.

"The subordination of Ireland is founded on conquest and consent. But America never was conquered by Britain. She never consented to be a state, dependent upon the British parliament. What religious, moral, or political obligations, then, are we under, to submit to parliament as supreme? None at all. If Great Britain will resort to force, all Europe will pronounce her a tyrant, and America never will submit to her, be the danger of disobedience as great as it will.

"If Great Britain has protected the colonies, all the profits of our trade centred in her lap. If she has been a nursing mother to us, we have, as nursed children commonly do, been very fond of her, and rewarded her all along tenfold for all her care.

"We New England men do not derive our laws from parliament, nor from common law, but from the law of nature and the compact made with the king in our charters. If our charters could be forfeited, and were actually forfeited, the only consequence would be, that the king would have no power over us at all. The connection would be broken between the crown and the natives of this country. The charter of London in an arbitrary reign was decreed forfeited; the charter of Massachusetts was declared forfeited also. But no American charter will ever be decreed forfeited again; or if any should, the decree will be regarded no more than a vote of the lower house of the Robinhood society. God forbid the privileges of millions of Americans should depend upon the discretion of a lord chancellor. It may as well be pretended that the people of Great Britain can forfeit their privileges, as the people of this province. If the contract of state is broken, the people and king of England must recur to nature. It is the same in this province. We shall never more submit to decrees in chancery, or acts of parliament, annihilating charters or 'abridging English liberties.'

CHAP. XXI. 1775 Feb.

"Should the nation suffer the minister to persevere in his madness and send fire and sword against us, we have men enough to defend ourselves. The colonies south of Pennsylvania have a back country, inhabited by a hardy robust people, many of whom are emigrants from New England, and habituated like multitudes of New England men, to carry their rifles on one shoulder to defend themselves against the savages, while they carry their axes, scythes, and hoes upon the other. We have manufacturers of fire-arms; powder has been made here; nor could the whole British navy prevent the importation of arms and ammunition. The new-fangled militia will have the discipline and subordination of regular troops. A navy might burn a seaport town, but will the minister be nearer his mark? At present we hold the power of the Canadians as nothing; their dispositions, moreover, are not unfriendly to us. The savages will be more likely to be our friends than our enemies.

"The two characteristics of this people, religion and humanity, are strongly marked in all their proceedings. We are not exciting a rebellion. Resist-

CHAP. XXI. 1775. Feb.

ance by arms against usurpation and lawless violence, is not rebellion by the law of God or the land. Resistance to lawful authority makes rebellion. Hampden, Russell, Sydney, Holt, Somers, Tillotson, were no rebels. If an act of parliament is null and void, it is lawful to resist it.

"This people under great trials and dangers, have discovered great abilities and virtues, and that nothing is so terrible to them as the loss of their liberties. They act for America and posterity. If there is no possible medium between absolute independence and subjection to the authority of parliament, all North America are convinced of their independence, and determined to defend it at all hazards."

CHAPTER XXII.

HAS NEW ENGLAND A RIGHT IN THE NEWFOUNDLAND FISHERIES?

February, 1775.

CHAP. XXII. 1775. Feb.

On the tenth of February, after the speaker reported to the house of commons the answer to their address, Lord North presented a message from the king, asking the required "augmentation to his forces." The minister, who still clung to the hope of reducing Massachusetts by the terrors of legislation, next proposed to restrain the commerce of New England and exclude its fishermen from the Banks of Newfoundland. The best shipbuilders in the world were at Boston, and their yards had been closed; the New England fishermen were now to be restrained from a toil in which they excelled the world. Thus the joint right to the fisheries was made a part of the great American struggle.

"God and nature," said Johnston, "have given that fishery to New England and not to Old." Dunning defended the right of the Americans to fish on the Banks. "If rebellion is resistance to government," said Sir George Savile, "it must sometimes be

CHAP. XXII. 1775. Feb. justifiable. May not a people, taxed without their consent, and their petitions against such taxation rejected, their charters taken away without hearing, and an army let loose upon them without a possibility of obtaining justice, be said to be in justifiable rebellion?" But the ministerial measure, which, by keeping the New England fishermen at home provoked discontent and provided recruits for an insurgent army, was carried through all its stages by great majorities. Bishop Newton, in the lords, reasoned "that rebellion is the sin of witchcraft, and that one so unnatural as that of New England, could be ascribed to nothing less than diabolical infatuation."

The minister of France took the occasion to request the most rigorous and precise orders to all British naval officers not to annoy the commerce of the French colonies. "Such orders," answered Rochford, "have been given; and we have the greatest desire to live with you on the best understanding and the most perfect friendship." A letter from Lord Stormont, the British ambassador at Paris, was also cited in the house of lords to prove that France equally wished a continuance of peace. "It signifies nothing," said Richmond; "you can put no trust in Gallic faith, except so long as it shall be their interest to keep their word." With this Rochford, the secretary of state, readily agreed; proving, however, from Raynal's History of the two Indies, that it was not for the interest of France that the English colonies should throw off the yoke. The next courier took to the king of France the report, that neither the opposition nor the British minister put faith in his sincerity; and the inference seemed justified that they themselves were insincere.

CHAP. XXII. 1775. Feb.

The English mind was in the process of change. The destruction of the tea at Boston had been condemned as a lawless riot, for which the pride of the nation demanded an indemnity. But the proposal to enter upon a civil war with a view to enforce for parliament a power of taxation which it could never render effective, or a mutilation of a charter to which the public was indifferent, was received by merchants, tradesmen, and the majority of the people with abhorrence. Lord North himself leaned far towards the Americans, and would gladly have escaped from his embarrassments by concession or resigning office; but George the Third, who liked his pliant minister too well to give him up, yielded just enough to his advice to retain him in his place and yet to baffle his design. "I am a friend to holding out the olive branch," wrote the king, "yet I believe that when once vigorous measures appear to be the only means, the colonies will submit. I shall never look to the right or to the left, but steadily pursue that track which my conscience dictates to be the right one." The preparations for war were, therefore, to proceed; but he consented, that the commanders of the naval and military forces might be invested with commissions for the restoration of peace according to a measure to be proposed by Lord North. From Franklin, whose aid in the scheme was earnestly desired, the minister once more sought to learn the least amount of concession that could be accepted.

No sooner was Franklin consulted, than he expressed his approbation of the proposed commission, and of Lord Howe as one of its members; and to smooth the way to conciliation, he offered at once the

CHAP. XXII. 1775. Feb.

payment of an indemnity to the India company, provided the Massachusetts acts should be repealed. "Without the entire repeal," said he, "the language of the proposal is, try on your fetters first, and then if you don't like them, we will consider." On the eighteenth of February, Franklin, by appointment, once more saw Lord Howe. "Consent," said he, "to accompany me, and co-operate with me in the great work of reconciliation:" and he coupled his request with a promise of ample appointments and subsequent rewards. "Accepting favors," said the American, "would destroy the influence you propose to use; but let me see the propositions, and if I approve of them, I will hold myself ready to accompany you at an hour's warning." His opinions, which he had purposely reduced to writing and signed with his own hand, were communicated to Lord Howe, and through him to Lord North, as his last words; and they were these: "The Massachusetts must suffer all the hazards and mischiefs of war, rather than admit the alteration of their charter and laws by parliament. They that can give up essential liberty to obtain a little temporary safety, deserve neither liberty nor safety."

The minister was disheartened; he stood almost alone, helpless for the want of a vigorous will, dreading the conflict with America, yet feebly and vainly resisting the impetuosity of his colleagues. Franklin was informed on the twentieth, that his principles and those of parliament were as yet too wide from each other for discussion; and on the same day, Lord North, armed with the king's consent in writing, proposed in the house of commons a plan of con-

CHAP. XXII. 1775. Feb.

ciliation. "Now," said Vergennes, as he heard of it, "now more than ever is the time for us to keep our eyes wide open."

The proposal was formed on the principle, that parliament, if the colonies would tax themselves to its satisfaction, would impose on them no duties except for the regulation of commerce. A wild opposition ensued. Lord North could not quell the storm, and for two hours he seemed in a considerable minority, more from the knowledge of his disposition to relent, than for the substance of his measure. "The plan should have been signed by John Hancock and Otis," said Rigby, in his inconsiderate zeal to condemn the minister. Welbore Ellis, and others, par- 12.
ticularly young Acland, angry at his manifest repugnance to cruelty, declared against him loudly and roughly. "Whether any colony will come in on these terms I know not," said Lord North; "but it is just and humane to give them the option. If one consents, a link of the great chain is broken. If not, it will convince men of justice and humanity at home, that in America they mean to throw off all dependence." Jenkinson reminded the house, that Lord North stood on ground chosen by Grenville; but the Bedford party none the less threatened to vote against the minister, till Sir Gilbert Elliot, the well known friend of the king, brought to his aid the royal influence, and secured for the motion a large majority.

Lord North must have fallen, but for the active interposition of the king. Yet the conciliation which he offered, could not lead to an agreement, for no confidence could be placed in its author, who was the

CHAP. XXII. 1775. Feb.

feeble head of an adverse ministry. "Chatham," wrote the French minister, "can say like Scanderbeg, 'I give my scimitar, but not the arm to wield it.'" The two systems, moreover, were essentially in contrast with each other. Chatham denied the right of parliament to tax; North asserted it; Chatham asked free grants from deliberative assemblies in the full exercise of the right to judge of their own ability to give; North put chains on the colonies, and invited them one by one to make a bid, each for its separate ransom; Chatham proposed to repeal the Massachusetts acts; North was silent about them. Yet even this semblance of humanity was grudged. To recover his lost ground with the extreme supporters of authority, North was obliged to join with Suffolk and Rochford in publishing "a paper declaring his intention to make no concessions."

The army in Boston was to be raised to ten thousand men, and the general to be superseded on account of his incapacity to direct such a force. "If fifty thousand men and twenty millions of money," said David Hume, "were intrusted to such a lukewarm coward as Gage, they never could produce any effect." Amherst declined the service, unless the army should be raised to twenty thousand men; the appointment of Sir William Howe was therefore made public. He possessed no one quality of a great general, and he was selected for his name. On receiving the offer of the command, "Is it a proposition?" he asked, "or an order from the king?" and when told an order, he replied, it was his duty to obey it. "You should have refused to go against this people," cried the voters of Nottingham, with whom he had broken

CHAP. XXII. 1775. Feb.

faith. "Your brother died there in the cause of freedom; they have shown their gratitude to your name and family by erecting a monument to him." "If you go," said many of them, "we hope you may fall." "We cannot wish success to the undertaking," said many more. "My going thither," wrote Howe in apology, "is not my seeking. I was ordered, and could not refuse. Private feelings ought to give way to the service of the public. There are many loyal and peaceable subjects in America; the insurgents are very few in comparison. When they find they are not supported in their frantic ideas by the more moderate, they will, from fear of punishment, subside to the laws. This country must now fix the foundation of its stability with America, by procuring a lasting obedience."

At the same time, Lord Howe, the admiral, was announced as commander of the naval forces and pacificator; for it was pretended that the olive branch and the sword were to be sent together.

Of the two major generals who attended Howe, the first in rank was Sir Henry Clinton, son of a former governor in New York, related to the families of Newcastle and Bedford, and connected by party with the ministry. The other was John Burgoyne. A bastard son of one peer, he had made a runaway match with the daughter of another. In the last war he served in Portugal with spirit, and was brave even to rashness. His talent for description made him respectable as a man of letters; as a dramatic writer, his place is not among the worst. He was also a ready speaker in the house of commons, inclining to the liberal side in politics; yet

CHAP. XXII. 1775. Feb. ready to risk life and political principles for the darling object of effacing the shame of his birth, by winning military glory with rank and fortune.

His service in America was preceded by a public parade of his principles. "I am confident," said the new devotee in the house of commons, "there is not an officer or soldier in the king's service who does not think the parliamentary right of Great Britain a cause to fight for, to bleed and die for." The assertion was extravagant; many of the best would not willingly bear arms against their kindred in America.

In reply to Burgoyne, Henry Temple Luttrell, whom curiosity once led to travel many hundreds of miles along the flourishing and hospitable provinces of the continent, bore testimony to their temperance, urbanity, and spirit, and predicted that, if set to the proof, they would evince the magnanimity of republican Rome. He saw in the aspect of infant America, features which at maturer years denoted a most colossal force. "Switzerland and the Netherlands," he reminded the house, "demonstrate what extraordinary obstacles a small band of insurgents may surmount in the cause of liberty."

While providing for a reinforcement to its army, England enjoined the strictest watchfulness on its consuls and agents in every part of Europe, to intercept all munitions of war destined for the colonies. To check the formation of magazines on the Dutch island of St. Eustatius, which was the resort of New England mariners, the British envoy, with dictatorial menaces, required the States General of Holland to forbid their subjects from so much as transporting military stores to the West Indies, beyond the absolute wants of their own colonies. Of the French government, preventive measures were requested in the most courteous words.

Meantime, an English vessel had set sail immediately to convey to the colonies news of Lord North's proposal, in the confident belief that, under the mediation of a numerous army, provinces which neither had the materials for war, nor the means of obtaining them, would be divided by the mere hint of giving up the point of taxation. "The plan," said Chatham, "will be spurned; and every thing but justice and reason, prove vain to men like the Americans." "It is impossible," said Fox, "to use the same resolution to make the Americans believe their government will give up the right of taxing, and the mother country that it will be maintained."

Franklin sent advice to Massachusetts by no means to begin war without the advice of the continental congress, unless on a sudden emergency; "but New England alone," said he, "can hold out for ages against this country, and if they are firm and united, in seven years will win the day." "By wisdom and courage, the colonies will find friends everywhere;" thus he wrote to James Bowdoin of Boston, as if predicting a French alliance. "The eyes of all Christendom are now upon us, and our honor as a people is become a matter of the utmost consequence. If we tamely give up our rights in this contest, a century to come will not restore us, in the opinion of the world; we shall be stamped with the character of dastards, poltroons, and fools; and be despised and trampled upon, not by this haughty, insolent nation only, but by all mankind. Present

CHAP. XXII. 1775. Feb. inconveniences are, therefore, to be borne with fortitude, and better times expected."

"Every negotiation which shall proceed from the present administration," wrote Garnier to Vergennes, "will be without success in the colonies. Will the king of England lose America rather than change his ministry? Time must solve the problem; if I am well informed, the submission of the Americans is not to be expected."

CHAPTER XXIII.

THE ANNIVERSARY OF THE BOSTON MASSACRE.

FEBRUARY—MARCH, 1775.

CHAP. XXIII. 1775. Feb.

THE French minister judged rightly; the English government had less discernment and was deceived by men who had undertaken to secure New York to the crown, if their intrigues could be supported by a small military force.

But the friends of the British system in that colony were not numerous, and were found only on the surface. The Dutch Americans formed the basis of the population, and were in a special manner animated by the glorious example of their fathers, who had proved to the world that a small people under great discouragements can found a republic. The story of their strife with Spain, their successful daring, their heroism during their long war for freedom, was repeated on the banks of the Hudson and the Mohawk. It was remembered, too, that England herself owed her great revolution, the renovation of her own political system, to Holland. How hard, then, that the superior power which had been the fruit of

CHAP. XXIII. 1775. Feb.

that restoration, should be employed to impair the privileges of colonists of Dutch descent! By temperament moderate but inflexible, little noticed by the government, they kept themselves noiselessly in reserve; but their patriotism was inflamed and guided by the dearest recollections of their nationality. Many of the Anglo-Americans of New York were from New England, whose excitement they shared; and the mechanics of the city were almost to a man enthusiasts for decisive measures. The landed aristocracy was divided; but the Dutch and the Presbyterians, especially Schuyler of Albany, and the aged Livingston of Rhinebeck, never hesitated to risk their vast estates in the cause of inherited freedom. The latter had once thought of emigrating to Switzerland, if he could nowhere else escape oppression. In no colony did English dominion find less of the sympathy of the people than in New York.

In Virginia the Blue Ridge answered British menaces with a mountain tone of defiance. "We cannot part with liberty but with our lives," said the inhabitants of Botetourt. "Our duty to God, our country, ourselves, and our posterity, all forbid it. We stand prepared for every contingency." The dwellers on the waters of the Shenandoah, meeting at Staunton, commended the Virginia delegates to the applause of succeeding ages, their example to the hearts of every Virginian and every American. "For my part," said Adam Stephen, "before I would submit my life, liberty, and property to the arbitrary disposal of a venal aristocracy, I would sit myself down with a few friends upon some rich and healthy spot, six hundred miles to the westward, and there form a settlement which in a short time would command attention and respect." CHAP. XXIII.

The valleys of Kentucky laughed as they heard the distant tread of clustering troops of adventurers, who, under a grant from the Cherokees, already prepared to take possession of the meadows and undulating table land that nature has clothed with its richest grasses. Their views extended to planting companies of honest farmers, and erecting iron works, a salt manufactory, grist-mills, and saw-mills; and the culture of the rich region was to be fostered by premiums for the heaviest crop of corn, and for the emigrant who should drive out the greatest number of sheep. The men who are now to occupy "that most desirable territory," will never turn back, but, as we shall see, will carry American independence to the Wabash, the Detroit, and the Mississippi. 1775. Feb.

At Charleston, South Carolina, the association was punctually enforced. A ship load of near three hundred slaves was sent out of the colony by the consignee; even household furniture and horses, though they had been in use in England, could not be landed; and on the twenty-fifth, the whole cargo of "the Charming Sally" was thrown into Hog Island Creek.

The winter at Boston was the mildest ever known; and in this "the gracious interposition of heaven was recognised." All the towns in Massachusetts, nearly all in New England, and all the colonies ministered to the wants of Boston. Some relief came even from England. "Call me an enthusiast," said Samuel Adams; "this union among the colonies and warmth of affection can be attributed to nothing less than the

CHAP. XXIII. 1775. Feb. agency of the Supreme Being. If we believe that he superintends and directs the affairs of empires, we have reason to expect the restoration and establishment of the public liberties."

On Sunday, the twenty-sixth of February, two or three hundred soldiers, under the command of Leslie, sailed from Castle William, landed clandestinely at Marblehead, and hurried to Salem in quest of military stores. Not finding them there, the officer marched towards Danvers; but at the river, he found the bridge drawn up, and was kept waiting for an hour and a half, whilst the stores, insignificant in amount, were removed to a place of safety. Then having pledged his honor not to advance more than thirty yards on the other side, he was allowed to march his troops across the bridge. The alarm spread through the neighborhood; but Leslie hastily retraced his steps, and re-embarked at Marblehead.

Mar. At this time the British ministry received news of the vote in the New York assembly, refusing to consider the resolutions of congress. The confidence of the king reached its climax; and he spared no pains to win the colony. In an ostensible letter from the secretary of state, New York was praised for its attempts towards a reconciliation with the mother country; in a private letter, Dartmouth enjoined upon Colden to exert his address to facilitate the acceptance of Lord North's conciliatory resolution. The same directions were sent to the governors of every colony except Connecticut and Rhode Island, and they were enjoined from the king to make proper explanations to those whose situations and connections were to give facility to the measure.

How complete was the general confidence, that the great majorities in parliament would overawe the colonies, appeared on Monday, the sixth of March, when the bill depriving New England of her fisheries was to be engrossed. Even Lord Howe advocated it as the means of bringing the disobedient provinces to a sense of their duty, without involving the empire in a civil war. "Now," replied Fox, "as by this act all means of acquiring a livelihood, or of receiving provisions, is cut off, no alternative is left, but starving or rebellion. If the act should not produce universal acquiescence, I defy any body to defend the policy of it. Yet America will not submit. New York only differs in the modes." "The act," said Dundas, the solicitor general of Scotland, "is just, because provoked by the most criminal disobedience; is merciful, because that disobedience would have justified the severest military execution. As to the famine, which is so pathetically lamented, I am afraid it will not be produced by this act. When it is said, no alternative is left to them but to starve or rebel, this is not the fact, for there is another way, to submit." The king, on receiving an account of "the languor of opposition" during the debate, wrote to Lord North: "I am convinced the line adopted in American affairs will be crowned with success."

These words fell from George the Third on the day on which Boston commemorated the "massacre" of its citizens. The orator was Joseph Warren, who understood the delusion of the king, and resolved to prove that "the Americans would make the last appeal, rather than submit to the yoke prepared for their necks; that their unexampled pa-

CHAP. XXIII. 1775. Mar. 6.

tience had no alloy of cowardice." The commemoration was a public affront to Gage both as general of the army, and as governor of the province; for the subject of the oration was the baleful effects of standing armies in time of peace; and it was to be delivered to the town in a town meeting, contrary to an act of parliament which he came to Boston to enforce. In the crowd which thronged to the Old South Meeting-house, appeared about forty British officers of the army and navy; these, Samuel Adams, the moderator, received with studied courtesy, placing them all near the orator, some of them on the platform above the pulpit stairs. There they sat conspicuously, and listened to a vivid picture of the night of the massacre, after which Warren proceeded:

"Our streets are again filled with armed men, our harbor is crowded with ships of war; but these cannot intimidate us; our liberty must be preserved; it is far dearer than life; we hold it even dear as our allegiance; we cannot suffer even Britons to ravish it from us. Should America be brought into vassalage, Britain must lose her freedom also; her liberty, as well as ours, will eventually be preserved by the virtue of America. The attempt of parliament to raise a revenue from America, and our denial of their right to do it, have excited an almost universal inquiry into the rights of British subjects and of mankind. The malice of the Boston port-bill has been defeated in a very considerable degree, by benefactions in this and our sister colonies; and the sympathetic feelings for a brother in distress, and the grateful emotions of him who finds relief, must forever endear each to the other, and form those indissoluble bonds of friendship and affection on which the preservation of our rights so evidently depends. The mutilation of our charter has made every other colony jealous for its own. Even the sending troops to put these acts in execution, is not without advantages to us. The exactness and beauty of their discipline inspire our youth with ardor in the pursuit of military knowlege. Charles the Invincible taught Peter the Great the art of war; the battle of Pultowa convinced Charles of the proficiency Peter had made.

"Our country is in danger. Our enemies are numerous and powerful; but we have many friends, determining to be free, and Heaven and earth will aid the resolution. You are to decide the important question, on which rests the happiness and liberty of millions yet unborn. Act worthy of yourselves. The faltering tongue of hoary age calls on you to support your country. The lisping infant raises its suppliant hands, imploring defence against the monster slavery. Your fathers look from their celestial seats with smiling approbation on their sons, who boldly stand forth in the cause of virtue.

"My fellow-citizens, I know you want not zeal or fortitude. You will maintain your rights or perish in the generous struggle. However difficult the combat, you will never decline it, when freedom is the prize. An independence of Great Britain is not our aim. No, our wish is, that Britain and the colonies may, like the oak and the ivy, grow and increase together. But if these pacific measures are ineffectual, and it appears that the only way to safety is through fields of blood, I know you will not turn your faces from your foes, but will undauntedly press forward, until tyranny is trodden under foot."

CHAP. XXIII. 1775. Mar. 6.

The officers of the army and navy who heard the oration gave no offence during its delivery; but at the motion for "appointing an orator for the ensuing year to commemorate the horrid massacre," they began to hiss. The assembly became greatly exasperated, and threatened vengeance for the insult; but Adams, with imperturbable calmness, soon restored order; the vote was taken, and the business of the meeting was regularly concluded.

The event of that day maddened the army, and both officers and soldiers longed for revenge. An honest countryman from Billerica inquiring for a firelock, bought an old one of a private; but as soon as he had paid the full price, he was seized by half a dozen of a company for having violated an act of parliament against trading with soldiers, and confined during the night in the guard-room. The next day he was labelled on his back, "American liberty, or a specimen of democracy," was tarred and feathered, and carted through the principal streets of the town, accompanied by all the drums and fifes of the forty-seventh, playing Yankee Doodle, by a guard of twenty men with fixed bayonets, and by a mob of officers, among whom was Lieutenant Colonel Nesbit himself.

"See what indignities we suffer, rather than precipitate a crisis," wrote Samuel Adams to Virginia. The soldiers seemed encouraged to provoke the people, that they might have some color for beginning hostilities.

CHAPTER XXIV.

PUBLIC OPINION IN ENGLAND.

March, 1775.

CHAP. XXIV. 1775. Mar.

While such was the state of angry opposition between the citizens and soldiers at Boston, Lord Howe at London finally broke off his negotiations with Franklin, and the ministry used the pen of Samuel Johnson, to inflame the public mind. Johnson was a poor man's son, and had himself tasted the bitter cup of extreme indigence. His father left no more than twenty pounds. To bury his mother and pay her little debts, he had written Rasselas. For years he had gained a precarious support as an author. He had paced the streets of London all night long, from not having where to lay his head; he had escaped a prison for a trifle he owed by begging an alms of Richardson, had broken his bread with poverty, and had even known what it is from sheer want to go without a dinner. When better days came, he loved the poor as few else love them; and he nursed in his house whole nests of the lame, the blind, the sick, and the sorrowful. A man who had thus sturdily battled

CHAP. XXIV. 1775. Mar. with social evils, and was so keenly touched by the wretchedness of the down-trodden, deserved to have been able to feel for an injured people; but he refused to do so. Having defined the word pension as "pay given to a state hireling for treason to his country," he was himself become a pensioner; and at the age of three score and six, with small hire, like a bravo who loves his trade, he set about the task of his work-masters. In a tract, which he called "Taxation no Tyranny," he echoed to the crowd the haughty rancor, which passed down from the king and his court, to his council, to the ministers, to the aristocracy, their parasites and followers, with nothing remarkable in his party zeal, but the intensity of its bitterness; or in his manner, but its unparalleled insolence; or in his argument, but its grotesque extravagance.

The Bostonians had declared to the general congress their willingness to resign their opulent town, and wander into the country as exiles. "Alas!" retorted Johnson, "the heroes of Boston will only leave good houses to wiser men." To the complaints of their liability to be carried out of their country for trial, he answered, "we advise them not to offend." When it was urged, that they were condemned unheard, he asserted, "there is no need of a trial; no man desires to hear that which he has already seen."

Franklin had remained in Great Britain for no reason but to promote conciliation; and with an implacable malice which was set off by a ponderous effort at mirth, Johnson pointed at him as the "master of mischief, teaching congress to put in motion the engine of political electricity, and to give the great stroke by the name of Boston."

Did the Americans claim a right of resistance, "Audacious defiance!" cried Johnson, "acrimonious malignity! The indignation of the English is like that of the Scythians, who returning from war, found themselves excluded from their own houses by their slaves."

Virginia and the Carolinas had shown impatience of oppression. "How is it," asked Johnson, "that we hear the loudest yelps for liberty among the drivers of negroes? The slaves should be set free; they may be more grateful and honest than their masters."

Lord North inclined to mercy: "Nothing," said Johnson, "can be more noxious to society than clemency which exacts no forfeiture;" and he proposed to arm the savage Indians, turn out the British soldiers on free quarters among the Americans, remodel all their charters, and take away their political privileges.

Dickinson of Pennsylvania had insisted, that the Americans complained only of innovations. "We do not put a calf into the plough," said the moralist; "we wait till he is an ox." This, however, the ministry bade him erase, not for its ribaldry, but as unwilling to concede that the calf had been spared; and Johnson obeyed, comparing himself to a mechanic for whom "the employer is to decide." Was he told that the Americans were increasing in numbers, wealth, and love of freedom; "This talk," said he, "that they multiply with the fecundity of their own rattlesnakes, disposes men accustomed to think themselves masters, to hasten the experiment of binding obstinacy before it is become yet more obdu-

CHAP. XXIV. 1775. Mar.

rate." He mocked at the rule of progression, which showed that America must in the end exceed Europe in population. "Then," said he in derision, not knowing how much truth he was uttering, "in a century and a quarter let the princes of the earth tremble in their palaces."

Had Johnson been truly a man of genius, he would have escaped the shame of having, in his old age, aimed at freedom the feeble shaft which was meant to have carried ruin. In spite of the ostentatious pomp of his morality, his own heart was riveted to the earth. At the last, he cowered under the fear of dissolution as though death were an enemy; scarifying his limbs in the vain hope of breathing though but a few hours more; unable in the moment of change to fix his eye on God, or to grasp eternity; the emblem of the old political system, which also lay on its deathbed, helplessly longing to live on. His name is never breathed as a watchword; his writings never thrill as oracles.

The pure-minded man, who in a sensual age, became the quickener of religious fervor, the preacher to the poor, John Wesley, also came forward to defend the system of the court with the usual arguments. He looked so steadily towards the world beyond the skies, that he could not brook the interruption of devout gratitude by bloody contests in this stage of being. Besides, he saw that the rupture between the English and the Americans was growing wider every day, and to him the total defection of America was the evident prelude of a conspiracy against monarchy. The thought of such a conspiracy made him shudder. "No governments under

Heaven," said he, "are so despotic as the republican; no subjects are governed in so arbitrary a manner as those of a commonwealth. The people never but once in all history gave the sovereign power, and that was to Masaniello of Naples. Our sins will never be removed, till we fear God and honor the king." Wesley's mental constitution was not robust enough to gaze on the future with unblenched calm. He could not foresee that the constellation of republics, so soon to rise in the wilds of America, would welcome the members of the society, which he was to found, as the pioneers of religion; that the breath of liberty would waft their messages to the masses of the people; would encourage them to collect the white and the negro, slave and master in the green wood, for counsel on divine love and the full assurance of grace; and would carry their consolation, and songs, and prayers to the furthest cabins in the wilderness. To the gladdest of glad tidings for the political regeneration of the world, Wesley listened with timid trembling, as to the fearful bursting of the floodgates of revolution; and he knew not, that God was doing a work, which should lead the nations of the earth to joy.

Mar. 16.

In the house of lords, Camden, on the sixteenth of March, took the occasion of the motion to commit the bill depriving New England of the fisheries, to reply not to ministers only, but to their pensioned apologist, in a speech which was admired in England, and gained applause of Vergennes. He justified the union of the Americans, and refuted the suggestion that New York was or could be detached from it. By the extent of America, the numbers of

CHAP. XXIV. 1775. Mar. 16. its people, their solid, firm, and indissoluble agreement on the great basis of liberty and justice, and the want of men and money on the part of England, he proved that England could not but fail in her attempt at coercion, and that the ultimate independence of America was inevitable. "I cannot think him serious," said Sandwich. "Suppose the colonies do abound in men; they are raw, undisciplined, and cowardly. I wish instead of forty or fifty thousand of these brave fellows, they would produce in the field at least two hundred thousand; the more the better; the easier would be the conquest. At the siege of Louisburg. Sir Peter Warren found what egregious cowards they were. Believe me, my lords, the very sound of a cannon would send them off, as fast as their feet could carry them." He then abused the Americans for not paying their debts, and ascribed their associations to a desire to defraud their creditors. It is memorable, that when on the twenty-first, the debate was renewed and the bill passed, both Rockingham and Shelburne, the heads of the old whigs, and the new, inserted in their protest against the act, that "the people of New England are especially entitled to the fisheries."

Franklin, as he heard the insinuations of Sandwich against the honesty of his countrymen, turned on his heel in wrath; nothing was left for him but to go home where duty called him. The French minister, who revered his supreme ability, sought with him one last interview. "I spoke to him," wrote Garnier to Vergennes, "of the part which our president Jeannin had taken in establishing the independence and forming the government of the United Provinces;" and the citation of the precedent cheered Franklin as a prediction. "But then," subjoined Garnier, "they have neither a marine, nor allies, nor a prince of Orange."

A large part of his last day in London, Franklin passed with Edmund Burke, and however much he may have been soured and exasperated by wrongs and insults to himself and his country, he still regarded the approaching independence as an event which gave him the greatest concern. He called up the happy days which America had passed under the protection of England; he said "that the British empire was the only instance of a great empire, in which the most distant members had been as well governed as the metropolis; but then," reasoned he, "the Americans are going to lose the means which secured to them this rare and precious advantage. The question with them, is not whether they are to remain as they had been before the troubles, for better, they could not hope to be; but whether they are to give up so happy a situation without a struggle. I lament the separation between Great Britain and her colonies; but it is inevitable."

So parted the great champion of the British aristocracy, and the man of the people. For what noble purpose will they two act together once more? When will an age again furnish minds like theirs? Burke revered Franklin to the last, foretold the steady brightening of his fame; and drew from his integrity the pleasing hope of ultimate peace.

On the morning after his conversation with Burke, Franklin posted to Portsmouth with all speed, and before his departure from London was

CHAP. XXIV. 1775. Mar. known, was embarked for Philadelphia. What tidings were to greet his landing?

"He has left with bad designs," said Hutchinson; "had I been the master, his embarkation would have been prevented."—"With his superiority," said Garnier, "and with the confidence of the Americans, he will be able to cut out work for the ministers who have persecuted him." Vergennes felt assured he would spread the conviction that the British ministry had irrevocably chosen its part; and that America had no choice but independence.

With personal friends, with merchants, with manufacturers, with the liberal statesmen of England, with supporters of the ministry, Franklin had labored on all occasions earnestly, disinterestedly, and long. With his disappearance from the scene, the last gleam of a compromise vanished. The administration and their followers called him insincere. They insisted on believing to the last, that he had private instructions which would have justified him in accepting the regulating act for Massachusetts, and they attributed his answers to an inflexible and subtle hostility to England. But nothing deceives like jealousy; he perseveringly endeavored to open the eyes of the king and his servants. At the bar of the house of commons he first revealed his conviction, that persistence in taxation would compel independence; it was for the use of the government, that once to Strahan and then to Lord Howe he explained the American question with frankness and precision. The British ministry overreached themselves by not believing him. "Speaking the truth to them in sincerity," said Franklin, "was my only finesse."

CHAP. XXIV. 1775. Mar.

The ability displayed by him in his intercourse with the British government has, in its way, never been exceeded. He contemplated the course of events as calmly as he would have watched a process of nature. His judgment was quick and infallible; his communications prompt, precise, and unequivocal; his frankness perfect. He never shunned responsibility, and never assumed too much. In every instance, his answers to the ministry and their emissaries, were those which the voice of America would have dictated, could he have taken her counsel. In him is discerned no deficiency and no excess. Full of feeling, even to passion, he observed, and reasoned, and spoke serenely. Of all men, he was a friend to peace; but the terrors of a sanguinary civil war did not confuse his perceptions or impair his decision. Neither Chatham, nor Rockingham, nor Burke, blamed Franklin for renouncing allegiance; and we shall see Fox once more claim his friendship, and Shelburne and the younger Pitt rest upon him with the confidence which he deserved. He went home to the work of independence, and, through independence, of peace.

Mar. 22.

He was sailing out of the British channel with a fair wind and a smooth sea, when on the twenty-second of March, on occasion of the bill prohibiting New England from the fisheries, Edmund Burke, for the vindication of his party, but with no hope of success, brought forward in the house of commons resolutions for conciliation. Beyond all others, he had asserted the right of parliament to tax America; and he could not wholly justify its uprising. He began, therefore, with censuring parliament for its many in-

CHAP. XXIV. 1775. Mar. 22.

consistencies in its legislation on the subject; and then entered upon a splendid eulogy of the colonies, whose rapid growth from families to communities, from villages to nations, attended by a commerce, great out of all proportion to their numbers, had added to England in a single life as much as England had been growing to in a series of seventeen hundred years.

"As to the wealth which the colonies have drawn from the sea by their fisheries," he continued, speaking specially of the bill then in its last stage before the house, "you had all that matter fully opened at your bar. And pray, sir, what in the world is equal to it? Pass by the other parts, and look at the manner in which the people of New England have of late carried on the whale fishery. Whilst we follow them among the tumbling mountains of ice, and behold them penetrating into the deepest frozen recesses of Hudson's Bay and Davis's Straits, whilst we are looking for them beneath the arctic circle, we hear that they have pierced into the opposite region of polar cold, that they are at the antipodes, and engaged under the frozen serpent of the south. Falkland Island, which seemed too remote and romantic an object for the grasp of national ambition, is but a stage and resting place in the progress of their victorious industry. Nor is the equinoctial heat more discouraging to them, than the accumulated winter of both the poles. We know that whilst some of them draw the line and strike the harpoon on the coast of Africa, others run the longitude, and pursue their gigantic game along the coast of Brazil. No sea but what is vexed by their fisheries. No climate that is not witness to their toils. Neither the perseverance of Holland, nor the activity of France, nor the dexterous and firm sagacity of English enterprise, ever carried this most perilous mode of hard industry to the extent to which it has been pushed by this recent people; a people who are still, as it were, but in the gristle, and not yet hardened into the bone of manhood. When I contemplate these things; when I know that the colonies in general owe little or nothing to any care of ours, and that they are not squeezed into this happy form by the constraints of watchful and suspicious government, but that, through a wise and salutary neglect, a generous nature has been suffered to take her own way to perfection; when I reflect upon these effects, when I see how profitable they have been to us, I feel all the pride of power sink, and all presumption in the wisdom of human contrivances melt and die away within me. My rigor relents. I pardon something to the spirit of liberty.

"From six capital sources, of descent; of form of government; of religion in the northern provinces; of manners in the southern; of education; of the remoteness of situation from the first mover of government; from all these causes a fierce spirit of liberty has grown up. It looks to me to be narrow and pedantic to prosecute that spirit as criminal; to apply the ordinary ideas of criminal justice to this great public contest. I do not know the method of drawing up an indictment against a whole people.

"My idea, therefore, without considering whether we yield as matter of right, or grant as matter of favor, is to admit the people of our colonies into an

CHAP. XXIV. 1775. Mar. 22.

interest in the constitution. A revenue from America! You never can receive it, no, not a shilling. For all service, whether of revenue, trade, or empire, my trust is in her interest in the British constitution. My hold of the colonies is in the close affection which grows from common names, from kindred blood, from similar privileges, and equal protection. These are ties, which though light as air, are as strong as links of iron. Let the colonies always keep the idea of their civil rights associated with your government—they will cling and grapple to you; and no force under heaven will be of power to tear them from their allegiance. But let it be once understood that your government may be one thing, and their privileges another; that these two things may exist without any mutual relation; the cement is gone; the cohesion is loosened; and every thing hastens to decay and dissolution. As long as you have the wisdom to keep the sovereign authority of this country as the sanctuary of liberty, the sacred temple consecrated to our common faith, wherever the chosen race and sons of England worship freedom, they will turn their faces towards you. The more they multiply, the more friends you will have; the more ardently they love liberty, the more perfect will be their obedience. Slavery they can have anywhere. It is a weed that grows in every soil. But until you become lost to all feeling of your true interest and your natural dignity, freedom they can have from none but you. This is the commodity of price, of which you have the monopoly. This is the true act of navigation, which binds to you the commerce of the colonies, and through them secures to you the

CHAP. XXIV. 1775. Mar. 22.

wealth of the world. Deny them this participation of freedom, and you break the unity of the empire. It is the spirit of the English constitution, which, infused through the mighty mass, pervades, feeds, unites, invigorates, vivifies every part of the empire, even down to the minutest member. Is it not the same virtue which does every thing for us here in England?

"All this, I know well enough, will sound wild and chimerical to the profane herd of those vulgar and mechanical politicians, who think that nothing exists but what is gross and material; and who, therefore, far from being qualified to be directors of the great movement of empire, are not fit to turn a wheel in the machine. But to men truly initiated and rightly taught, these ruling and master principles, which, in the opinion of such men as I have mentioned, have no substantial existence, are in truth every thing, and all in all. Magnanimity in politics is not seldom the truest wisdom; and a great empire and little minds go ill together. If we are conscious of our situation, and glow with zeal to fill our places as becomes our station and ourselves, we ought to auspicate all our public proceedings on America, with the old warning of the church, LIFT UP YOUR HEARTS! We ought to elevate our minds to the greatness of that trust to which the order of Providence has called us. By adverting to the dignity of this high calling, our ancestors have turned a savage wilderness into a glorious empire; and have made the most extensive, and the only honorable conquests, not by destroying, but by promoting the

CHAP. XXIV. wealth, the number, the happiness of the human race."

1775. Mar. 22. For three hours, Burke was heard with attention; but after a reply by Jenkinson, his deep wisdom was scoffed away by a vote of more than three to one. It was the moment of greatest depression to the friends of liberty in England; their efforts in parliament only exposed their want of power. Ministers anticipated as little resistance in the colonies.

CHAPTER XXV.

VIRGINIA PREPARES FOR SELF-DEFENCE.

MARCH—APRIL, 1775.

CHAP. XXV. 1775. Mar. 20.

FROM prejudice, habit, and affection, the members of the convention of Virginia, in which even the part of Augusta county, west of the Alleghany mountains, was represented, cherished the system of limited monarchy under which they had been born and educated in their land of liberty. They were accustomed to associate all ideas of security in their political rights with the dynasty of Hanover, and had never, even in thought, desired to renounce their allegiance. They loved to consider themselves an integral part of the great British empire. The distant life of landed proprietors in solitary mansion houses, favored independence of thought; but it also generated an aristocracy, which differed widely from the simplicity and equality of New England. Educated in the Anglican church, no religious zeal had imbued them with a fixed hatred of kingly power; no deep seated antipathy to a distinction of ranks, no theoretic zeal for the introduction of a republic, no speculative

CHAP. XXV. 1775. Mar. 20. fanaticism drove them to a restless love of change. They had, on the contrary, the greatest aversion to a revolution, and abhorred the dangerous experiment of changing their form of government without some absolute necessity.

Virginia was, moreover, wholly unprepared for war. Its late expedition against the Shawanese Indians had left a debt of one hundred and fifty thousand pounds; its currency was of paper and it had no efficient system of revenue. Its soil, especially in the low country, was cultivated by negro slaves, so that the laborers in the field could not furnish recruits for an army. Except a little powder in a magazine near Williamsburg, it was destitute of warlike stores; and it had no military defences. Of all the colonies it was the most open to attack; the magnificent bay of the Chesapeake and the deep water of the James, the Potomac, and other rivers, bared it to invasions from the sea.

The people had been quick to resent aggressions, but they had not been willing to admit the thought of making that last appeal which would involve independence. Such was the state of Virginia, when on the twentieth of March its second convention assembled. The place of meeting was the old church in Richmond. The proceedings of the continental congress were approved, and the delegates of the colony in congress were applauded with perfect unanimity. On the twenty-third, thê mediating interposition of the assembly of Jamaica was considered, and was recognised as a proof of their generous and affectionate interest, and "their patriotic endeavors to fix the just claims of the colonists upon permanent constitutional principles;" and the convention of the Old Dominion renewed their assurances, "that it was the most ardent wish of their colony and of the whole continent of North America, to see a speedy return of those halcyon days when they lived a free and happy people." CHAP. XXV. 1775. Mar.

To Patrick Henry this language seemed likely to lull the public mind into confidence, at a time when the interruption of the sessions of the general assembly left them "no opportunity, in their legislative capacity, of making any provision to secure their rights from the further violations with which they were threatened." He therefore proposed "that this colony be immediately put into a posture of defence, and that a committee prepare a plan for the embodying, arming, and disciplining such a number of men, as may be sufficient for that purpose." The resolution was opposed by Bland, Harrison, and Pendleton, three of the delegates of Virginia in congress, and by Nicholas, who had been among the most resolute in the preceding May. The thought of an actual conflict in arms with England was new; they counted on the influence of the friends of liberty in the parent country, the interposition of the manufacturing interests, or the relenting of the sovereign himself. "Are we ready for war?" they asked; "are we a military people? Where are our stores, our soldiers, our generals, our money? We are defenceless; yet we talk of war against one of the most formidable nations in the world. It will be time enough to resort to measures of despair when every well-founded hope has vanished."

"What," rejoined Henry, "has there been in the conduct of the British ministry for the last ten years to

CHAP. XXV. 1775. Mar.

justify hope? Are fleets and armies necessary to a work of love and reconciliation? These are the implements of subjugation, sent over to rivet upon us the chains which the British ministry have been so long forging. And what have we to oppose to them? Shall we try argument? We have been trying that for the last ten years; have we any thing new to offer? Shall we resort to entreaty and supplication? We have petitioned—we have remonstrated—we have supplicated—and we have been spurned from the foot of the throne. In vain may we indulge the fond hope of reconciliation. There is no longer room for hope. If we wish to be free, we must fight! I repeat it sir, we must fight! An appeal to arms and to the God of Hosts is all that is left us!

"They tell me, that we are weak; but shall we gather strength by irresolution? We are not weak. Three millions of people, armed in the holy cause of liberty, and in such a country, are invincible by any force which our enemy can send against us. We shall not fight alone. A just God presides over the destinies of nations; and will raise up friends for us. The battle is not to the strong alone; it is to the vigilant, the active, the brave. Besides, we have no election. If we were base enough to desire it, it is too late to retire from the contest. There is no retreat, but in submission and slavery. The war is inevitable—and let it come! let it come!

"Is life so dear, or peace so sweet, as to be purchased at the price of chains and slavery? Forbid it, Almighty God!—I know not what course others may take; but as for me, give me liberty, or give me death."

His transfigured features glowed as he spoke, and his words fell like a doom of fate. He was supported by Richard Henry Lee, who made an estimate of the force which Britain could employ against the colonies, and after comparing it with their means of resistance, proclaimed, that the auspices were good; adding, that

Thrice is he armed, who hath his quarrel just!

The resolutions were adopted. To give them effect, a committee was raised, consisting of Patrick Henry, Richard Henry Lee, Washington, Jefferson, and others, who in a few days reported a plan for the establishment of a well-regulated militia by forming in every county one or more volunteer companies and troops of horse, to be in constant training and readiness to act on any emergency. Whatever doubts had been before expressed, the plan was unanimously accepted. Nicholas would even have desired the more energetic measure of organizing an army. The convention also voted to encourage the manufacture of woollen, cotton, and linen; of gunpowder; of salt, and iron, and steel; and recommended to the inhabitants to use colonial manufactures in preference to all others. Before dissolving their body, they elected their former delegates to the general congress, in May, adding to the number Thomas Jefferson, "in case of the non-attendance of Peyton Randolph."

To intimidate the Virginians, Dunmore issued various proclamations, and circulated a rumor that he would excite an insurrection of their slaves. He also sent a body of marines in the night preceding the twenty-first of April, to carry off the gunpowder, stored at Williamsburg in the colony's magazine. The party

CHAP. XXV. 1775. April 21. succeeded; but as soon as it was known, drums were sent through the city to alarm the inhabitants, the independent company got under arms, and the people assembled for consultation. At their instance the mayor and corporation asked the governor upon what motives the powder had been carried off privately "by an armed force, particularly at a time when they were apprehensive of an insurrection among their slaves;" and they peremptorily demanded that it should be restored.

The governor at first answered evasively; but on hearing that the citizens had reassembled under arms, he abandoned himself to passion. "The whole country," said he, "can easily be made a solitude, and by the living God! if any insult is offered to me, or those who have obeyed my orders, I will declare freedom to the slaves, and lay the town in ashes."

The offer of freedom to the negroes came very oddly from the representative of the nation which had sold them to their present masters, and of the king who had been displeased with the colony for its desire to tolerate that inhuman traffic no longer; and it was but a sad resource for a commercial metropolis, to keep a hold on its colony by letting loose slaves against its own colonists.

The seizure of the powder startled Virginia. "This first public insult is not to be tamely submitted to," wrote Hugh Mercer and others from Fredericksburg to Washington; and they proposed, as a body of light-horsemen, to march to Williamsburg for the honor of Virginia. Gloucester county would have the powder restored. The Henrico committee would be content with nothing less. Bedford offered a premium for the manufacture of gunpowder. The independent company of Dumfries could be depended upon for any service which respected the liberties of America. The Albemarle volunteers "were ready to resent arbitrary power, or die in the attempt." "I expect the magistrates of Williamsburg, on their allegiance," such was Dunmore's message, "to stop the march of the people now on their way, before they enter this city; otherwise it is my fixed purpose to arm all my own negroes, and receive and declare free all others that will come to me. I do enjoin the magistrates and all loyal subjects, to repair to my assistance, or I shall consider the whole country in rebellion, and myself at liberty to annoy it by every possible means; and I shall not hesitate at reducing houses to ashes, and spreading devastation wherever I can reach." To the secretary of state he wrote: "With a small body of troops and arms, I could raise such a force from among Indians, negroes, and other persons, as would soon reduce the refractory people of this colony to obedience."

On Saturday, the twenty-ninth of April, there were at Fredericksburg upwards of six hundred well armed men. A council of one hundred and two weighed the moderating advice received from Washington and Peyton Randolph, and they agreed to disperse; yet not till they had pledged to each other their lives and fortunes, to reassemble at a moment's warning, and by force of arms to defend the law, the liberty, and rights of Virginia, or any sister colony, from unjust and wicked invasion. Did they forebode that the message from a sister colony was already on the wing?

CHAPTER XXVI.

THE KING WAITS TO HEAR OF THE SUCCESS OF LORD NORTH'S PROPOSITION.

April—May, 1775.

CHAP. XXVI. 1775. April. Even so late as the first day of April, the provincial congress of Massachusetts, still fondly hoping for a peaceful end of all their troubles, so far recognised the authority of Gage, as to vote, that if he would issue writs in the usual form for the election of a general assembly, to be held on the last Wednesday in May, the towns ought to obey the precepts, and elect members; but in case such writs should not be issued, they recommended the choice of delegates for a third provincial congress. On Sunday, the second, two vessels arrived at Marblehead with the tidings, that both houses of parliament had pledged to the king their lives and fortunes for the reduction of America, that New England was prohibited from the fisheries, and that the army of Gage was to be largely reinforced. April 3. The next morning, congress required the attendance of all absent members, and desired the towns not yet represented to send members without delay.

"If America," wrote Joseph Warren on that day, "is an humble instrument of the salvation of Britain, it will give us the sincerest joy; but if Britain must lose her liberty, she must lose it alone. America must, and will be free. The contest may be severe—the end will be glorious. United and prepared as we are, we have no reason to doubt of success, if we should be compelled to the last appeal; but we mean not to make that appeal until we can be justified in doing it in the sight of God and man. Happy shall we be, if the mother country will allow us the free enjoyment of our rights, and indulge us in the pleasing employment of aggrandizing her."

The most appalling danger proceeded from the Indians of the northwest, whom it was now known Canadian emissaries were seeking to influence. The hateful office fell naturally into the hands of La Corne, Hamilton, the lieutenant governor for Detroit, and others, who were most ready to serve the bad passions of those from whom they expected favors. Guy Johnson was also carefully removing the American missionaries from the Six Nations.

Countervailing measures were required for immediate security. Dartmouth college, "a new and defenceless" institution of charity on the frontier, where children of the Six Nations received Christian training, was "threatened with an army of savages;" its president, Eleazer Wheelock, sent, therefore, as the first envoy from New England, the young preacher James Dean, who was a great master of the language of the Iroquois, "to itinerate as a missionary among the tribes in Canada, and brighten the chain of friendship."

CHAP. XXVI. 1775. April.

To the Mohawks, whose ancient territory included the passes from Canada and the war-paths from the more remote western nations, the Massachusetts congress despatched the humane and thoughtful Kirkland, who had lived among them as a missionary; and who was now instructed to prevail with them either to take part with the Americans, or "at least to stand neuter, and not assist their enemies." To each of the converted Indians who were domiciled at Stockbridge, the congress voted a blanket and a ribbon as a testimony of affection, saying, "we are all brothers." The Stockbridge Indians, after deliberating in council for two days, promised in their turn to intercede with the Six Nations in behalf of the colonists among whom they dwelt.

Meantime the Green Mountain Boys formally renounced the government of New York, which was virtually renouncing their allegiance to the king; and agreed to seize the fort at Ticonderoga as soon as the king's troops should commit hostilities. Their purpose was communicated in profound secrecy to Thomas Walker, a restless Anglo-Canadian, at Montreal. In my opinion," wrote Walker to Samuel Adams and Joseph Warren, "they are the most proper persons for this job, which will effectually curb the province of Quebec."

The congress of Massachusetts adopted a code for its future army, and authorized the committee of safety to form and pay six companies of artillery; yet they refused to take into pay any part of the militia or minute men. They enjoined every town to have its committee of correspondence; they ordered a day of fasting and prayer for the union of the American colonies, and their direction to such measures as God would approve; they encouraged the poor of Boston to move into the country; they sent special envoys to each of the other New England states to concert measures for raising an army of defence; and they urged "the militia and minute men" in the several towns to be on the alert. They forbade every act that could be interpreted as a commencement of hostilities; but they resolved unanimously that the militia might act on the defensive. If the forces of the colony should be called out, the members of the congress agreed to repair instantly to Concord. Then, on the fifteenth of April, they adjourned, expecting a long and desperate war with the mighty power of Great Britain, yet with no treasury but the good-will of the people; not a soldier in actual service; hardly ammunition enough for a parade day; as for artillery, having scarce more than ten cannon of iron, four of brass, and two cohorns; with no executive but the committee of safety; no internal government but by committees of correspondence; no visible centre of authority; and no distinguished general officer to take the command of the provincial troops. Anarchy must prevail, unless there lives in the heart of the people an invisible, resistless, formative principle, that can organize and guide.

CHAP. XXVI. 1775. April.

Gage, who himself had about three thousand effective men, learned through his spies the state of the country and the ludicrously scanty amount of stores, collected by the provincial committees at Worcester and Concord. The report increased his confidence as well as the insolence of his officers; and as soon as the members of the congress had gone to

CHAP. XXVI. their homes, he resolved on striking a blow, as the king desired.

1775. April 10. On the tenth of April, the lord mayor Wilkes, with the aldermen and livery of London, approached the throne, to complain to the king that the real purpose of his ministers, whom they earnestly besought him to dismiss, was, "to establish arbitrary power over all America;" the king answered: "It is with the utmost astonishment that I find any of my subjects capable of encouraging the rebellious disposition which unhappily exists in some of my colonies;" and by a letter from the lord chamberlain, he announced his purpose never again to receive on the throne any address from the lord mayor and aldermen, but in their corporate capacity.

If more troops were sent, the king's standard erected, and a few of the leaders taken up, Hutchinson was ready to stake his life for the submission of the colonies. Some of the ministry believed that they were getting more and more divided, and that there would be no great difficulty in bringing the contest to a conclusion. The sending reinforcements was treated as almost a matter of indifference.

To assist in disjoining the colonies, New York, North Carolina, and Georgia, were excepted from restraints imposed on the trade and fisheries of all the rest. That North Carolina could be retained in obedience, through a part of its own people, was believed in England, on the authority of its governor. With the utmost secrecy, the king sent over Allan Maclean of Torloish, to entice to the royal standard the Highlanders of the old forty-seventh regiment, now settled in that province; at the very time when its convention, which met on the third of April, were expressing a perfect agreement with the general congress; and were heartily seconded by its assembly.

CHAP. XXVI. 1775. April. 10.

New York was the pivot of the policy of ministers. The defection of its assembly from the acts of the general congress was accepted as conclusive proof that the province would adhere to the king. But if Rivington's gazette quoted texts of Scripture in favor of passive obedience, Holt's paper replied by other texts and examples. The New York merchants who furnished supplies to the British army at Boston, were denounced at the liberty pole as enemies to the country. When Sears, who moved that every man should provide himself with four and twenty rounds, was carried before the mayor and refused to give bail, he was liberated on his way to prison, and with flying colors, a crowd of friends, and loud huzzas for him and for MacDougal, was conducted through Broadway to a meeting in the Fields. If the assembly, by a majority of four, refused to forbid importations, the press taunted them for taking gifts, and when they would have permitted a ship to discharge its cargo, the committee laughed at their vote and enforced the association. As they refused to choose delegates to another congress, a poll was taken throughout the city, and against one hundred and sixty-three, there appeared eight hundred and twenty-five in favor of being represented. The rural counties co-operated with the city; and on the twentieth of April, forty-one delegates met in convention, chose Philip Livingston unanimously their president; re-elected all their old members to congress, except the lukewarm Isaac Low; and unani-

April 15.

April 20.

CHAP. XXVI. 1775. April. mously added five others, among them Philip Schuyler, George Clinton, and Robert R. Livingston; not to hasten a revolution, but to "concert measures for the preservation of American rights, and for the restoration of harmony between Great Britain and the colonies."

This happened at a time when the king believed New York won over by immunities and benefactions, and the generals who were on the point of sailing were disputing for the command at that place. "Burgoyne would best manage a negotiation," said the king; but Howe would not resign his right to the post of confidence. Vergennes saw things just as they were; the British ministry, with a marvellous blindness that but for positive evidence would be incredible, thought it easy to subdue Massachusetts, and corrupt New York. On the fifteenth day of April, letters were written to Gage, to take possession of every colonial fort; to seize and secure all military stores of every kind, collected for the rebels; to arrest and imprison all such as should be thought to have committed treason; to repress rebellion by force; to make the public safety the first object of consideration; to substitute more coercive measures for ordinary forms of proceeding, without pausing "to require the aid of a civil magistrate." Thurlow and Wedderburn had given their opinion that the Massachusetts congress was a treasonable body. The power of pardon, which was now conferred on the general, did not extend to the president of "that seditious meeting," nor to "its most forward members," who, as unfit subjects for the king's mercy, were to be brought "to condign punishment" by prosecution either in America or in England.

While the king, through Lord Dartmouth, confidently issued these sanguinary instructions which a numerous army could hardly have enforced, four of the regiments at first destined to Boston, received orders to proceed directly to New York, where their presence was to aid the progress of intrigue. At the same time the "Senegal" carried out six packages, each containing a very large number of copies of "An address of the people of Great Britain to the inhabitants of America," written in the blandest terms by Sir John Dalrymple at Lord North's request, to coöperate with his conciliatory resolution.

"The power of taxation over you," said the pamphleteer, "we desire to throw from us as unworthy of you to be subject to, and of us to possess. We wished to make the concession. From the late differences it is the fault of us both, if we do not derive future agreement by some great act of state. Let the colonies make the first advance; if not, parliament will do so by sending a commission to America. The first honor will belong to the party which shall first scorn punctilio in so noble a cause. We give up the disgraceful and odious privilege of taxing you. As to the judges dependent on the king's pleasure, if you suspect us, appoint your own judges, pay them your own salaries. If we are wrong in thinking your charters formed by accident, not by forethought, let them stand as they are. Continue to share the liberty of England. With such sentiments of kindness in our breasts, we cannot hear without the deepest concern a charge, that a system has been formed to enslave you by means of parliament."

The mild and affectionate language of this pam-

CHAP. XXVI. 1775. April. phlet, composed for the ministers, printed at the public cost, and sent out by public authority to be widely distributed, formed a strange contrast to that written by Samuel Johnson for England, and clashed discordantly with the vengeful orders transmitted to Boston. Yet Lord North was false only as he was weak and uncertain. He really wished to concede and conciliate, but he had not force enough to come to a clear understanding even with himself. When he encountered the opposition in the house of commons, he sustained his administration by speaking confidently for vigorous measures; when alone his heart sank within him from dread of civil war.

The remonstrance and memorial of the assembly of New York, which Burke, their agent, presented to
May. 15. parliament on the fifteenth of May, was rejected, because they questioned the right of parliament to tax America. Three days later, Lord North avowed the orders for raising Canadian regiments of French Papists; "however," he continued, "the dispute with America is not so alarming as some people apprehend. I have not the least doubt it will end speedily, happily, and without bloodshed."

May 23. On the twenty-third of May, secret advices from Philadelphia confirmed Dartmouth and the king in their confidence, that North's conciliatory resolution "would remove all obstacles to the restoration of public tranquillity," through "the moderation and loyal disposition of the assembly of New York." The king, in proroguing parliament on the twenty-sixth, no longer introduced the rebel people of Massachusetts, but spoke only of "his subjects in America, whose wishes were to be gratified and apprehensions removed as far as the constitution would allow." The court gazette of the day was equally moderate. The members of parliament dispersed, and as yet no tidings came from the colonies of a later date than the middle of April. All America, from Lake Champlain to the Altamaha; all Europe, Madrid, Paris, Amsterdam, Vienna, hardly less than London, were gazing with expectation towards the little villages that lay around Boston.

CHAP. XXVI. 1775. May. 27.

CHAPTER XXVII.

LEXINGTON.

April 19, 1775.

CHAP. XXVII. 1775. April 19.

On the afternoon of the day on which the provincial congress of Massachusetts adjourned, Gage took the light infantry and grenadiers off duty, and secretly prepared an expedition to destroy the colony's stores at Concord. But the attempt had for several weeks been expected; a strict watch had been kept; and signals were concerted to announce the first movement of troops for the country. Samuel Adams and Hancock, who had not yet left Lexington for Philadelphia, received a timely message from Warren, and in consequence, the committee of safety removed a part of the public stores and secreted the cannon.

On Tuesday the eighteenth, ten or more sergeants in disguise dispersed themselves through Cambridge and further west, to intercept all communication. In the following night, the grenadiers and light infantry, not less than eight hundred in number, the flower of the army at Boston, commanded by the incompetent Lieutenant Colonel Smith, crossed in the boats of

CHAP. XXVII. 1775. April 19.

the transport ships from the foot of the common to East Cambridge. There they received a day's provisions, and near midnight, after wading through wet marshes, that are now covered by a stately town, they took the road through West Cambridge to Concord.

"They will miss their aim," said one of a party who observed their departure. "What aim?" asked Lord Percy, who overheard the remark. "Why, the cannon at Concord," was the answer. Percy hastened to Gage, who instantly directed that no one should be suffered to leave the town. But Warren had already, at ten o'clock, despatched William Dawes through Roxbury to Lexington, and at the same time desired Paul Revere to set off by way of Charlestown.

Revere stopped only to engage a friend to raise the concerted signals, and five minutes before the sentinels received the order to prevent it, two friends rowed him past the Somerset man of war across Charles river. All was still, as suited the hour. The ship was winding with the young flood; the waning moon just peered above a clear horizon; while from a couple of lanterns in the tower of the North Church, the beacon streamed to the neighboring towns, as fast as light could travel.

A little beyond Charlestown Neck, Revere was intercepted by two British officers on horseback; but being himself well mounted, he turned suddenly, and leading one of them into a clay pond, escaped from the other by the road to Medford. As he passed on, he waked the captain of the minute men of that town, and continued to rouse almost every house on the way to Lexington.

CHAP. XXVII. 1775. April 19. The troops had not advanced far, when the firing of guns and ringing of bells announced that their expedition had been heralded before them; and Smith sent back to demand a reinforcement.

On the morning of the nineteenth of April, between the hours of twelve and one, the message from Warren reached Adams and Hancock, who divined at once the object of the expedition. Revere, therefore, and Dawes, joined by Samuel Prescott, "a high son of liberty" from Concord, rode forward, calling up the inhabitants as they passed along, till in Lincoln they fell upon a party of British officers. Revere and Dawes were seized and taken back to Lexington, where they were released; but Prescott leaped over a low stone wall, and galloped on for Concord.

There at about two in the morning, a peal from the belfry of the meeting-house called the inhabitants of the place to their town hall. They came forth, young and old, with their firelocks, ready to make good the resolute words of their town debates. Among the most alert was William Emerson the minister, with gun in hand, his powder-horn and pouch for balls slung over his shoulder. By his sermons and his prayers, he had so hallowed the enthusiasm of his flock, that they held the defence of their liberties a part of their covenant with God; his presence with arms, proved his sincerity and strengthened their sense of duty.

From daybreak to sunrise, the summons ran from house to house through Acton. Express messengers and volleys from minute men spread the alarm. How children trembled as they were scared out of sleep by the cries! How wives with heaving breasts, bravely seconded their husbands; how the countrymen, forced suddenly to arm, without guides or counsellors, took instant counsel of their courage. The mighty chorus of voices rose from the scattered farm-houses, and as it were from the very ashes of the dead. Come forth, champions of liberty; now free your country; protect your sons and daughters, your wives and homesteads; rescue the houses of the God of your fathers, the franchises handed down from your ancestors. Now all is at stake; the battle is for all.

CHAP. XXVII. 1775. April 19.

Lexington, in 1775, may have had seven hundred inhabitants; forming one parish, and having for their minister the learned and fervent Jonas Clark, the bold inditer of patriotic state papers that may yet be read on their town records. In December, 1772, they had instructed their representative to demand "a radical and lasting redress of their grievances, for not through their neglect should the people be enslaved." A year later, they spurned the use of tea. In 1774, at various town meetings, they voted "to increase their stock of ammunition," "to encourage military discipline, and to put themselves in a posture of defence against their enemies." In December, they distributed to "the train band and alarm list" arms and ammunition, and resolved to "supply the training soldiers with bayonets."

At two in the morning, under the eye of the minister, and of Hancock and Adams, Lexington common was alive with the minute men; and not with them only, but with the old men also, who were exempts, except in case of immediate danger to the town. The roll was called, and of militia and alarm men, about

CHAP. XXVII. 1775. April 19. one hundred and thirty answered to their names. The captain, John Parker, ordered every one to load with powder and ball, but to take care not to be the first to fire. Messengers, sent to look for the British regulars, reported that there were no signs of their approach. A watch was therefore set, and the company dismissed with orders to come together at beat of drum. Some went to their own homes; some to the tavern, near the southeast corner of the common.

Adams and Hancock, whose proscription had already been divulged, and whose seizure was believed to be intended, were compelled by persuasion to retire towards Woburn.

The last stars were vanishing from night, when the foremost party, led by Pitcairn, a major of marines, was discovered, advancing quickly and in silence. Alarm guns were fired, and the drums beat, not a call to village husbandmen only, but the reveille to humanity. Less than seventy, perhaps less than sixty, obeyed the summons, and in sight of half as many boys and unarmed men, were paraded in two ranks, a few rods north of the meeting-house.

How often in that building had they, with renewed professions of their faith, looked up to God as the stay of their fathers, and the protector of their privileges! How often on that village green, hard by the burial place of their forefathers, had they pledged themselves to each other to combat manfully for their birthright inheritance of liberty! There they now stood side by side, under the provincial banner, with arms in their hands, silent and fearless, willing to fight for their privileges, scrupulous not to begin civil war, and as yet unsuspicious of immediate danger. The ground on which they trod was the altar of freedom, and they were to furnish its victims. CHAP. XXVII.

The British van, hearing the drum and the alarm guns, halted to load; the remaining companies came up; and at half an hour before sunrise, the advance party hurried forward at double quick time, almost upon a run, closely followed by the grenadiers. Pitcairn rode in front, and when within five or six rods of the minute men, cried out: "Disperse, ye villains, ye rebels, disperse; lay down your arms; why don't you lay down your arms and disperse?" The main part of the countrymen stood motionless in the ranks, witnesses against aggression; too few to resist, too brave to fly. At this Pitcairn discharged a pistol, and with a loud voice cried, "Fire." The order was instantly followed, first by a few guns, which did no execution, and then by a heavy, close, and deadly discharge of musketry. 1775. April 19.

In the disparity of numbers, the common was a field of murder, not of battle; Parker, therefore, ordered his men to disperse. Then, and not till then, did a few of them, on their own impulse, return the British fire. These random shots of fugitives or dying men did no harm, except that Pitcairn's horse was perhaps grazed, and a private of the tenth light infantry was touched slightly in the leg.

Jonas Parker, the strongest and best wrestler in Lexington, had promised never to run from British troops; and he kept his vow. A wound brought him on his knees. Having discharged his gun, he was preparing to load it again, when as sound a heart as ever throbbed for freedom was stilled by a bayo-

CHAP. XXVII. 1775. April 19. net, and he lay on the post which he took at the morning's drum beat. So fell Isaac Muzzey, and so died the aged Robert Munroe, the same who in 1758 had been an ensign at Louisburg. Jonathan Harrington, junior, was struck in front of his own house on the north of the common. His wife was at the window as he fell. With the blood gushing from his breast, he rose in her sight, tottered, fell again, then crawled on hands and knees towards his dwelling; she ran to meet him, but only reached him as he expired on their threshold. Caleb Harrington, who had gone into the meeting-house for powder, was shot as he came out. Samuel Hadley and John Brown were pursued, and killed after they had left the green. Asahel Porter, of Woburn, who had been taken prisoner by the British on the march, endeavoring to escape, was shot within a few rods of the common.

Day came in all the beauty of an early spring. The trees were budding; the grass growing rankly a full month before the season; the blue bird and the robin gladdening the genial season, and calling forth the beams of the sun which on that morning shone with the warmth of summer; but distress and horror gathered over the inhabitants of the peaceful town. There on the green, lay in death the gray-haired and the young; the grassy field was red "with the innocent blood of their brethren slain," crying unto God for vengeance from the ground.

Seven of the men of Lexington were killed; nine wounded; a quarter part of those who stood in arms on the green. These are the village heroes, who were more than of noble blood, proving by their spirit that they were of a race divine. They gave their lives in testimony to the rights of mankind, bequeathing to their country an assurance of success in the mighty struggle which they began. Their names are had in grateful remembrance, and the expanding millions of their countrymen renew and multiply their praise from generation to generation. They fulfilled their duty not from the accidental impulse of the moment; their action was the slowly ripened fruit of Providence and of time. The light that led them on, was combined of rays from the whole history of the race; from the traditions of the Hebrews in the gray of the world's morning; from the heroes and sages of republican Greece and Rome; from the example of Him who laid down his life on the cross for the life of humanity; from the religious creed which proclaimed the divine presence in man, and on this truth as in a life-boat, floated the liberties of nations over the dark flood of the middle ages; from the customs of the Germans transmitted out of their forests to the councils of Saxon England; from the burning faith and courage of Martin Luther; from trust in the inevitable universality of God's sovereignty as taught by Paul of Tarsus, and Augustine, through Calvin and the divines of New England; from the avenging fierceness of the Puritans, who dashed down the mitre on the ruins of the throne; from the bold dissent and creative self assertion of the earliest emigrants to Massachusetts; from the statesmen who made, and the philosophers who expounded, the revolution of England; from the liberal spirit and analyzing inquisitiveness of the eighteenth century; from the cloud of witnesses of all the ages to the

CHAP. XXVII. 1775. April 19.

CHAP. XXVII. 1775. April 19.

reality and the rightfulness of human freedom. All the centuries bowed themselves from the recesses of a past eternity to cheer in their sacrifice the lowly men who proved themselves worthy of their forerunners, and whose children rise up and call them blessed.

Heedless of his own danger, Samuel Adams, with the voice of a prophet, exclaimed, "Oh! what a glorious morning is this!" for he saw that his country's independence was rapidly hastening on, and, like Columbus in the tempest, knew that the storm did but bear him the more swiftly towards the undiscovered world.

CHAPTER XXVIII.

TO CONCORD AND BACK TO BOSTON.

April Nineteenth, 1775.

CHAP. XXVIII 1775. April 19.

The British troops drew up on the village green, fired a volley, huzzaed thrice by way of triumph, and after a halt of less than thirty minutes, marched on for Concord. There, in the morning hours, children and women fled for shelter to the hills and the woods, and men were hiding what was left of cannon and military stores.

The minute companies and militia formed on the usual parade, over which the congregation of the town, for near a century and a half, had passed on every day of public worship; the freemen to every town meeting; and lately the patriot members of the provincial congress twice a day to their little senate house. Near that spot Winthrop, the father of Massachusetts, had given counsel; and Eliot, the apostle of the Indians, had spoken words of benignity and wisdom. The people of Concord, of whom about two hundred appeared in arms on that day, were unpretending men, content in their humil-

CHAP. XXVIII. ity; their energy was derived from their sense of the divine power. This looking to God as their sovereign, brought the fathers to their pleasant valley; this controlled the loyalty of the sons; and this has made the name of Concord venerable throughout the world.

1775. April 19.

The alarm company of the place rallied near the liberty pole on the hill, to the right of the Lexington road, in the rear of the meeting-house. They went to the perilous duties of the day, "with seriousness and acknowledgment of God," as though they were to be engaged in acts of worship. The minute company of Lincoln, and a few from Acton, pressed in at an early hour; but the British, as they approached, were seen to be four times as numerous as the Americans. The latter, therefore, retreated, first to an eminence eighty rods further north, then across the Concord river by the North bridge, till just beyond it, by a back road they gained high ground, about a mile from the centre of the town. There they waited for aid.

About seven o'clock, the British marched with rapid step under the brilliant sunshine into Concord, the light infantry along the hills, and the grenadiers in the lower road. Left in undisputed possession of the hamlet, they made search for stores. To this end, one small party was sent to the South bridge over Concord river; and of six companies under Captain Laurie, three, comprising a hundred soldiers or more, were stationed as a guard at the North bridge, while three others advanced two miles further, to the residence of Barrett, the highest military officer of the neighborhood, where arms were thought to have been concealed. But they found there nothing to destroy except some carriages for cannon. His wife at their demand gave them refreshment; but refused pay, saying: "We are commanded to feed our enemy, if he hunger."

CHAP. XXVIII

1775. April 19.

At daybreak, the minute men of Acton crowded at the drumbeat to the house of Isaac Davis, their captain, who "made haste to be ready." Just thirty years old, the father of four little ones, stately in his person, a man of few words, earnest even to solemnity, he parted from his wife, saying, "Take good care of the children," as though he had foreseen that his own death was near; and while she gazed after him with resignation, he led off his company to the scene of danger.

Between nine and ten, the number of Americans on the rising ground above Concord bridge had increased to more than four hundred. Of these there were twenty-five minute men from Bedford, with Jonathan Wilson for their captain; others were from Westford, among them Thaxter, a preacher; others from Littleton, from Carlisle, and from Chelmsford. The Acton company came last, and formed on the right. The whole was a gathering not so much of officers and soldiers, as of brothers and equals; of whom every one was a man well known in his village, observed in the meeting-house on Sundays, familiar at town meetings, and respected as a freeholder or a freeholder's son.

Near the base of the hill, Concord river flows languidly in a winding channel, and was approached by a causeway over the wet ground of its left bank. The by-road from the hill on which the Americans

CHAP. XXVIII. 1775. April 19. had rallied, ran southerly till it met the causeway at right angles. The Americans saw before them within gunshot British troops holding possession of their bridge; and in the distance a still larger number occupying their town, which, from the rising smoke, seemed to have been set on fire.

In Concord itself, Pitcairn had fretted and fumed with oaths and curses at the tavern-keeper for shutting against him the doors of the inn, and exulted over the discovery of two twenty-four pounders in the tavern yard, as though they reimbursed the expedition. These were spiked; sixty barrels of flour were broken in pieces, but so imperfectly, that afterwards half the flour was saved; five hundred pounds of ball were thrown into a mill-pond. The liberty pole and several carriages for artillery were burned; and the court house took fire, though the fire was put out. Private dwellings were rifled; but this slight waste of public stores was all the advantage for which Gage precipitated a civil war.

The Americans had as yet received only uncertain rumors of the morning's events at Lexington. At the sight of fire in the village, the impulse seized them "to march into the town for its defence." But were they not subjects of the British king? Had not the troops come out in obedience to constituted and acknowledged authorities? Was resistance practicable? Was it justifiable? By whom could it be authorized? No union had been formed; no independence proclaimed; no war declared. The husbandmen and mechanics who then stood on the hillock by Concord river, were called on to act, and their action would be war or peace, submission or independence. Had they doubted, they must have despaired. CHAP. XXVIII

But duty is bolder than theory, more confident than the understanding, older and more imperative than speculative science; existing from eternity, and recognised in its binding force from the first morning of creation. Prudent statesmanship would have asked anxiously for time to ponder, and would have missed the moment for decision by delay. Wise philosophy would have compared the systems of government, and would have lost from hesitation the glory of opening a new era on mankind. The humble train-bands at Concord acted, and God was with them. 1775. April 19.

"I never heard from any person the least expression of a wish for a separation," Franklin, not long before, had said to Chatham. In October, 1774, Washington wrote, "No such thing as independence is desired by any thinking man in America." "Before the nineteenth of April, 1775," relates Jefferson, "I never had heard a whisper of a disposition to separate from Great Britain." Just thirty-seven days had passed, since John Adams in Boston published to the world: "That there are any who pant after independence, is the greatest slander on the province."

The American revolution did not proceed from precarious intentions. It grew out of the soul of the people, and was an inevitable result of a living affection for freedom, which actuated harmonious effort as certainly as the beating of the heart sends warmth and color and beauty to the system. The rustic heroes of that hour obeyed the simplest, the highest, and the surest instincts, of which the seminal principle

CHAP. XXVIII 1775. April 19. existed in all their countrymen. From necessity they were impelled by a strong endeavor towards independence and self-direction; this day revealed the plastic will which was to attract the elements of a nation to a centre, and by an innate force to shape its constitution.

The officers, meeting in front of their men, spoke a few words with one another, and went back to their places. Barrett, the colonel, on horseback in the rear, then gave the order to advance, but not to fire unless attacked. The calm features of Isaac Davis, of Acton, became changed; the town schoolmaster, who was present, could never afterwards find words strong enough to express, how his face reddened at the word of command. "I have not a man that is afraid to go," said Davis, looking at the men of Acton; and drawing his sword, he cried, "March." His company, being on the right, led the way towards the bridge, he himself at their head, and by his side Major John Buttrick, of Concord, with John Robinson, of Westford, lieutenant colonel in Prescott's regiment, but on this day a volunteer without command.

Thus these three men walked together in front, followed by minute men and militia, in double file, trailing arms. They went down the hillock, entered the by-road, came to its angle with the main road, and there turned into the causeway that led straight to the bridge. The British began to take up the planks; the Americans, to prevent it, quickened their step. At this, the British fired one or two shots up the river; then another, by which Luther Blanchard and Jonas Brown were wounded. A volley followed, and Isaac Davis and Abner Hosmer, the latter a son of the deacon of the Acton church, fell dead. Three hours before, Davis had bid his wife and children farewell. That afternoon, he was carried home and laid in her bedroom. His countenance was little altered and pleasant in death. The bodies of two others of his company who were slain that day were brought also to her house, and the three were followed to the village graveyard by a concourse of the neighbors from miles around. God gave her length of days in the land which his generous self-devotion assisted to redeem. She lived to see her country touch the gulf of Mexico and the Pacific, and when it was grown great in numbers, wealth, and power, the United States in congress paid honors to her husband's martyrdom, and comforted her under the double burden of sorrow and more than ninety years.

As the British fired, Emerson, who was looking on from his chamber window near the bridge, was for one moment uneasy, lest the fire should not be returned. It was only for a moment; Buttrick, leaping into the air, and at the same time partially turning round, cried aloud, as if with his country's voice, "Fire, fellow-soldiers, for God's sake fire;" and the cry, "fire, fire, fire," ran from lip to lip. Two of the British fell; several were wounded. In two minutes, all was hushed. The British retreated in disorder towards their main body; the countrymen were left in possession of the bridge. This is the world renowned BATTLE OF CONCORD; more eventful than Agincourt or Blenheim.

The Americans had acted from impulse, and stood

CHAP. XXVIII. 1775. April 19.

astonished at what they had done. They made no pursuit and did no further harm, except that one wounded soldier, attempting to rise as if to escape, was struck on the head by a young man with a hatchet. The party at Barrett's might have been cut off, but was not molested. As the Sudbury company, commanded by the brave Nixon, passed near the South bridge, Josiah Haynes, then eighty years of age, deacon of the Sudbury church, urged an attack on the British party stationed there; his advice was rejected by his fellow-soldiers as premature, but the company in which he served proved among the most alert during the rest of the day.

In the town of Concord, Smith, for half an hour, showed by marches and countermarches, his uncertainty of purpose. At last, about noon, he left the town, to retreat the way he came, along the crooked and hilly road that wound through forests and thickets. The minute men and militia, who had taken part in the fight, ran over the hills opposite the battle field into the east quarter of the town, crossed the pasture known as the "Great Fields," and acting each from his own impulse, placed themselves in ambush a little to the eastward of the village, near the junction of the Bedford road. There they were reinforced by men who were coming in from all around, and at that point the chase of the English began.

Among the foremost were the minute men of Reading, led by John Brooks, and accompanied by Foster the minister of Littleton as a volunteer. The company of Billerica, whose inhabitants, in their just indignation at Nesbit and his soldiers, had openly resolved to "use a different style from that of petition and complaint," came down from the north, while the East Sudbury company appeared on the south. A little below the Bedford road, at Merriam's corner, the British faced about; but after a sharp encounter, in which several of them were killed, they were compelled to resume their retreat.

CHAP. XXVIII

1775. April 19.

At the high land in Lincoln, the old road bent towards the north; just where great trees on the west, thickets on the east, and stone walls in every direction, offered cover to the pursuers. The men from Woburn came up in great numbers, and well armed. Along these defiles, eight of the British were left. Here Pitcairn was forced to quit his horse, which was taken with his pistols in their holsters. A little further on, Jonathan Wilson, captain of the Bedford minute men, too zealous to keep on his guard, was killed by a flanking party. At another defile in Lincoln, the minute men of Lexington, commanded by John Parker, renewed the fight. Every piece of wood, every rock by the wayside, served as a lurking-place. Scarce ten of the Americans were at any time seen together; yet the hills on each side seemed to the British to swarm with "rebels," as if they had dropped from the clouds, and "the road was lined" by an unintermitted fire from behind stone walls and trees.

At first the invaders moved in order; as they drew near Lexington, their flanking parties became ineffective from weariness; the wounded were scarce able to get forward. In the west of Lexington, as the British were rising Fiske's hill, a sharp contest ensued. It was at the eastern foot of the same hill,

CHAP. XXVIII. 1775. April 19. that James Hayward, son of the deacon of Acton church, encountered a regular, and both at the same moment fired; the regular was instantly killed, James Hayward was mortally wounded. A little further on fell the octogenarian Josiah Haynes, of Sudbury, who had kept pace by the side of the swiftest in the pursuit, with a rugged valor which age had not tempered.

The British troops, "greatly exhausted and fatigued, and having expended almost all their ammunition," began to run rather than retreat in order. The officers vainly attempted to stop their flight. "They were driven before the Americans like sheep." At last, about two in the afternoon, after they had hurried with shameful haste through the middle of the town, about a mile below the field of the morning's murder, the officers got to the front, and by menaces of death, began to form them under a very heavy fire.

At that moment Lord Percy came in sight with the first brigade, consisting of Welsh fusiliers, the fourth, the forty-seventh, and the thirty-eighth regiments, in all about twelve hundred men, with two field pieces. Insolent as usual, they marched out of Boston to the tune of Yankee Doodle; but they grew alarmed at finding every house on the road deserted. They met not one person to give them tidings of the party whom they were sent to rescue; and now that they had made the junction, they could think only of their own safety.

While the cannon kept the Americans at bay, Percy formed his detachment into a square, enclosing the fugitives, who lay down for rest on the ground, "their tongues hanging out of their mouths like those of dogs after a chase."

CHAP. XXVIII

1775. April 19.

From this time the Americans had to contend against nearly the whole of the British army in Boston. Its best troops, fully two-thirds of its whole number, and more than that proportion of its strength, were now with Percy. And yet delay was sure to prove ruinous. The British must fly speedily and fleetly, or be overwhelmed. Two wagons sent out to them with supplies, were waylaid and captured by Payson, the minister of Chelsea. From far and wide minute men were gathering. The men of Dedham, even the old men, received their minister's blessing and went forth, in such numbers that scarce one male between sixteen and seventy was left at home. That morning William Prescott mustered his regiment, and though Pepperell was so remote that he could not be in season for the pursuit, he hastened down with five companies of guards. Before noon, a messenger rode at full speed into Worcester, crying "To arms;" a fresh horse was brought, and the tidings went on; while the minute men of that town, joining hurriedly on the common in a fervent prayer from their minister, did not halt even for rest till they reached Cambridge.

Aware of his perilous position, Percy, after resting but half an hour, renewed the retreat. The light infantry marched in front, the grenadiers next, while the first brigade, which now furnished the very strong flanking parties, brought up the rear. They were exposed to a fire on each flank, in front and from behind. The Americans, who were good marksmen, would lie down concealed to load their guns at one place, and discharge them at another, running from front to flank, and from flank to rear. Rage

CHAP. XXVIII 1775. April 19. and revenge and shame at their flight led the regulars to plunder houses by the wayside, to destroy in wantonness windows and furniture, to set fire to barns and houses.

Beyond Lexington the troops were attacked by men chiefly from Essex and the lower towns. The fire from the rebels slackened, till they approached West Cambridge, where Joseph Warren and William Heath, both of the committee of safety, the latter a provincial general officer, gave for a moment some little appearance of organization to the resistance, and the fight grew sharper and more determined. Here the company from Danvers, which made a breastwork of a pile of shingles, lost eight men, caught between the enemy's flank guard and main body. Here, too, a musket ball grazed the hair of Warren, whose heart beat to arms, so that he was ever in the place of greatest danger. The British became more and more "exasperated;" and indulged themselves in savage cruelty. In one house they found two aged, helpless, unarmed men, and butchered them both without mercy, stabbing them, breaking their skulls, and dashing out their brains. Hannah Adams, wife of Deacon Joseph Adams of Cambridge, lay in child-bed with a babe of a week old, but was forced to crawl with her infant in her arms and almost naked to a corn shed, while the soldiers set her house on fire. At Cambridge, an idiot, perched on a fence to gaze at the regular army, was wantonly shot at and killed. Of the Americans there were never more than four hundred together at any one time; but as some grew tired or used up their ammunition, others took their places, and though there was not much concert or discipline, the pursuit never flagged. CHAP. XXVIII

Below West Cambridge, the militia from Dorchester, Roxbury, and Brookline came up. Of these, Isaac Gardner of the latter place, one on whom the colony rested many hopes, fell about a mile west of Harvard college. The field pieces began to lose their terror, so that the Americans pressed upon the rear of the fugitives, whose retreat could not become more precipitate. Had it been delayed a half hour longer, or had Pickering with his fine regiment from Salem and Marblehead been alert enough to have intercepted them in front, it was thought that, worn down as they were by fatigue and exhausted of ammunition, they must have surrendered. But a little after sunset, the survivors escaped across Charlestown neck. 1775. April 19.

The troops of Percy had marched thirty miles in ten hours; the party of Smith, in six hours, had retreated twenty miles; the guns of the ships of war and a menace to burn the town of Charlestown saved them from annoyance during their rest on Bunker Hill, and while they were ferried across Charles river.

During the day, forty-nine Americans were killed, thirty-four wounded, and five missing. The loss of the British in killed, wounded, and missing, was two hundred and seventy-three. Among the wounded were many officers; Smith himself was hurt severely.

All the night long, the men of Massachusetts streamed in from scores of miles around, old men as well as young. They had scarce a semblance of artillery, or warlike stores; no powder, nor organiza-

CHAP. XXVIII. 1775. April 19. tion, nor provisions; but there they were, thousands with brave hearts, determined to rescue the liberties of their country. "The night preceding the outrages at Lexington, there were not fifty people in the whole colony that ever expected any blood would be shed in the contest;" the night after, the king's governor and the king's army found themselves closely beleaguered in Boston.

"The next news from England must be conciliatory, or the connection between us ends," said Warren. "This month," so William Emerson of Concord, who had been chaplain to the provincial congress, chronicled in a blank leaf of his almanac, "is remarkable for the greatest events of the present age." "From the nineteenth of April, 1775," said Clark, of Lexington, on its first anniversary, "will be dated the liberty of the American world."

CHAPTER XXIX.

EFFECTS OF THE DAY OF LEXINGTON AND CONCORD: THE ALARM.

APRIL, 1775.

DARKNESS closed upon the country and upon the town, but it was no night for sleep. Heralds on swift relays of horses transmitted the war-message from hand to hand, till village repeated it to village; the sea to the backwoods; the plains to the highlands; and it was never suffered to droop, till it had been borne north, and south, and east, and west, throughout the land. It spread over the bays that receive the Saco and the Penobscot. Its loud reveille broke the rest of the trappers of New Hampshire, and ringing like bugle-notes from peak to peak, overleapt the Green Mountains, swept onward to Montreal, and descended the ocean river, till the responses were echoed from the cliffs of Quebec. The hills along the Hudson told to one another the tale. As the summons hurried to the south, it was one day at New York; in one more at Philadelphia; the next it lighted a watchfire at Baltimore; thence it waked an answer at Annapolis. Crossing

CHAP. XXIX. 1775. April 19.

CHAP. XXIX. 1775. April. the Potomac near Mount Vernon, it was sent forward without a halt to Williamsburg. It traversed the Dismal Swamp to Nansemond along the route of the first emigrants to North Carolina. It moved onwards and still onwards through boundless groves of evergreen to Newbern and to Wilmington. "For God's sake, forward it by night and by day," wrote Cornelius Harnett by the express which sped for Brunswick. Patriots of South Carolina caught up its tones at the border, and despatched it to Charleston, and through pines and palmettoes and moss-clad live oaks, still further to the south, till it resounded among the New England settlements beyond the Savannah. Hillsborough and the Mecklenburg district of North Carolina rose in triumph, now that their wearisome uncertainty had its end. The Blue Ridge took up the voice and made it heard from one end to the other of the valley of Virginia. The Alleghanies, as they listened, opened their barriers that the "loud call" might pass through to the hardy riflemen on the Holston, the Watauga, and the French Broad. Ever renewing its strength, powerful enough even to create a commonwealth, it breathed its inspiring word to the first settlers of Kentucky; so that hunters who made their halt in the matchless valley of the Elkhorn, commemorated the nineteenth day of April by naming their encampment LEXINGTON.

With one impulse the colonies sprung to arms: with one spirit they pledged themselves to each other "to be ready for the extreme event." With one heart, the continent cried "Liberty or Death."

The first measure of the Massachusetts committee of safety after the dawn of the twentieth of April,

CHAP XXIX. 1775. April.

was a circular to the several towns in Massachusetts. "We conjure you," they wrote, "by all that is dear, by all that is sacred; we beg and entreat, as you will answer it to your country, to your consciences, and above all, to God himself, that you will hasten and encourage by all possible means the enlistment of men to form the army; and send them forward to head-quarters at Cambridge with that expedition which the vast importance and instant urgency of the affair demands."

The people of Massachusetts had not waited for the call. The country people, as soon as they heard the cry of innocent blood from the ground, snatched their firelocks from the walls; and wives, and mothers, and sisters took part in preparing the men of their households to go forth to the war. The farmers rushed to "the camp of liberty," often with nothing but the clothes on their backs, without a day's provisions, and many without a farthing in their pockets. Their country was in danger; their brethren were slaughtered; their arms alone employed their attention. On their way, the inhabitants gladly opened their hospitable doors and all things were in common. For the first night of the siege, Prescott of Pepperell with his Middlesex minute men kept the watch over the entrance to Boston, and while Gage was driven for safety to fortify the town at all points, the Americans already talked of nothing but driving him and his regiments into the sea.

At the same time the committee by letter gave the story of the preceding day to New Hampshire and Connecticut, whose assistance they entreated. "We shall be glad," they wrote, "that our brethren

CHAP. XXIX. 1775. April. who come to our aid, may be supplied with military stores and provisions, as we have none of either, more than is absolutely necessary for ourselves." And without stores, or cannon, or supplies even of powder, or of money, Massachusetts by its congress, on the twenty-second of April, resolved unanimously that a New England army of thirty thousand men should be raised, and established its own proportion at thirteen thousand six hundred. The term of enlistment was fixed for the last day of December.

Long before this summons the ferries over the Merrimack were crowded by men from New Hampshire. "We go," said they, "to the assistance of our brethren." By one o'clock of the twentieth upwards of sixty men of Nottingham assembled at the meeting-house with arms and equipments, under Cilley and Dearborn; before two they were joined by bands from Deerfield, and Epsom; and they set out together for Cambridge. At dusk they reached Haverhill ferry, a distance of twenty-seven miles, having run rather than marched; they halted in Andover only for refreshments, and traversing fifty-five miles in less than twenty hours, by sunrise of the twenty-first, paraded on Cambridge common.

The veteran John Stark, skilled in the ways of the Indian, the English, and his countrymen, able to take his rest on a bearskin with a roll of snow for a pillow, frank and humane, eccentric but true, famed for coolness, and courage, and integrity, had no rival in the confidence of his neighbors, and was chosen colonel of their regiment by their unanimous vote. He rode in haste to the scene of action, on the way encouraging the volunteers to rendezvous at Medford. So many followed, that on the morning of the twenty-second, he was detached with three hundred to take post at Chelsea, where his battalion, which was one of the fullest in the besieging army, became a model for its discipline.

By the twenty-third, there were already about two thousand men from the interior parts of New Hampshire, desirous "not to return before the work was done." Many who remained near the upper Connecticut, threw up the civil and military commissions held from the king, for said they: "The king has forfeited his crown, and all commissions from him are therefore vacated of course."

In Connecticut, Trumbull, the governor, sent out writs to convene the legislature of the colony at Hartford on the Wednesday following the battle. Meantime the people could not be restrained. On the morning of the twentieth, Israel Putnam, of Pomfret, in leather frock and apron, was assisting hired men to build a stone wall on his farm, when he heard the cry from Lexington. Leaving them to continue their task, he set off instantly to rouse the militia officers of the nearest towns. On his return, he found hundreds who had mustered and chosen him their leader. Issuing orders for them to follow, he himself pushed forward without changing the checked shirt he had worn in the field, and reached Cambridge at sunrise the next morning, having rode the same horse a hundred miles within eighteen hours. He brought to the service of his country courage which, during the war, was never questioned; and a heart than which none throbbed more honestly or warmly for American freedom.

CHAP. XXIX. 1775. April.

From Weathersfield, a hundred young volunteers marched for Boston on the twenty-second, well armed and in high spirits. From the neighboring towns, men of the largest estates, and the most esteemed for character, seized their firelocks and followed. By the second night, several thousands from the colony were on their way. Some fixed on their standards and drums the colony arms, and round it in letters of gold, the motto, that God who brought over their fathers would sustain the sons.

In New Haven, Benedict Arnold, captain of a volunteer company, agreed with his men to march the next morning for Boston. "Wait for proper orders," was the advice of Wooster; but the self-willed commander, brooking no delay, extorted supplies from the committee of the town; and on the twenty-ninth, reached the American head-quarters with his company. There was scarcely a town in Connecticut that was not represented among the besiegers.

The nearest towns of Rhode Island were in motion before the British had finished their retreat. At the instance of Hopkins and others, Wanton, the governor, though himself inclined to the royal side, called an assembly. Its members were all of one mind; and when Wanton, with several of the council, showed hesitation, they resolved, if necessary, to proceed alone. The council yielded, and confirmed the unanimous vote of the assembly which authorized raising an army of fifteen hundred men. "The colony of Rhode Island," wrote Bowler, the speaker, to the Massachusetts congress, "is firm and determined; and a greater unanimity in the lower house scarce ever prevailed." Companies of the men of Rhode Island preceded this early message. CHAP. XXIX.

The conviction of Massachusetts gained the cheering confidence that springs from sympathy, now that New Hampshire and Connecticut and Rhode Island had come to its support. The New England volunteers were men of substantial worth, of whom almost every one represented a household. The members of the several companies were well known to each other, as to brothers, kindred, and townsmen; known to the old men who remained at home, and to all the matrons and maidens. They were sure to be remembered weekly in the exercises of the congregations; and morning and evening in the usual family devotions, they were commended with fervent piety to the protection of Heaven. Every young soldier lived and acted, as it were, under the keen observation of all those among whom he had grown up, and was sure that his conduct would occupy the tongues of his village companions while he was in the field, and perhaps be remembered his life long. The camp of liberty was a gathering in arms of schoolmates, neighbors, and friends; and Boston was beleaguered round from Roxbury to Chelsea by an unorganized, fluctuating mass of men, each with his own musket and his little store of cartridges, and such provisions as he brought with him, or as were sent after him, or were contributed by the people round about. 1775. April.

The British officers, from the sense of their own weakness, and from fear of the American marksmen, dared not order a sally. Their confinement was the more irksome, for it came of a sudden before their magazines had been filled; and was followed by

CHAP. XXIX. 1775. April. "an immediate stop to supplies of every kind." The troops, in consequence, suffered severely from unwholesome diet; and their commanders fretted with bitter mortification. They had scoffed at the Americans as cowards who would run at their sight; and they had saved themselves from destruction only by the rapidity of their retreat. Reinforcements and three new general officers were already on the Atlantic, and these would have to be received into straitened quarters by a defeated army. They knew that England, and even the ministers, would condemn the inglorious expedition which had brought about so sudden and so fatal a change. As if to brand in their shame, the officers shrunk from avowing their own acts; and though no one would say that he had seen the Americans fire first, they tried to make it pass current, that a handful of countrymen at Lexington had begun a fight with a detachment that outnumbered them as twelve to one. "They did not make one gallant attempt during so long an action," wrote Smith, who was smarting under his wound, and escaped captivity only by the opportune arrival of Percy.

Men are prone to fail in equity towards those whom their pride regards as their inferiors. The Americans, slowly provoked and long suffering, treated the prisoners with tenderness, and nursed the wounded as though they had been members of their own families. They even invited Gage to send out British surgeons for their relief. Yet Percy could degrade himself so far as to calumniate the countrymen who gave him chase, and officially lend himself to the falsehood, that "the rebels scalped and cut off

April.

the ears of some of the wounded who fell into their hands." He should have respected the name which he bore; famed as it is in history and in song; and he should have respected the men before whom he fled. The falsehood brings dishonor on its voucher; the people whom he reviled, were among the mildest and most compassionate of their race.

CHAPTER XXX.

EFFECTS OF THE DAY OF LEXINGTON AND CONCORD CONTINUED: THE CAMP OF LIBERTY.

APRIL—MAY, 1775.

CHAP. XXX. 1775. April.

THE inhabitants of Boston suffered an accumulation of sorrows, brightened only by the hope of the ultimate relief of all America. Gage made them an offer that if they would promise not to join in an attack on his troops, and would lodge their arms with the selectmen at Faneuil Hall, the men, women, and children, with all their effects, should have safe conduct out of the town. The proposal was accepted. For several days the road to Roxbury was thronged with wagons and trains of wretched exiles; but they were not allowed to take with them any provisions; and nothing could be more affecting than to see the helpless families come out without any thing to eat. The provincial congress took measures for distributing five thousand of the poor among the villages of the interior. But the loyalists of Boston, of whom two hundred volunteered to enter the king's service, desired to detain the people as hostages; Gage therefore soon violated his pledge; and many respected citizens, children whose fathers were absent, widows, unemployed mechanics, persons who had no protectors to provide for their escape, remained in town to share the hardships of a siege, ill provided, and exposed to the insults of an exasperated enemy. Words cannot describe their sufferings.

Connecticut still hoped for "a cessation of hostilities," and for that purpose, Johnson, so long its agent abroad, esteemed by public men in England for his moderation and ability, repaired as one of its envoys to Boston; but Gage only replied by a narrative which added new falsehoods to those of Smith and Percy. By a temperate answer he might have confused New England; the effrontery of his assertions, made against the clearest evidence, shut out the hope of an agreement.

No choice was left to the Massachusetts committee of safety but to drive out the British army, or perish in the attempt; even though every thing conspired to make the American forces incapable of decisive action. There was no unity in the camp. At Roxbury, John Thomas had command, and received encomiums for the good order which prevailed in his division; but Ward, the general who was at Cambridge, had the virtues of a magistrate rather than of a soldier. He was old, unused to a separate military command, and so infirm, that he was not fit to appear on horseback; and he never could introduce exact discipline among free men, whom even the utmost vigor and ability might have failed to control, and who owned no superiority but that of merit, no

CHAP. XXX. 1775. April.

obedience but that of willing minds. Nor had he received from the provincial congress his commission as commander in chief; nor was his authority independent of the committee of safety. Moreover, the men from other colonies did not as yet form an integral part of one "grand American" army, but appeared as independent corps from their respective provinces under leaders of their own.

Of the men of Massachusetts who first came down as volunteers, the number varied from day to day; and was never at any one time ascertained with precision. Many of them returned home almost as soon as they came, for want of provisions or clothes, or because they had not waited to put their affairs in order. Of those who enlisted in the Massachusetts army, a very large number absented themselves on furlough. It was feared by Ward that it would be impossible for him to keep the army together; and that he should be left alone. As for artillery, it was found, on inquiry, that there were altogether no more than six three-pounders and one six-pounder in Cambridge, besides sixteen pieces in Watertown, of different sizes, some of them good for nothing. But even these were more than could be used. There was no ammunition but for the six three-pounders, and very little for them. In the scarcity of powder, the most anxious search was made for it throughout the colony; and after scouring five principal counties, the whole amount that could be found was less than sixty-eight barrels. The other colonies, to which the most earnest entreaties were addressed for a supply, were equally unprovided. In the colony of New York, there were not more than one hundred pounds of powder for sale. CHAP. XXX.

Notwithstanding these obstacles, the scheming genius of New England was in the highest activity. While the expedition against Ticonderoga was sanctioned by a commission granted to Benedict Arnold, the congress, which was then sitting in Watertown, received from Jonathan Brewer, of Waltham, a proposition to march with a body of five hundred volunteers to Quebec, by way of the rivers Kennebeck and Chaudiere, in order to draw the governor of Canada, with his troops, into that quarter, and thus secure the northern and western frontiers from inroads. He was sure it "could be executed with all the facility imaginable." The design was not then favored, but it did not pass out of mind. 1775. May 1.

Now that Massachusetts had entered into war with Great Britain, next to the want of military stores, the poverty of her treasury, which during the whole winter had received scarcely five thousand pounds of currency to meet all expenses, gave just cause for apprehension. For more than twenty years, she had endeavored by legislative penalties to exclude the paper currency of other provinces, and had issued no notes of her own but certificates of debt, in advance of the revenue. These certificates were for sums of six pounds and upwards, bearing interest, and had no forced circulation, and were kept at par by the high condition of her credit and her general prosperity. The co-operation of neighboring colonies compelled her congress in May to legalize the paper money of Connecticut and Rhode Island; and from fiscal necessity to issue her own treasury notes. Of May 5.

CHAP. XXX. 1775. May. her first emission of one hundred thousand pounds, there were no notes under four pounds, and they all preserved the accustomed form of certificates of public debt, of which the use was not made compulsory. But in less than three weeks, an emission of twenty-six thousand pounds was authorized for the advance pay to the soldiers, and these "soldiers' notes," of which the smallest was for one dollar, were made a legal tender "in all payments without discount or abatement." Rhode Island put out twenty thousand pounds in bills, of which the largest was for forty shillings, the smallest for sixpence.

On the fifth of May, the provincial congress resolved: "that General Gage had disqualified himself for serving the colony in any capacity, that no obedience was in future due to him, that he ought to be guarded against as an unnatural and inveterate enemy." To provide for order was an instant necessity; but the patriots of the colony checked their eagerness to renovate the ancient custom of annually electing their chief magistrate, and resolved to wait till they could receive from the continental congress "explicit advice respecting the taking up and exercising the powers of civil government." They were ready to receive a plan, or with the consent of congress, to establish a form for themselves.

"After the termination of the present struggle," wrote Warren, "I hope never more to be obliged to enter into a political war. I would, therefore, wish the government here to be so happily constituted, that the only road to promotion may be through the affections of the people. I would have such a government as should give every man the greatest liberty to do what he pleases, consistent with restraining him from doing any injury to another, or such a government as would most contribute to the good of the whole, with the least inconvenience to individuals."

To form the grand American army, New Hampshire agreed to raise two thousand men, of whom perhaps twelve hundred reached the camp. Folsom was their brigadier, but John Stark was the most trusty officer. Connecticut offered six thousand men, and about twenty-three hundred remained at Cambridge, with Spenser as their chief commander, and Putnam as second brigadier.

Rhode Island voted an army of fifteen hundred men, and probably about a thousand of them appeared round Boston, under Nathaniel Greene as their commander. He was one of eight sons, born in a house of a single story, near the Narragansett Bay in Warwick. In that quiet seclusion, Gorton and his followers, untaught of universities, had reasoned on the highest questions of being. They had held, that in America Christ was coming to his temple, that outward ceremonies, baptism and the eucharist, and also kings and lords, bishops and chaplains, were all but carnal ordinances, sure to have an end; that humanity must construct its church by "the voice of the Son of God," the voice of reason and love. The father of Greene, descended from ancestry of this school, was at once an anchor smith, a miller, a farmer, and, like Gorton, a preacher. The son excelled in diligence and in manly sports. None of his age could wrestle, or skate, or run better than he; or stand before him as a neat ploughman and a skilful mechanic.

CHAP. XXX. 1775. May.

Aided by intelligent men of his own village, or of Newport, he read Euclid, and learned to apply geometry to surveying and navigation; he studied Watts's logic, Locke on the human understanding, Ferguson on civil society, pored over English versions of the Lives of Plutarch, the Commentaries of Cæsar, and became familiar with some of the best English classics.

When the stamp-act was resisted, he and his brothers never feared to rally at the drum-beat. Simple in his tastes, temperate as a Spartan, and a great lover of order, he rose early, and was indefatigable at study or at work. He married, and his home became the abode of peace and hospitality. His neighbors looked up to him as an extraordinary man, and from 1770, he was their representative in the colonial legislature. Once in 1773, he rode to Plainfield in Connecticut, to witness a grand military parade; and the spectacle was for him a good commentary on Sharp's military guide. In 1774, in a coat and hat of the Quaker fashion, he was seen watching the exercise and manœuvres of the British troops at Boston, where he used to buy of Henry Knox, a bookseller, treatises on the art of war.

On the day of Lexington, Greene started to share in the conflict; but being met by tidings of the retreat of the British, he went back to take his seat in the Rhode Island legislature. He next served as a commissioner to concert military plans with Connecticut, and when in May the Rhode Island brigade of fifteen hundred men was enlisted, he was elected its general. None murmured at the advancement of the unassuming man whom nature had so gifted with readiness to oblige, and gentleness of disposition, and the mildest manners, that every one loved him. "I hope," said he meekly, " God will preserve me in the bounds of moderation, and enable me to support myself with proper dignity, neither rash nor timorous." He loved to serve his country more than the honor of serving it; and if its good had required it, would have exchanged his command for that of a sergeant, or the place of a soldier in the ranks, without a murmur. As he became familiar with his duty, he never forgot that he was keeping guard for the interests of mankind, looking to the continental congress as the friend of the liberty of the world, and the support of the rights of human nature.

CHAPTER XXXI.

EFFECTS OF THE DAY OF LEXINGTON AND CONCORD CONTINUED: THE GENERAL RISING.

APRIL—MAY, 1775.

CHAP. XXXI. 1775. April 23.

On Sunday the twenty-third of April, the day after the dissolution of the provincial congress of New York, the news from Lexington suddenly burst upon the city. The emissaries who had undertaken to break the chain of union by intrigue, saw with dismay the arrest of their schemes by the beginning of war. The inhabitants, flushed with resentment, threw off restraints. Though it was Sunday, two sloops which lay at the wharves laden with flour and supplies for the British at Boston, of the value of eighty thousand pounds, were speedily unloaded. The next day Dartmouth's despatches arrived with Lord North's conciliatory resolve, and with lavish promises of favor. But the royal government was already prostrate, and could not recover its consideration. Isaac Sears concerted with John Lamb to stop all vessels going to Quebec, Newfoundland, Georgia, or Boston; where British authority was still supreme. The people who came together at beat of drum shut up the custom-house; and the merchants whose vessels were cleared out, dared not let them sail. CHAP. XXXI. 1775. April 24.

In the following days the city arms and ammunition of New York were secured; and volunteer companies paraded in the streets. Small cannon were hauled from the city to Kingsbridge; churchmen as well as presbyterians, without regard to creeds, took up arms. As the old committee of fifty-one lagged behind the prevailing excited zeal of the multitude, on Monday, the first of May, the people, at the usual places of election, chose for the city and county, a new general committee of one hundred, who "resolved in the most explicit manner to stand or fall with the liberty of the continent." All parts of the colony were summoned to choose delegates to a provincial convention, to which the city and county of New York deputed one and twenty as their representatives.

Eighty-three members of the new general committee met as soon as they were chosen; and on the motion of John Morin Scott, seconded by Alexander MacDougall, an association was set on foot, engaging under all the ties of religion, honor, and love of country, to submit to committees and to congress, to withhold supplies from British troops, and at the risk of lives and fortunes, to repel every attempt at enforcing taxation by parliament. The royalists had desired the presence of a considerable body of British soldiery; the blood shed at Lexington left them no hope but in a change of policy. Accordingly, fourteen members of the New York assembly, most of them stanch supporters of the

CHAP. XXXI. 1775. May. plans of the ministry, entreated General Gage that hostilities might cease till fresh orders could be received from the king, and especially that no military force might be permitted to land or be stationed in the province of New York.

May 5. On the day for the sailing of the packet, all parties made their appeal to England. The royal council despatched two agents to represent to the ministry how severely the rash conduct of the army at Boston had injured the friends of the king; while the New York committee thus addressed the Lord Mayor and corporation of London, and through them the capital of the British empire, and the people of Great Britain:

"Born to the bright inheritance of English freedom, the inhabitants of this extensive continent can never submit to slavery. The disposal of their own property with perfect spontaneity is their indefeasible birthright. This they are determined to defend with their blood, and transfer to their posterity. The present machinations of arbitrary power, if unremittedly pursued, will, by a fatal necessity, terminate in a dissolution of the empire. This country will not be deceived by measures conciliatory in appearance. We cheerfully submit to a regulation of commerce by the legislature of the parent state, excluding in its nature every idea of taxation. When our unexampled grievances are redressed, our prince will find his American subjects testifying by as ample aids as their circumstances will permit, the most unshaken fidelity to their sovereign. America is grown so irritable by oppression, that the least shock in any part is, by the most powerful sympathetic affection, instantaneously felt through the whole continent. This city is as one man in the cause of liberty; our inhabitants are resolutely bent on supporting their committee and the intended provincial and continental congresses; there is not the least doubt of the efficacy of their example in the other counties. In short, while the whole continent are ardently wishing for peace upon such terms as can be acceded to by Englishmen, they are indefatigable in preparing for the last appeal.

CHAP. XXXI. 1775. May 5.

"We speak the real sentiments of the confederated colonies, from Nova Scotia to Georgia, when we declare, that all the horrors of civil war will never compel America to submit to taxation by authority of parliament."

The letter was signed by the chairman and eighty-eight others of the committee, of whom the first was John Jay. They did this, knowing that at the time there were not five hundred pounds of powder in all the city, that several regiments were already ordered to New York, that it was commanded by Brooklyn heights, and that the deep water of its harbor exposed it on both sides to ships of war.

The packet for England had hardly passed Sandy Hook, when on Saturday, the sixth of May, the delegates to the continental congress from Massachusetts and Connecticut, drew near. Three miles from the city, they were met by a company of grenadiers and a regiment of the city militia under arms, by carriages and a cavalcade, and by many thousands of persons on foot. Along roads which were crowded as if the whole city had come out to meet them, they

CHAP. XXXI. made their entry, amidst loud acclamations, the ringing of bells, and every demonstration of joy.

1775. May 8. On Monday the delegation from Massachusetts, with a part of that of New York, were escorted across the Hudson River by two hundred of the militia under arms, and three hundred citizens; and triumphal honors awaited them at Newark and Elizabethtown.

The governor of New Jersey could not conceal his chagrin, that Gage "had risked commencing hostilities," before the experiment had been tried of attempting to cajole the several colonial legislatures into an acquiescence in Lord North's propositions.

The committee of Newark were willing to hazard their lives and fortunes in support of their brethren of the Massachusetts Bay. Princeton and Perth Amboy advised a provincial congress; to which Morris county promptly appointed delegates. "All ranks of men" in Woodbridge greatly applauded and admired the conduct and bravery of Massachusetts. On the second of May the New Jersey committee of correspondence called a provincial congress for the twenty-third at Trenton. To anticipate its influnece, the governor convened the regular assembly eight days earlier at Burlington, and laid before them the project of Lord North. The assembly could see in the proposition no avenue to reconciliation; and declared their intention to "abide by the united voice of the continental congress."

Such too was the spirit of Pennsylvania. "Let us not be bold in declarations and cold in action; nor have it said of Philadelphia that she passed noble resolutions and neglected them," were the words of

Mifflin, youngest of the orators who on the twenty-fifth of April, addressed the town-meeting called in Philadelphia on receiving the news from Lexington. Thousands of the inhabitants of the city were present, and agreed "to associate for the purpose of defending with arms, their lives, their property, and liberty." Each township in Berks county, resolved to raise and discipline its company. Reading formed a company of its old men also, who wore crape in lieu of a cockade, in token of sorrow for the slaughter of their brethren. In Philadelphia thirty companies, with fifty to one hundred in each, daily practised the manual exercise of the musket.

The Pennsylvania assembly which met on the first day of May, would not listen to the ministerial terms. "We can form," say they, "no prospect of any lasting advantages for Pennsylvania but what must arise from a communication of rights and property with the other colonies." The fifth of May saw the arrival of Franklin after a placid voyage over the smoothest seas; and the next morning he was unanimously elected a deputy to the congress. It was the signal for Galloway to retire; but the delegation, to which Thomas Wilson and James Wilson were added, were still instructed to combine if possible a redress of grievances with "union and harmony between Great Britian and the colonies."

May 5.

The little colony of Delaware was behind no one in public spirit. In Maryland, at the request of the colonels of militia, Eden at Annapolis gave up the arms and ammunition of the province to the freemen of the county. Pleased with his concession, the provincial convention distinguished itself by its dis-

CHAP. XXXI. passionate moderation; and "its delegates to congress went determined to bring about a reconciliation."

1775. May 2. Virginia was still angry at the seizure of its provincial magazine and at the menace of Dunmore to encourage an insurrection of slaves, when on the second day of May, at the cry from Lexington, the independent company of Hanover and its county committee were called together by Patrick Henry. The soldiers, most of them young men, kindled at his words, elected him their chief, and marched for Williamsburg. On the way it was thought that his army increased to five thousand.

"There is scarce a county of the whole colony," wrote Dunmore, "wherein part of the people have not taken up arms, and declared their intention of forcing me to make restitution of the powder." Alarmed by the "insurrections," he convened the council of Virginia, and in a proclamation of the
May 3. third of May did not scruple to utter the falsehood that he had removed the ammunition lest it should be seized by insurgent slaves. Message after message could not arrest the march or change the purpose of Henry. Lady Dunmore, who need have feared nothing for herself, professed to dread being retained as a hostage, and with her family retired to the Fowey man-of-war. The governor first resolved to resist and then thought it best to yield.
May 4. On the morning of the fourth, at about sunrise, a messenger met Patrick Henry at Doncastle's Ordinary in New Kent, and as a compensation for the gunpowder taken out of the magazine, paid him three hundred and thirty pounds, for which he was to account to the provincial congress of Virginia. When

it was afterwards found that the sum exceeded the value of the powder, the next Virginia convention directed the excess to be restored.

Two days after the return of the volunteers, Dunmore issued a proclamation against "a certain Patrick Henry," and his "deluded followers;" and secretly denounced him to the ministry as "a man of desperate circumstances, one who had been very active in encouraging disobedience and exciting a spirit of revolt among the people for many years past." On the other hand, the interior resounded with the praise of the insurgents. On the eighth, Louisa county sent them its hearty thanks. On the ninth, Spottsylvania cordially approved their prudent, firm, and spirited conduct; and Orange county in a letter signed among others by the young and studious James Madison, a recent graduate of Princeton college, applauded their zeal for the honor and interest of the country. "The blow struck in Massachusetts," they add, "is a hostile attack on this and every other colony, and a sufficient warrant to use reprisal."

May 11.

On the eleventh, Patrick Henry set off for the continental congress; and his progress was a triumph. Amidst salutes and huzzas, a volunteer guard accompanied him to the Maryland side of the Potomac; and as they said farewell, they invoked God's blessing on the champion of their "dearest rights and liberties."

CHAPTER XXXII.

EFFECTS OF THE DAY OF LEXINGTON AND CONCORD CONTINUED: TICONDEROGA TAKEN.

MAY, 1775.

CHAP. XXXII. 1775. May. THE people of South Carolina, who had hoped relief through the discontinuance of importations from Britain, had received the decision of parliament with bitter disappointment. The tidings from Lexington foretold an inevitable conflict. South Carolina was insulated by her remoteness; yet she did not falter. On the very night after receiving the news, men of Charleston took possession of the royal arsenal, and distributed twelve hundred stand of arms. On the second day of June, the members of her provincial congress, Henry Laurens being their president, associated themselves for defence against every foe; "ready to sacrifice their lives and fortunes to secure her freedom and safety." They resolved to raise two regiments of infantry, and a regiment of rangers. To this end, one hundred and forty thousand pounds sterling were issued in bills of credit, which for a year and a half the enthusiasm of the people did not suffer to fall in value. "We are ready to give freely half or the whole of our estates for the security of our liberties," was the universal language.

The militia officers threw up their commissions from the royal governor, and submitted to the orders of congress. A council of safety was charged with executive powers. In the midst of these proceedings, Lord William Campbell, their new governor, arrived, and the provincial congress waited on him with an address: "No lust of independence has had the least influence upon our counsels; no subjects more sincerely desire to testify their loyalty and affection. We deplore the measures, which, if persisted in, must rend the British empire. Trusting the event to Providence, we prefer death to slavery."

"The people of Charleston are as mad as they are here in Boston," was the testimony of Gage.

The skirmish at Lexington became known in Savannah on the tenth of May, and added Georgia to the union. At that time she had about seventeen thousand white inhabitants and fifteen thousand Africans. Her militia was not less than three thousand. Her frontier, which extended from Augusta to St. Mary's, was threatened by the Creeks with four thousand warriors; the Chickasaws, with four hundred and fifty; the Cherokees, with three thousand; the Choctaws, with twenty-five hundred. But danger could not make her people hesitate. On the night of the eleventh, Noble Wimberley Jones, Joseph Habersham, Edward Telfair, and others, broke open the king's magazine in the eastern part of the city, and took from it over five hundred pounds of powder.

CHAP. XXXII. 1775. May.

In writing to the committee for Boston, they acknowledged the noble stand taken by Massachusetts; and to the Boston wanderers, they sent sixty-three barrels of rice and one hundred and twenty-two pounds in specie. On the king's birthday the patriots erected a liberty pole; as if to express the wish still to combine allegiance to the king with their devotion to American liberty.

"A general rebellion throughout America is coming on suddenly and swiftly," reported their governor. "Matters will go to the utmost extremity."

Meantime, great deeds had been achieved by the mountaineers of the north. To hold the city of New York, its harbor, and the river Hudson, and by means of the fortresses on the lakes to keep open a free communication with Canada, was the scheme by which it was hoped to insulate and reduce New England. On Saturday, the twenty-ninth of April, Samuel Adams and Hancock, as they passed through Hartford, had secretly met the governor and council of Connecticut, to promote the surprise of Ticonderoga, which had been planned by the Green Mountain Boys. Ethan Allen was encouraged by an express messenger to hold them in readiness; and the necessary funds were furnished from the treasury of Connecticut. Sixteen men of that colony leaving Salisbury, were joined in Massachusetts by John Brown, who had first proposed the enterprise in a letter from Montreal, by Colonel James Easton, and by not so many as fifty volunteers from Berkshire. At Bennington they found Ethan Allen, who was certainly "the proper man to head his own people." Repairing to the north, he sent the alarm through the hills of Vermont; and on Sunday, the seventh of May, about one hundred Green Mountain Boys and near fifty soldiers from Massachusetts, under the command of Easton, rallied at Castleton. Just then arrived Benedict Arnold, with only one attendant. He brought a commission from the Massachusetts committee of safety, which was disregarded, and the men unanimously elected Ethan Allen their chief.

CHAP. XXXII. 1775. May.

On the eighth of May, the party began the march; late on the ninth, they arrived at Orwell. With the utmost difficulty, a few boats were got together, and eighty-three men crossing the lake with Allen, landed near the garrison. The boats were sent back for Seth Warner and the rear guard; but if they were to be waited for, there could be no surprise. The men were, therefore, at once drawn up in three ranks, and as the first beams of morning broke upon the mountain peaks, Allen addressed them: "Friends and fellow-soldiers: We must this morning quit our pretensions to valor, or possess ourselves of this fortress; and inasmuch as it is a desperate attempt, I do not urge it on, contrary to will. You that will undertake voluntarily, poise your firelock."

At the word every firelock was poised. "Face to the right," cried Allen; and placing himself at the head of the centre file, Arnold keeping emulously at his side, he marched to the gate. It was shut, but the wicket was open. The sentry snapped a fuzee at him. The Americans rushed into the fort, darted upon the guards, and raising the Indian war whoop, such as had not been heard there since the days of Montcalm, formed on the parade in hollow

CHAP. XXXII. 1775. May 10. square, to face each of the barracks. One of the sentries, after wounding an officer, and being slightly wounded himself, cried out for quarter and showed the way to the apartment of the commanding officer. "Come forth instantly, or I will sacrifice the whole garrison," cried Ethan Allen, as he reached the door. At this, Delaplace, the commander, came out undressed, with his breeches in his hand. "Deliver to me the fort instantly," said Allen. "By what authority?" asked Delaplace. "In the name of the great Jehovah, and the continental congress!" answered Allen. Delaplace began to speak again, but was peremptorily interrupted, and at sight of Allen's drawn sword near his head, he gave up the garrison, ordering his men to be paraded without arms.

Thus was Ticonderoga taken in the gray of the morning of the tenth of May. What cost the British nation eight millions sterling, a succession of campaigns and many lives, was won in ten minutes by a few undisciplined men, without the loss of life or limb.

The Americans gained with the fortress nearly fifty prisoners, more than a hundred pieces of cannon, one thirteen inch mortar, and a number of swivels, stores, and small arms. To a detachment under Seth Warner, Crown Point, with its garrison of twelve men, surrendered upon the first summons. Another party succeeded in making a prisoner of Skeene, a dangerous British agent; and in getting possession of the harbor of Skeenesborough.

Messengers carried to the continental congress news of the great acquisition which inaugurated the day of its assembling. "A war has begun," wrote

Joseph Warren from the Massachusetts congress; "but I hope after a full conviction, both of our ability and resolution to maintain our rights, Britain will act with necessary wisdom; this I most heartily wish, as I feel a warm affection still for the parent state."

CHAP. XXXII.

1775. May.

CHAPTER XXXIII.

EFFECTS OF THE DAY OF LEXINGTON AND CONCORD IN EUROPE.

May to July, 1775.

CHAP. XXXIII 1775. May.

The news from Lexington surprised London in the last days of May. The people had been lulled into a belief, that the ministry indulged in menaces only to render the olive branch acceptable; and the measures of parliament implied confidence in peace. And now it was certain that war had begun, that Britain was at war with herself.

The Massachusetts congress, by a swift packet in its own service, had sent to England a calm and accurate statement of the events of the nineteenth of April, fortified by depositions, with a charge to Arthur Lee their agent, to give it the widest circulation. These were their words to the inhabitants of Britain: "Brethren, we profess to be loyal and dutiful subjects, and so hardly dealt with as we have been, are still ready, with our lives and fortunes, to defend the person, family, crown, and dignity of our royal sovereign. Nevertheless, to the persecution and tyranny of his cruel ministry we will not submit;

appealing to Heaven for the justice of our cause, we determine to die or be free." CHAP. XXXIII

Granville Sharpe, who was employed in the ordnance department, declined to take part in sending stores to America, and after some delay, threw up his employment. 1775. May.

Lord Chatham was the real conqueror of Canada for England; and Carleton had been proud to take to Quebec as his aide de camp Chatham's eldest son. But it was impossible for the offspring of the elder Pitt to draw his sword against the Americans; and his resignation was offered, as soon as it could be done without a wound to his character as a soldier.

Admiral Keppel, one of the most gallant officers in the British navy, expressed his readiness to serve, if required, against the ancient enemies of England, but asked not to be employed in America.

An inhabitant of London, after reading morning prayers in his family as usual, closed the book with a face of grief, and to his children, of whom Samuel Rogers, the poet, was one, told the sad tale of the murder of their American brethren.

The recorder of London put on a full suit of mourning, and being asked if he had lost a relative or friend, answered, "Yes, many brothers at Lexington and Concord."

Ten days before the news arrived, Lord Effingham, who in his youth had been prompted by military genius to enter the army, and had lately served as a volunteer in the war between Russia and Turkey, finding that his regiment was intended for America, renounced the profession which he loved, as the only means of escaping the obligation of fight-

CHAP. XXXIII 1775. June. ing against the cause of freedom. This resignation gave offence to the court, and was a severe rebuke to the officers who did not share his scruple; but at London the Common Hall, in June, thanked him publicly as "a true Englishman;" and the guild of merchants in Dublin addressed him in the strongest terms of approbation.

June 24. On the twenty-fourth of June, the citizens of London, agreeing fully with the letter received from New York, voted an address to the king, desiring him to consider the situation of the English people, "who had nothing to expect from America but gazettes of blood, and mutual lists of their slaughtered fellow-subjects." And again they prayed for the dissolution of parliament, and a dismission for ever of the present ministers. As the king refused to receive this address on the throne, it was never presented; but it was entered in the books of the city and published under its authority.

The society for constitutional information, after a special meeting on the seventh of June, raised a hundred pounds, "to be applied," said they, "to the relief of the widows, orphans, and aged parents of our beloved American fellow-subjects, who, faithful to the character of Englishmen, preferring death to slavery, were, for that reason only, inhumanly murdered by the king's troops at Lexington and Concord." Other sums were added; and an account of what had been done was laid before the world by Horne Tooke in the "Public Advertiser." The publication raised an implacable spirit of revenge. Three printers were fined in consequence one hundred pounds each; and Horne was pursued unrelentingly by Thurlow, till in a later year he was convicted before Lord Mansfield of a libel, and sentenced to pay a fine of two hundred pounds and to be imprisoned twelve months. Thurlow even asked the judge to punish him with the pillory.

CHAP. XXXIII

1775. June.

It was Hutchinson, whose false information had misled the government. The moment was come when he was to lose his distinction as chief counsellor to the ministers, and to sink into insignificance. A continent was in arms, and the prize contended for was the liberty of mankind; but Hutchinson saw nothing of the grandeur of the strife, saying: "The country people must soon disperse, as it is the season for planting their Indian corn, the chief sustenance of New England."

With clearer vision Garnier took notice, that the Americans had acted on the nineteenth of April, after a full knowledge of the address of the two houses of parliament to the king, pledging lives and fortunes for the reduction of America, and of the king's answer. "The Americans," he wrote to Vergennes, "display in their conduct, and even in their errors, more thought than enthusiasm, for they have shown in succession, that they know how to argue, to negotiate, and to fight." "The effects of General Gage's attempt at Concord are fatal," said Dartmouth, who just began to wake from his dream of conciliation. "By that unfortunate event, the happy moment of advantage is lost."

The condemnation of Gage was universal. Many people in England were from that moment convinced, that the Americans could not be reduced, and that England must concede their independence. The

CHAP. XXXIII 1775. June. British force, if drawn together, could occupy but a few insulated points, while all the rest would be free; if distributed, would be continually harassed and destroyed in detail.

These views were frequently brought before Lord North. That statesman was endowed with strong affections, and was happy in his family, in his fortune and abilities. In his public conduct, he, and he alone among ministers, was sensible to the reproaches of remorse; and he cherished the sweet feelings of human kindness. Appalled at the prospect, he wished to resign. But the king would neither give him a release, nor relent towards the Americans. Every question of foreign policy was made subordinate to that of their reduction. The enforcement of the treaty of Paris respecting Dunkirk, was treated as a small matter. The complaints of France for the wrongs her fishermen had suffered, and the curtailment of her boundary in the fisheries of Newfoundland, were uttered with vehemence, received with suavity, and recognised as valid. How to subdue the rebels was the paramount subject of consideration.

The people of New England had with one impulse rushed to arms; the people of England quite otherwise stood aghast, doubtful and saddened, unwilling to fight against their countrymen; languid and appalled; astonished at the conflict, which they had been taught to believe never would come; in a state of apathy; irresolute between their pride and their sympathy with the struggle for English liberties. The king might employ emancipated negroes, or Indians, or Canadians, or Russians, or Germans;

Englishmen enough to carry on the war were not to be engaged. CHAP. XXXIII

The ministers, as they assembled in the cabinet, on the evening of the fourteenth of June, were in very bad humor; Lord North grieved at the prospect of further disagreeable news. The most prominent person at the meeting was Sandwich, who had been specially sent for; a man of talents, greedy alike of glory and of money, but incapable of taking the lead, for he was incapable of awakening enthusiasm. There was no good part for them to choose, except to retire, and leave Chatham to be installed as conciliator; but they clung to their places, and the stubborn king, whatever might happen, was resolved not to change his government. There existed no settled plan, no reasonable project; the conduct of the administration hardly looked beyond the day. A part of them threw all blame on the too great lenity of North. 1775. June 14.

As there were no sufficient resources in England for the subjugation of America, some proposed to blockade its coast, hold its principal ports, and reduce the country by starvation and distress. But zeal for energetic measures prevailed, and the king's advisers cast their eyes outside of England for aid. They counted with certainty upon the inhabitants of Canada; they formed plans to recruit in Ireland; they looked to Hanover for regiments to take the place of British garrisons in Europe. The Landgrave of Hesse began to think his services as a dealer in troops might be demanded; but a more stupendous scheme was contemplated. Russia had just retired from the war with Turkey, with embarrassed finances, and an army

CHAP. XXXIII 1775. June. of more than three hundred thousand men. England had courted an alliance with that power, as a counterpoise to the Bourbons; had assented to the partition of Poland; had invited and even urged a former Czar to exercise a controlling influence over the politics of Germany; by recent demonstrations and good offices, had advanced the success of the Russian arms against the Ottoman Porte. The empress was a woman of rare ability; ambitious of conquest; equally ambitious of glory. Her army, so Potemkin boasted, might alone spare troops enough to trample the Americans under foot. To the Russian empress, the king resolved to make a wholesale application; and to the extent of his wants, to buy at the highest rate battalions of Russian serfs, just emancipated by their military service; Cossack rangers; Sclavonian infantry; light troops from fifty semi-barbarous nationalities, to crush the life of freedom in America. The thought of appearing as the grand arbitress of the world, with paramount influence in both hemispheres, was to dazzle the imagination of Catherine; and lavish largesses were to purchase the approval of her favorites.

This plan was not suddenly conceived; at New York, in the early part of the previous winter, it had been held up in terror to the Americans. Success in the negotiation was believed to be certain.

But the contracting for Russian troops, their march to convenient harbors in the north, and their transport from the Baltic to America, would require many months; the king was impatient of delay. A hope still lingered that the Highlanders and others in the interior of North Carolina, might be induced to rise, and be formed into a battalion. Against Virginia, whose people were thought to exceed all bounds in their madness, it was intended to employ a separate squadron, and a small detachment of regular troops. Three thousand stand of arms, with two hundred rounds of powder and ball for each musket, together with four pieces of light artillery, were instantly shipped for the use of Dunmore; and as white men could not be found in sufficient numbers to use them, the king rested his confidence of success in checking the rebellion on the ability of his governor to arm Indians and negroes enough to make up the deficiency. This plan of operations bears the special impress of George the Third.

At the north, the king called to mind that he might "rely upon the attachment of his faithful allies, the Six Nations of Indians," and he turned to them for immediate assistance. To insure the fulfilment of his wishes, the order to engage them was sent directly in his name to the unscrupulous Indian agent, Guy Johnson, whose functions were made independent of Carleton. "Lose no time," it was said; "induce them to take up the hatchet against his majesty's rebellious subjects in America. It is a service of very great importance; fail not to exert every effort that may tend to accomplish it; use the utmost diligence and activity."

It was also the opinion at court, that "the next word from Boston would be that of some lively action, for General Gage would wish to make sure of his revenge."

The sympathy for America which prevailed more and more in England, reached the king's own brother,

CHAP. XXXIII 1775. July.

the weak but amiable duke of Gloucester. In July he crossed the channel, with the view to inspect the citadels along the eastern frontier of France. When he left Dover, nothing had been heard from America later than the retreat of the British from Concord, and the surprise of Ticonderoga. Metz, the strongest place on the east of France, was a particular object of his journey; and as his tour was made with the sanction of Louis the Sixteenth, he was received there by the Count de Broglie as the guest of the king. Among the visitors on the occasion, came a young man not yet eighteen, whom de Broglie loved with parental tenderness, Gilbert Motier de la Fayette. His father had fallen in his twenty-fifth year, in the battle of Minden, leaving his only child less than two years old. The boyish dreams of the orphan had been of glory and of liberty; at the college in Paris, at the academy of Versailles, no studies charmed him like tales of republics; rich by vast inheritances, and married at sixteen, he was haunted by a passion to rove the world as an adventurer in quest of fame, and the opportunity to strike a blow for freedom. A guest at the banquet in honor of the duke of Gloucester, he listened with avidity to an authentic version of the uprising of the New England husbandmen. The reality of life had now brought before him something more wonderful than the brightest of his visions; the youthful nation insurgent against oppression and fighting for the right to govern themselves, took possession of his imagination. He inquired; he grew warm with enthusiasm; and before he left the table, the men of Lexington and Concord had won for America a volunteer in Lafayette.

In Paris, wits, philosophers, and coffee-house politicians, were all to a man warm Americans, considering them as a brave people, struggling for natural rights, and endeavoring to rescue those rights from wanton violence. Their favorite mode of reasoning was, that as the Americans had no representatives in parliament, they could owe no obedience to British laws. This argument they turned in all its different shapes, and fashioned into general theories.

CHAP. XXXIII

1775. July.

The field of Lexington, followed by the taking of Ticonderoga, fixed the attention of the government of France. From the busy correspondence between Vergennes and the French embassy at London, it appeared, that the British ministry were under a delusion in persuading themselves that the Americans would soon tire; that the system of an exclusively maritime war was illusory, since America could so well provide for her wants within herself. Franklin was known to be more zealous than ever, and perfectly acquainted with the resources of Great Britain; and at Versailles he enjoyed the reputation of being endowed by Heaven with qualities that made him the most fit to create a free nation, and to become the most celebrated among men.

The sagacity of Vergennes traced the relation of the American revolution to the history of the world. "The spirit of revolt," said he, "wherever it breaks out, is always a troublesome example. Moral maladies, as well as those of the physical system, can become contagious. We must be on our guard, that the independence which produces so terrible an explosion in North America, may not communicate itself to points that interest us in the hemispheres.

CHAP. XXXIII. 1775. July. We long ago made up our own mind to the results which are now observed; we saw with regret that the crisis was drawing near; we have a presentiment that it may be followed by more extensive consequences. We do not disguise from ourselves the aberrations which enthusiasm can encourage, and which fanaticism can effectuate."

The subject, therefore, grew in magnitude and interest for the king and his cabinet. The contingent danger of a sudden attack on the French possessions in the West Indies, required precaution; and Louis the Sixteenth thought it advisable at once to send an emissary to America, to watch the progress of the revolution. This could best be done from England; and the embassy at London, as early as the
July. 10. tenth of July, began the necessary preliminary inquiries. "All England," such was the substance of its numerous reports to Vergennes, "is in a position, from which she never can extricate herself. Either all rules are false, or the Americans will never again consent to become her subjects."

So judged the statesmen of France, on hearing of the retreat from Concord, and the seizure of Ticonderoga.

CHAPTER XXXIV.

THE SECOND CONTINENTAL CONGRESS.

May, 1775.

CHAP. XXXIV

1775. May 10.

A few hours after the surrender of Ticonderoga, the second continental congress met at Philadelphia. There among the delegates, appeared Franklin and Samuel Adams; John Adams, and Washington, and Richard Henry Lee; soon joined by Patrick Henry, and by George Clinton, Jay, and Jay's college friend, the younger Robert R. Livingston, of New York.

Whom did they represent? and what were their functions? They were committees from twelve colonies, deputed to consult on measures of conciliation, with no means of resistance to oppression beyond a voluntary agreement for the suspension of importations from Great Britain. They formed no confederacy; they were not an executive government; they were not even a legislative body. They owed the use of a hall for their sessions to the courtesy of the carpenters of the city; there was not a foot of land on which they had the right to execute their decisions; and they had not one civil officer to carry out

CHAP. XXXIV. 1775. May. 10. their commands, nor the power to appoint one. Nor was one soldier enlisted, nor one officer commissioned in their name. They had no treasury; and neither authority to lay a tax, nor to borrow money. They had been elected, in part at least, by tumultuary assemblies, or bodies which had no recognised legal existence; they were intrusted with no powers but those of counsel; most of them were held back by explicit or implied instructions; and they represented nothing more solid than the unformed opinion of an unformed people. Yet they were encountered by the king's refusal to act as a mediator, the decision of parliament to enforce its authority, and the actual outbreak of civil war. The waters had risen; the old roads were obliterated; and they must strike out a new path for themselves and for the continent.

The exigency demanded the instant formation of one great commonwealth and the declaration of independence. "They are in rebellion," said Edmund Burke; "and have done so much as to necessitate them to do a great deal more." Independence had long been the desire of Samuel Adams, and was already the reluctant choice of Franklin, and of John Adams, from a conviction that it could not ultimately be avoided. But its immediate declaration was not possible. American law was the growth of necessity, not of the wisdom of individuals. It was not an acquisition from abroad; it was begotten from the American mind, of which it was a natural and inevitable, but also a slow and gradual development. It is truly the child of the people, an emanation from its will. The sublime thought that there existed a united nation, was yet to spring into being, to liberate the public

CHAP. XXXIV. 1775. May. 10.

spirit from allegiance to the past, and summon it to the creation of a state. But before this could be well done, the new directing intelligence must represent the sum of the intelligence of twelve or thirteen provinces, inhabited by men not of English ancestry only, but intermixt with French, still more with Swedes, and yet more with Dutch and Germans; a state of society where Quakers, who held it wickedness to fight, stood over against Calvinists, whose religious creed encouraged resistance to tyranny; where freeholders, whose pride in their liberties and confidence in their power to defend the fields which their own hands had subdued, were checked by merchants whose treasures were afloat, and who feared a war as the foreshadowing of their own bankruptcy. Massachusetts might have come to a result with a short time for reflection; but congress must respect masses of men, composed of planters and small manufacturers, of artisans and farmers; one-fifth of whom had for their mother tongue some other language than the English. Nor were they only of different nationalities. They were not exclusively Protestant; and those who were Protestants, professed the most different religious creeds. To all these congress must have regard; and wait for the just solution from a sentiment superior to race and language, planted by God in the heart of mankind. The American constitution came from the whole people, and expresses a community of its thought and will. The nation proceeded not after the manner of inventors of mechanisms, but like the divine architect; its work is self-made; and is neither a copy of any thing past, nor a product of external force, but an unfolding of its own internal nature.

CHAP. XXXIV.

1775. May. 10.

The Americans were persuaded that they were set apart for the increase and diffusion of civil and religious liberty; chosen to pass through blessings and through trials, through struggles and through joy, to the glorious fulfilment of their great duty of establishing freedom in the new world, and setting up an example to the old. But by the side of this creative impulse, the love of the mother country lay deeply seated in that immense majority who were the descendants of British ancestry, and this love was strongest in the part of the country where the collision had begun. The attachment was moreover justified; for the best part of their culture was derived from England, which had bestowed on them milder, more tolerant, and more equal governments, than the distant colonies of other European powers had ever known.

When congress met, it was as hard to say of its members as of their constituents, whether they were most swayed by regard for the country from which the majority of them sprung, or by the sense of oppression. The parent land which they loved was an ideal England, preserving as its essential character, through all accidents of time and every despotic tendency of a transient ministry, the unchanging attachment to liberty. Of such an England they cherished the language, the laws, and the people; and they would not be persuaded that independence of her was become the only security for the preservation of their own inherited rights. In this divided state of their affections, the unpreparedness of the country for war, and the feeble and narrow powers with which they were intrusted, devotedness to the old relations weighed against the call of freedom to the new. The conservative feeling still maintained its energy, and forbade any change, except where a change was demanded by instant necessity.

1775. May. 10.

They came together thus undecided, and they long remained undecided. They struggled against every forward movement, and made none but by compulsion. Not by foresight, nor by the preconceived purpose of themselves or their constituents, but by the natural succession of inevitable events, it became their office to cement a union and constitute a nation.

The British troops from Boston had invaded the country, had wasted stores which were the property of the province, had burned and destroyed private property, had shed innocent blood; the people of Massachusetts had justly risen in arms, accepted aid from the neighboring colonies, and besieged the British army. At once, on the eleventh, the consideration of the report of the agents of congress on their petition to the king, gave way to the more interesting and more important narrative of the events of the nineteenth of April, and their consequences. The members listened with sympathy, and their approval of the conduct of Massachusetts was unanimous. But as that province, without directly asking the continent to adopt the army which she had assembled, entreated direction and assistance; and as the answer might involve an ultimate declaration of independence, as well as the immediate use of the credit and resources of all the colonies, the subject was reserved for careful deliberation in a committee of the whole.

May 11.

On the thirteenth, Lyman Hall presented himself

CHAP. XXXIV. from Georgia as a delegate for the parish of St. John's, and was gladly admitted with the right to
1775. May 13. vote, except when the question should be taken by colonies.

The first important decision of congress related
May. 15. to New York. The city and county on the fifteenth asked how to conduct themselves with regard to the regiments which were known to be under orders to that place; and with the sanction of Jay and his colleagues, they were instructed, not to oppose the landing of the troops, but not to suffer them to erect fortifications; to act on the defensive, but to repel force by force, in case it should become necessary for the protection of the inhabitants and their property.

When Edmund Burke heard of this advice, he expressed surprise at the scrupulous timidity which could suffer the king's forces to possess themselves of the most important post in America. But in the want of an effective military organization, of artillery, and ammunition, no means existed to prevent the disembarkation of British regiments. The city was at the mercy of the power which commanded the water; and which, on any sudden conflict, could have sent an army into its streets, and have driven the patriots from their homes.

But the advice of the continental congress was pregnant with embarrassments, for it recognised the existing royal government of New York, and tolerated its governor and all naval and military officers, contractors, and Indian agents, in the peaceful discharge of their usual functions. The rule was laid down for the province, before its own congress could come together; and when they assembled, they could but conform to it. All parties seemed tacitly to agree to a truce, which was to adjourn the employment of force. Towards the royal government the colonists manifested courteous respect; avoiding every decision which should specially invite attack or make reconciliation impossible. They allowed the British vessel of war, "the Asia," to be supplied with provisions; but adopted measures of restraint in the intercourse between the ship and the shore. They disapproved the act of the people in seizing the king's arms. To Guy Johnson, the superintendent of the Indians, they offered protection, if he and the Indians under his superintendency would promise neutrality. They sent to Massachusetts their warmest wishes in the great cause of American liberty, and made it their first object "to withstand the encroachments of ministerial tyranny;" but they, at the same time, "labored for the restoration of harmony between the colonies and the parent state," and were willing to defer decisive action till every opportunity for the recovery of peace by an accommodation should have been exhausted. In this manner the aristocratic portion of the friends of American rights in the province exercised a controlling influence. They stood before God and the world free from the responsibility of war, having done every thing to avoid it, except to surrender their rights. Of all the provinces, New York was in its acts the most measured; consistently reluctant to believe in the fatal necessity of war, but determined if necessary to defy the worst, for the preservation of liberty; confident that in the hour of need, its forbearance and moderation would secure the union of its people.

CHAP. XXXIV. 1775. May.

These were the considerations which swayed the continental congress in the policy which it dictated to New York. They also induced John Jay of that colony to make the motion in congress for a second petition to the king.

CHAPTER XXXV.

THE REVOLUTION EMANATES FROM THE PEOPLE.

MAY, 1775.

CHAP. XXXV. 1775. May 18.

THE motion of Jay was for many days the subject of private and earnest discussion; but the temper of the congress was still irresolute, when on the eighteenth of May they received the news of the taking of Ticonderoga. The achievement was not in harmony with their advice to New York; they for the time rejected the thought of invading Canada, and they were inclined even to abandon the conquest already made; though as a precaution they proposed to withdraw to the head of Lake George all the captured cannon and munitions of war, which on the restoration of peace were to be scrupulously returned.

For many days the state of the union continued to engage the attention of congress in a committee of the whole. The bolder minds, yet not even all the delegates from New England, discerned the tendency of events towards an entire separation of the colonies from Britain. In the wide division of opinions the decision appeared for a time to rest on South

CHAP. XXXV. 1775. May. Carolina; but the delegates from that province, no less than from the others of the south, like the central colonies, nourished the hope of peace, for which they desired to make one more petition.

Vain illusion! The unappeasable malice of the supporters of the ministry was bent on the most desperate and cruel efforts, while every part of the continent rung the knell of colonial subjection. A new nation was bursting into life. Boston was so strictly leaguered, that it was only from the islands in and near the harbor that fodder, or straw, or fresh meat could be obtained for the British army. On Sunday
May 21. morning, the twenty-first of May, about sunrise, it was discovered, that they were attempting to secure the hay on Grape Island. Three alarm guns were fired; the drums beat to arms; the bells of Weymouth and Braintree were set a ringing; and the men of Weymouth, and Braintree, and Hingham, and of other places, to the number of two thousand, swarmed to the sea side. Warren, ever the bravest among the brave, ever present where there was danger, came also. After some delay, a lighter and a sloop were obtained; and the Americans eagerly jumped on board. The younger brother of John Adams was one of the first to push off and land on the island. The English retreated, while the Americans set fire to the hay.

May 25. On the twenty-fifth of May, Howe, Clinton, and Burgoyne, arrived with reinforcements. They brought their angling rods, and they found themselves pent up in a narrow peninsula; they had believed themselves sure of taking possession of a continent with a welcome from the great body of the people, and they had no reception but as enemies, and no outlet from town but by the sea. CHAP. XXXV.

Noddle's Island, now East Boston, and Hog Island were covered with hay and cattle, with sheep and horses. About eleven in the morning of the twenty-seventh, twenty or thirty men passed from Chelsea to Hog Island and thence to Noddle's Island, and drove off or destroyed a great deal of stock. A schooner and a sloop, followed by a party of marines in boats, were sent from the British squadron to arrest them. The Americans retreated to Hog Island and cleared it of more than three hundred sheep, besides cows and horses. They then drew up on Chelsea Neck, and by nine in the evening received reinforcements, with two small four pounders. Warren was among his countrymen, of whom Putnam took the command. Cheered on by the presence of such leaders, they kept up an attack till eleven at night, when the schooner was deserted. At daybreak it was boarded by the provincials, who carried off four four-pounders and twelve swivels, and then set it on fire. The English lost twenty killed and fifty wounded; the provincials had but four wounded, and those slightly. 1775. May 27.

The New Englanders were so encouraged by these successes, that they stripped every island between Chelsea and Point Alderton of cattle and forage; and the light-house at the entrance of Boston harbor was burned down. They were as ready for partisan enterprises on the water as on land; if they could only get gunpowder, they were confident of driving off the British.

The same daring prevailed on the northern fron-

CHAP. XXXV. 1775. May. tier. The possession of Ticonderoga and Crown Point, the fortresses round which hovered the chief American traditions and recollections of military service, inflamed the imagination and stimulated the enterprise of the brave settlers of Vermont. A schooner, called for the occasion, "Liberty," was manned and armed; and Arnold, who had had experience at sea, took the command. With a fresh southerly wind he readily passed the lake; early on
May 18. the morning of the eighteenth, at the head of a party in boats, he surprised a sergeant and twelve men, and captured them, their arms, two serviceable brass field pieces, and a British sloop which lay in the harbor of St. John's. In about an hour the wind suddenly shifted, and, with a strong breeze from the north, Arnold returned with his prizes.

Ethan Allen, who desired not to be outdone, thought with one hundred men to take possession of St. John's. The scheme was wild, and he was compelled to retire before a superior force; but preserving his boastful courage, he wrote to congress: "Had I but five hundred men with me, I would have marched to Montreal."

The whole population west of the Green Mountains was interested to keep possession of Ticonderoga. Every man within fifty miles was desired by Arnold to repair to that post or to Crown Point with intrenching tools and all the powder and good arms that could be found. At the rumor of the proposed abandonment of their conquest, a loud protest was uttered unanimously by the foresters. "It is bad policy," said Ethan Allen, "to fear the resentment of an enemy." "Five hundred families," wrote Ar-

CHAP. XXXV. 1775. May.

nold, "would be left at the mercy of the king's troops and the Indians." The Massachusetts congress remonstrated; while Connecticut, with the consent of New York, ordered one thousand of her sons to march as speedily as possible to the defence of the two fortresses. The command of Lake Champlain was the best security against an attack from Indians and Canadians. Carleton, the governor of Canada, was using his utmost efforts to form a body capable of protecting the province. Officers from the French Canadian nobility were taken into pay; the tribes nearest to the frontiers of the English settlements were tampered with; in north-western New York, Guy Johnson was employing all his activity in insulating the settlers in Cherry Valley, winning the favor and support of the Six Nations, and duping the magistrates of Schenectady and Albany; while La Corne St. Luc, the old French superintendent of the Indians of Canada, a man who joined the reflective malice of civilization to the remorseless cruelty of the savage, sent belts to the northern tribes as far as the falls of St. Mary and Michilimackinack, to engage the ruthless hordes to take up arms, and distress the people along their extended frontier, till they should be driven to the British for protection.

Beyond the Alleghanies a commonwealth was rising on the banks of the Kentucky river, and by the very principles on which it was formed, it unconsciously renounced dependence on Britain.

Henderson and his associates had, during the winter, negotiated a treaty with the Cherokees for the land between the Ohio, the Cumberland mountains, the Cumberland river, and the Kentucky river; on the seventeenth of March they received their deed.

CHAP. XXXV. 1775. May. To this territory, Daniel Boone, with a body of enterprising companions, proceeded at once to mark out a path up Powell's valley; and through mountains and cane-brakes beyond. On the twenty-fifth of the month they were waylaid by Indians, who killed two men and wounded another very severely. Two days later the savages killed and scalped two more. "Now," wrote Daniel Boone, "is the time to keep the country while we are in it. If we give way now, it will ever be the case," and he pressed forward to the Kentucky river. There, on the first day of April, at the distance of about sixty yards from its west bank, near the mouth of Otter Creek, he began a stockade fort; which took the name of Boonesborough. At that place, while the congress at Philadelphia was groping irresolutely in the dark, seventeen men assembled as representatives of the four "towns" that then formed the seed of the state. May 25. Among these children of nature was Daniel Boone, the pioneer of the party. His colleague, Richard Calloway, was one of the founders of Kentucky and one of its early martyrs. The town of St. Asaph sent John Floyd, a surveyor who emigrated from southwestern Virginia; an able writer, respected for his culture and dignity of manner; of innate good breeding; ready to defend the weak; to follow the trail of the savage; heedless of his own life if he could recover women and children who had been made captive; destined to do good service, and survive the dangers of western life till American independence should be fought for and won.

From the settlement at Boiling Spring came James Harrod, the same who, in 1774, had led a party of forty-one to Harrodsburg, and during the summer of that year, had built the first log-cabin in Kentucky; a tall, erect, and resolute backwoodsman; unlettered but not ignorant; intrepid yet gentle; revered for energy and for benevolence; always caring for others, as a father, brother, and protector; unsparing of himself; never weary of kind offices to those around him; the first to pursue a stray horse, or to go to the rescue of prisoners; himself a skilful hunter, for whom the rifle had a companionship, and the wilderness a charm; so that in age his delight was in excursions to the distant range of the receding buffaloes, till at last he plunged into the remote forest, and was never heard of more.

CHAP. XXXV. 1775. May.

These and their associates, the fathers of Kentucky, seventeen in all, met on the twenty-third of May, beneath the great elm tree of Boonesborough, outside of the fort, on the thick sward of the fragrant white clover. The convention having been organized, prayers were read by a minister of the church of England. A speech was then delivered to the convention in behalf of the proprietary purchasers of the land from the Cherokees:

May 23.

"You are assembled for a noble purpose, however ridiculous it may seem to superficial minds; a work of the utmost importance to the well-being of this country in general, and of each and every individual. As justice is and must be eternally the same, so your laws, founded in wisdom, will gather strength by time.

"You are placing the corner-stone of an edifice, whose superstructure can only become great and glorious in proportion to the excellence of its foundation.

CHAP. XXXV. These considerations, gentlemen, will inspire you with sentiments worthy of the grandeur of the subject.

1775. May. "One common danger must secure to us harmony in opinion. If any doubt remain amongst you with respect to the force or efficacy of whatever laws you now or hereafter make, be pleased to consider, that all power is originally in the people."

"We represent the good people of this infant country," replied the convention on the twenty-fifth, in the words of a committee of which Calloway was
May 25. the head. "Deeply impressed with a sense of the importance of the trust our constituents have reposed in us, we will attempt the task with vigor, not doubting but unanimity will insure us success. That we have a right as a political body, without giving umbrage to Great Britain, or any of the colonies, to frame rules for the government of our little society, cannot be doubted by any sensible or unbiassed mind."

So reasoned the fathers of Kentucky. In their legislation, it was their chief care "to copy after the happy pattern of the English laws." Their colony they called Transylvania. Their titles to their lands they rested on a deed from the head warriors of the Cherokees as the first owners of the soil. Dunmore had taunted them with opening "an asylum for debtors and disorderly persons;" they repelled the calumny by instituting courts of justice. For defence against the savages, they organized a militia; they discountenanced profane swearing and sabbath breaking; they took thought for preventing the waste of game, and improving the breed of horses; and by solemn agreement they established as the basis of their constitution, the annual choice of dele-

CHAP. XXXV. 1775. May.

gates; taxes to be raised by the convention alone; salaries to be fixed by statute; land offices to be always open; and "a perfect religious freedom, and general toleration." Thus the pioneer law-givers for the west provided for freedom of conscience. A little band of hunters put themselves at the head of the countless hosts of civilization, in establishing the great principle of intellectual freedom. Long as the shadows of the western mountains shall move round with the sun, long as the rivers that gush from those mountains shall flow towards the sea, long as seed time and harvest shall return, that rule shall remain the law of the West. When Sunday dawned, the great tree which had been their council chamber became their church. Penetrated with a sense of the Redeemer's love, they lifted up their hearts to God in prayer and thanksgiving, and the forest that was wont to echo only the low of the buffalo and the whoop of the savage, was animated by the voices of their devotion. Thus began the commonwealth of Kentucky; it never knew any other system than independence, and was incapable of any thing else.

The state, now that it has become great and populous, honors the memory of the plain, simple-hearted man, who is best known as its pioneer. He was kindly in his nature, and never wronged a human being, not even an Indian, nor, indeed, animal life of any kind. "I with others have fought Indians," he would say, "but I do not know that I ever killed one; if I did, it was in battle, and never knew it." He was no hater of them, and never desired their extermination. In woodcraft he was acknowledged to be the first among men. This led him to love soli-

CHAP. XXXV. 1775. May.

tude, and habitually to hover on the frontier, with no abiding place; accompanied by the wife of his youth, who was the companion of his long life and travel. When at last death put them both to rest, Kentucky reclaimed their bones from their graves far up the Missouri, and now they lie buried on the hill above the cliffs of the Kentucky river, overlooking the lovely valley of the capital of that commonwealth. Around them are emblems of wilderness life; the turf of the blue grass lies lightly above them; and they are laid with their faces turned upward and westward, and their feet toward the setting sun.

A similar spirit of independence prevailed in the highlands which hold the head springs of the Yadkin and the Catawba. The region was peopled chiefly by Presbyterians of Scotch Irish descent, who brought to the new world the creed, the spirit of resistance, and the courage of the covenanters.

The people of the county of Mecklenburg had carefully observed the progress of the controversy with Britain; and during the winter, political meetings had repeatedly been held in Charlotte. That town had been chosen for the seat of the Presbyterian college, which the legislature of North Carolina had chartered, but which the king had disallowed; and it was the centre of the culture of that part of the province. The number of houses in the village was not more than twenty; but the district was already well settled by herdsmen who lived apart on their farms.

Some time in May, 1775, they received the news of the address, which in the preceding February had been presented to the king by both houses of parliament, and which declared the American colonies to be in a state of actual rebellion. This was to them the evidence that the crisis in American affairs was come, and the people proposed among themselves to abrogate all dependence on the royal authority. But the militia companies were sworn to allegiance; and "how," it was objected, "can we be absolved from our oath?" "The oath," it was answered, "binds only while the king protects." At the instance of Thomas Polk, the commander of the militia of the county, two delegates from each company were called together in Charlotte, as a representative committee. Before their consultations had ended, the message of the innocent blood shed at Lexington came up from Charleston, and inflamed their zeal. They were impatient that their remoteness forbade their direct activity; had it been possible, they would have sent a hundred bullocks from their fields to the poor of Boston. No minutes of the committee are known to exist, but the result of their deliberations, framed with superior skill, precision of language, and calm comprehensiveness, remains as the monument of their wisdom and their courage. Of the delegates to that memorable assembly, the name of Ephraim Brevard should be remembered with honor by his countrymen. He was one of a numerous family of patriot brothers, and himself in the end fell a martyr to the public cause. Trained in the college at Princeton, ripened among the brave Presbyterians of Middle Carolina, he digested the system which was then adopted, and which formed in effect a declaration of independence, as well as a complete system of government. "All laws and commissions confirmed by

CHAP. XXXV. 1775. May. or derived from the authority of the king or parliament," such are the bold but well considered words of these daring statesmen, "are annulled and vacated; all commissions, civil and military, heretofore granted by the crown to be exercised in the colonies, are void; the provincial congress of each province, under the direction of the great continental congress, is invested with all legislative and executive powers within the respective provinces, and no other legislative or executive power does or can exist at this time, in any part of these colonies. As all former laws are now suspended in this province, and the congress has not yet provided others, we judge it necessary for the better preservation of good order, to form certain rules and regulations for the internal government of this county, until laws shall be provided for us by the congress."

In accordance with these principles the freemen of the county formed themselves into nine military companies, and elected their own officers. Judicial powers were conferred on men to be singled out by the vote of the companies, two from each of them; the whole number of eighteen constituting a court of appeal. The tenure alike of military and civil officers was "the pleasure of their several constituents." All public and county taxes, all quitrents to the crown were sequestered; and it was voted that persons receiving new commissions from the king, or exercising old ones, should be dealt with as enemies of the country.

The resolves were made binding on all, and were to be enforced till the provincial congress should provide otherwise, or, what they knew would never take place, till the British parliament should resign its arbitrary pretensions with respect to America. At the same time the militia companies were directed to provide themselves with arms, and Thomas Polk and Joseph Kenedy were specially appointed to purchase powder, lead and flints.

CHAP. XXXV.

1775. May.

Before the month of May had come to an end, the resolutions were signed by Ephraim Brevard, as clerk of the committee, and were adopted by the people with the determined enthusiasm which springs from the combined influence of the love of liberty and of religion. Thus was Mecklenburg county, in North Carolina, separated from the British empire. The resolves were transmitted with all haste to be printed in Charleston, and as they spread through the South, they startled the royal governors of Georgia and North Carolina. They were despatched by a messenger to the continental congress, that the world might know their authors had renounced their allegiance to the king of Great Britain, and had constituted a government for themselves.

May. 31.

The messenger stopped on his way at Salisbury, and there, to a crowd round the court-house, the resolves were read and approved. The western counties were the most populous part of North Carolina; and the royal governor had flattered himself and the king, with the fullest assurances of their support. "I have no doubt," said he, "that I might command their best services at a word on any emergency. I consider I have the means in my own hands to maintain the sovereignty of this country to my royal master in all events." And now he was obliged to trans-

CHAP. XXXV. 1775. May.

mit the deliberate, consistent, and well-considered resolutions of Mecklenburg, which he described as the boldest of all, "most traitorously declaring the entire dissolution of the laws and constitution, and setting up a system of rule and regulation subversive of his Majesty's government."

CHAPTER XXXVI.

CONGRESS OFFERS TO NEGOTIATE WITH THE KING.

MAY, 1775.

FAR different was the spirit of the continental congress. The unexpected outbreak of war compelled them to adopt some system of defence; but many of its members still blinded themselves with the hope of reconciliation, and no measure for the vigorous prosecution of hostilities could be carried with unanimity, except after the concession of a second petition to the king. CHAP. XXXVI. 1775. May.

Washington foresaw the long and bloody contest which must precede the successful vindication of the liberties of America. Before the excursion to Concord he had avowed to his friends "his full intention to devote his life and fortune" to the cause; and he manifested his conviction of the imminence of danger by appearing at the debates in his uniform as an officer. He had read with indignation the taunts uttered in parliament on the courage of his countrymen; he now took a personal pride in the rising of

CHAP. XXXVI 1775. May. New England, and the precipitate retreat of Percy, which he thought might "convince Lord Sandwich that the Americans would fight for their liberties and property." "Unhappy it is," said he, "to reflect, that a brother's sword has been sheathed in a brother's breast, and that the once happy and peaceful plains of America are either to be drenched with blood, or inhabited by slaves. Sad alternative! But can a virtuous man hesitate in his choice?" Washington never hesitated in his choice; but he was too modest to demand a deference to his opinion, and too sincerely a friend to peace to suppress any movement that promised its restoration.

The delegates from New England, especially those from Massachusetts, could bring no remedy to the prevailing indecision; for they suffered from insinuations, that they represented a people who were republicans in their principles of government and fanatics in their religion; and they wisely avoided the appearance of importunity or excess in their demands.

As the delegates from South Carolina declined the responsibility of a decision, which would have implied an abandonment of every hope of peace, there could be no efficient opposition to the policy of again seeking the restoration of American liberty through the mediation of the king. This plan had the great advantage over the suggestion of an immediate separation from Britain, that it could be boldly promulgated, and was in harmony with the general wish; for the people of the continent, taken collectively, had not as yet ceased to cling to their old relations with their parent land, and so far from scheming independence, now that independence was become inevitable, they postponed the irrevocable decree and still longed that the necessity for it might pass by. CHAP. XXXVI.

In this state of things the man for the occasion was Dickinson, who wanted nothing but energy to secure to him one of the highest places among the statesmen of the world. Deficient in that great element of character which forms the junction between intelligence and action, his theoretic views on the rights of America and the just extent of her claims, coincided with those of the most zealous. Now that the charter of Massachusetts had been impaired, he did not ask merely relief from parliamentary taxation; he required security against the encroachments of parliament on charters and laws. The distinctness with which he spoke, satisfied Samuel Adams himself, who has left on record that the Farmer was a thorough Bostonian. 1775. May.

Moreover, the province of which he was the representative, was the third in rank for numbers, wealth, and importance; its system of government was eminently democratic; its capital city, distinguished by the presence of the congress, was the largest in the land. The honest scruples of the Quakers merited consideration. The proprietary and his numerous and powerful friends, rallied a party which offered all its influence to promote a successful intercession with the king; and the instructions of Pennsylvania to its delegates in congress looked primarily to a continued union with Britain.

It was in vain that the fiery Mifflin, who was likewise a member from Pennsylvania, expressed impatience. Franklin also knew that every method of peaceful entreaty had been exhausted. But though

CHAP. XXXVI. 1775. May. decided in his opinions, and open in expressing them, he betrayed no desire to rule the intention of congress, wishing rather to leave that body to pursue its own plans, unbiassed by his complaints or persuasions. Yet he never hesitated to support the boldest measures, and to reprove irresoluteness and delay. "Make yourselves sheep," he would say, "and the wolves will eat you." And again, "God helps them who help themselves;" and insisting on the absolute necessity of armed resistance, "united," he said, "we are well able to repel force by force." Thus "he encouraged the revolution," yet wishing independence, not as a victory of one party over another, but as the spontaneous action of a united people.

Dickinson, therefore, for the time, exercised an unbounded sway over the deliberations of congress, and had no cause to fear an effective opposition, when he seconded the motion of Jay for one more petition to the king. For a succession of days the state of the colonies continued to be the subject of earnest discussion; but through all the vacillations of hesitancy, the determination to sustain Massachusetts was never for a moment in doubt. This appeared on the twenty-fourth. On that day the chair of the president becoming vacant by the departure of Peyton Randolph for the legislature of Virginia, John Hancock, of Massachusetts, was elected unanimously in his stead, and Harrison, of Virginia, who was classed among the conservative members, conducted him to the chair, saying: "We will show Britain how much we value her proscriptions." For the proscription of Samuel Adams and Hancock had long been known, though it had not yet been proclaimed.

CHAP XXXVI. 1775. May.

No progress could be made in authorizing vigorous measures of defence, until the long deliberations in the committee of the whole had resulted in a compromise. Then, on Thursday, the twenty-fifth, directions were given to the provincial congress in New York to preserve the communication between the city of New York and the country, by fortifying posts at the upper end of the island, near King's Bridge, and on each side of Hudson river, in the Highlands. A post was also to be taken at or near Lake George.

On that same day, while Howe, Clinton and Burgoyne were entering Boston harbor, Duane, a delegate from New York, moved in the committee of the whole, "the opening of a negotiation in order to accommodate the unhappy disputes subsisting between Great Britain and the colonies, and that this be made a part of the petition to the king." "A negotiation once begun," said Colden, on hearing the news, "will give the people time to cool and feel the consequence of what they have already done, before the whole colonies become equally desperate." The dangerous proposal produced a warm debate, which, at the adjournment, was not concluded.

On the morning of the twenty-sixth, the delegates from New Jersey presented the vote of the assembly of that colony, refusing to consider Lord North's proposition as contained in the resolution of the house of commons, and consigning the subject to the continental congress. The communication was referred to the committee of the whole; which was thus officially in possession of the offer of the minister. The debate of the preceding day was renewed, and the timid party prevailed. The committee rose and

CHAP. XXXVI. 1775. May. submitted their report; upon which it was resolved, "that for the purpose of preserving the colonies in safety against every attempt to carry the unconstitutional and oppressive acts into execution by force of arms, these colonies be immediately put into a state of defence; but that with a sincere desire of contributing by all the means, not incompatible with a just regard for the undoubted rights and true interests of these colonies, to the promotion of this most desirable reconciliation, an humble and dutiful petition be presented to his majesty."

To this extent the vote was unanimous. But the additional motion of Duane was carried against an unyielding opposition, and did not advance the prospect of a peaceful solution. The acts altering the charter and laws of Massachusetts, were among those which the king was determined never to give up; and from the first commencement of the conflict, he declared himself more ready to concede independence to victorious arms, than wound his own sentiment of honor by a voluntary surrender of the measures which he had adopted for the government of a rebellious colony. The motion of Duane had no practical significance, unless it was intended to accept the proposition of Lord North as the basis for an agreement; but the majority would never consent to sacrifice the charter of Massachusetts. The position which they chose was, therefore, weak and untenable. By their wavering they led the people to neglect that steady system of resistance, which nothing but independence could justify or reward, and to wait listlessly for an accommodation; while the king gained a respite, which he employed with singleness of purpose in collecting forces for subduing his revolted subjects. They directed preparations for defence, and yet they would not authorize the several colonies to institute governments of their own. As a consequence, the people were not fully roused to the necessity of immediate and united action; and the officers of the crown, wherever they practised the duplicity of moderation, were able to maintain themselves in authority and continue their intrigues.

CHAP. XXXVI. 1775. May.

All this while, congress had misgivings that all their forbearance would be fruitless. They counselled New York to arm and train its militia, and with vigorous perseverance to embody men for the protection of the inhabitants of that city against the invasion of troops, alleging as a reason that "it was very uncertain whether their earnest endeavors to accommodate the unhappy differences between Great Britain and the colonies, by conciliatory measures, would be successful."

The support of the Canadians was also entreated, for it was recognised that the impending conflict was not a war of protestantism, but of humanity. On the first day of May, the Quebec act went into effect; and on the twenty-ninth, the American congress, by the hand of Jay, addressed the Canadians: "We most sincerely condole with you on the arrival of that day, in the course of which the sun could not shine on a single freeman in all your extensive dominions. By the introduction of your present form of government, or rather present form of tyranny, you and your wives and your children are made slaves." Appeals were also directed to their pride, their affection for France, their courage, and their re-

CHAP. XXXVI. 1775. May. gard for the common welfare; but no adequate motive for rising was set before them. As the congress intended still to petition the king, they could only request some vague co-operation in imploring the attention of their sovereign; a request which at most was only fitted to secure neutrality. The Canadians, as Frenchmen, feared not taxation by parliament, but the haughty dominion of their conquerors; as Catholics they dreaded the exclusive rule of Protestants. A union for independence with a promise of institutions of their own, might have awakened their enthusiasm; but to them the Quebec act was an improvement on their former condition; and they abhorred it less than a fraudulent representative system like that of Ireland. Their sympathy for the insurgents sprung mainly from a recollection of their own sufferings under the twelve years' tyranny which had gone by; and could be revived and sustained by nothing less than a total separation from English rule.

The day after the adoption of Jay's address to the Canadians, Willing of Philadelphia, one of those who most struggled to thwart every step towards independence, brought before congress a paper, containing propositions from Lord North, in the handwriting of Grey Cooper, his under secretary of the treasury. As the king had refused to treat with an American congress, the writing had no signature; but its authenticity was not questioned. By an appeal to affection for the king and country, it pressed earnestly the acceptance of the overture contained in the resolution of the house of commons. It was declared that the terms were honorable for Great Britain and safe for the colonies; and that neither

CHAP. XXXVI. 1775. May.

king, nor ministry, nor parliament, nor the nation, would admit of further relaxation; but that "a perfectly united ministry would, if necessary, employ the whole force of the kingdom to reduce the rebellious and refractory provinces and colonies." The arrogance of the language in which this ultimatum was couched, should have ensured its prompt and unanimous rejection, and have nerved congress to immediate decision. But it was laid on the table of the body, which was bent on a petition to the king, and "a negotiation" with his ministers. The month of May went by, and congress had not so much as given to Massachusetts its advice that that province should institute a government of its own; it authorized no invasion of Canada, and only yielded its assent to the act of Connecticut in garrisoning Ticonderoga and Crown Point. If great measures are to be adopted, the impulse must come from without.

CHAPTER XXXVII.

MASSACHUSETTS ASKS FOR GEORGE WASHINGTON AS COMMANDER IN CHIEF.

JUNE 1—JUNE 17, 1775.

CHAP. XXXVII
1775. June.

IN obedience to the injunctions of Lord North and Lord Dartmouth, who earnestly wished that the effort should be made to reconcile some one of the several colonial assemblies to their insidious offer, the first day of June, 1775, saw the house of burgesses of Virginia convened for the last time by a British governor. Peyton Randolph, the speaker, who had been attending as president the congress at Philadelphia, arrived at Williamsburg with an escort of independent companies of horse and foot, which eclipsed the pomp of the government, and in the eyes of the people raised the importance of the newly created continental power. The session was opened by a speech recommending accommodation on the narrow basis of the resolve which the king had accepted. But the moment chosen for the discussion was inopportune; Dunmore's menace to raise the standard of a servile insurrection, and set the slaves upon their masters, with British arms in their hands,

CHAP. XXXVII 1775. June.

filled the South with horror and alarm. Besides, the retreat from Concord raised the belief that the American forces were invincible; and the spirit of resistance had grown so strong, that some of the burgesses appeared in the uniform of the recently instituted provincial troops, wearing a hunting shirt of coarse linen over their clothes, and a woodman's axe by their sides.

The great civilian of Virginia came down from Albemarle with clear perceptions of the path of public duty. When parliament oppressed the colonies by the imposing of taxes, Jefferson would have been content with their repeal; when the charter and laws of Massachusetts were mutilated and set aside by the same authority, he still hoped for conciliation through the wisdom of Chatham. But after Lexington green had been stained with blood, Jefferson would no longer accept acts of repeal, unless accompanied by security against future aggression.

The finances of Virginia were at this time much embarrassed; beside her paper currency afloat, she was burdened with the undischarged expenses of the Indian war of the last year. The burgesses approved the conduct of that war, and provided the means of defraying its cost; but the governor would not pass their bill, because it imposed a specific duty of five pounds on the head, about ten per cent. on the value, of every slave imported from the West Indies. The last exercise of the veto power by the king's representative in Virginia was in favor of the slave trade.

The assembly, having on the fifth thanked the delegates of the colony to the first congress, prepared

CHAP. XXXVII 1775. June. to consider the proposal of the ministers. The governor grew uneasy, and sent them an apology for his removal of the fifteen half barrels of powder belonging to the province. "I was influenced in this," said he, in a written message, "by the best of motives," and he reminded them that he had ventured his life in the service of Virginia. But the burgesses took testimony relating to the transaction, which proved conclusively his open avowal of an intention to raise, free, and arm slaves. Meantime their consultations extended through several days, and Jefferson was selected to draft their reply.

While the house was thus engaged, Dunmore received an express from Gage to acquaint him of his intention to publish a proclamation, proscribing Samuel Adams and Hancock; and fearing he might be seized and detained as a hostage, he suddenly, in the night following the seventh of June, withdrew from the capital, and went on board the "Fowey" man-of-war, at York. He thus left the Ancient Dominion in the undisputed possession of its own inhabitants, as effectually as if he had abdicated all power for the king; giving as a reason for his flight, his apprehension of "falling a sacrifice to the daringness and atrociousness, the blind and unmeasurable fury of great numbers of the people."

The burgesses paid no heed to his angry words, but when they had brought their deliberations to a close, they, on the twelfth of June, addressed to him as their final answer, that "next to the possession of liberty, they should consider a reconciliation as the greatest of all human blessings, but that the resolution of the house of commons only changed the form of

CHAP. XXXVII. 1775. June

oppression, without lightening its burdens; that government in the colonies was instituted not for the British parliament, but for the colonies themselves; that the British parliament had no right to meddle with their constitution, or prescribe either the number, or the pecuniary appointments of their officers; that they had a right to give their money without coercion, and from time to time; that they alone were the judges, alike of the public exigencies and the ability of the people; that they contended, not merely for the mode of raising their money, but for the freedom of granting it; that the resolve to forbear levying pecuniary taxes still left unrepealed the acts restraining trade, altering the form of government of Massachusetts, changing the government of Quebec, enlarging the jurisdiction of courts of admiralty, taking away the trial by jury, and keeping up standing armies; that the invasion of the colonies with large armaments by sea and land was a style of asking gifts not reconcilable to freedom; that the resolution did not propose to the colonies to lay open a free trade with all the world; that as it involved the interest of all the other colonies, they were bound in honor to share one fate with them; that the bill of Lord Chatham on the one part, and the terms of congress on the other, would have formed a basis for negotiation and a reconciliation; that leaving the final determination of the question to the general congress, they will weary the king with no more petitions, the British nation with no more appeals." "What then," they ask, "remains to be done?" and they answer: "That we com-

CHAP. XXXVII 1775 June. mit our injuries to the justice of the evenhanded Being who doth no wrong."

"In my life," said Shelburne, as he read Jefferson's report, "I was never more pleased with a state paper, than with the assembly of Virginia's discussion of Lord North's proposition. It is masterly. But what I fear is, that the evil is irretrievable." At Versailles, Vergennes was equally attracted by the wisdom and dignity of the document; he particularly noticed the insinuation, that a compromise might be effected on the basis of the modification of the navigation acts; and saw so many ways opened of settling every difficulty, that it was long before he could persuade himself, that the infatuation of the British ministry was so blind as to neglect them all. From Williamsburg, Jefferson repaired to Philadelphia; but before he arrived there, decisive communications had been received from Massachusetts.

That colony still languished in anarchy, from which they were ready to relieve themselves, if they could but wring the consent of the continental congress. "We hope," wrote they, in a letter which was read to that body on the second of June, "you will favor us with your most explicit advice respecting the taking up and exercising the powers of civil government, which we think absolutely necessary for the salvation of our country." The regulation of the army was a subject of equal necessity. Uncounted and ungoverned, it was already in danger of vanishing like dew, or being dissolved by discontents. The incompetency of Ward for his station was observed by Joseph Warren, now president of the congress, by James Warren of Plymouth, by Gerry and others;

every hour made it more imperative, that he should be superseded; and yet his private virtues and the fear of exciting dissensions in the province, required the measure to be introduced with delicacy and circumspection. The war was to become a continental war; the New England army a continental army; and that change in its relations offered the opportunity of designating a new commander in chief. To this end, the congress of Massachusetts formally invited the general congress "to assume the regulation and direction of the army, then collecting from different colonies for the defence of the rights of America." At the same time Samuel Adams received a private letter from Joseph Warren, interpreting the words as a request that the continent should "take the command of the army by appointing a generalissimo." The generalissimo whom Joseph Warren, Warren of Plymouth, Gerry and others desired, was Washington. The bearer of the letter who had been commissioned to explain more fully the wishes of Massachusetts, was then called in. His communication had hardly been finished, when an express arrived with further news from the camp; that Howe, and Clinton, and Burgoyne, had landed in Boston; that British reinforcements were arriving; that other parts of the continent were threatened with war. A letter was also received and read, from the congress of New Hampshire, remotely intimating that "the voice of God and nature" was summoning the colonies to independence.

CHAP. XXXVII. 1775. June.

It was evident that congress would hesitate to adopt an army of New England men under a Massachusetts commander in chief. Virginia was the

CHAP. XXXVII 1775. June. largest and oldest colony, and one of her sons was acknowledged to surpass all his countrymen in military capacity and skill. The choice of Washington as the general, would at once be a concession to prejudice and in itself the wisest selection. On the earliest occasion John Adams explained the composition and character of the New England army; its merits and its wants; the necessity of its being adopted by the continent, and the consequent propriety that congress should name its general. Then speaking for his constituents, he pointed out Washington as the man, above all others, fitted for that station, and best able to promote union. Samuel Adams seconded his colleague. The delegates from the Ancient Dominion, especially Pendleton, Washington's personal friend, disclaimed any wish that the officer whom Massachusetts had advanced, should be superseded by a Virginian. Washington himself had never aspired to the honor; though for some time he had been "apprehensive that he could not avoid the appointment."

The balloting for continental officers was delayed, that the members from New York might consult their provincial congress on the nominations from that colony.

With an empire to found and to defend, congress had not, as yet, had the disposal of one penny of money. The army which beleaguered Boston had sent for gunpowder to every colony in New England, to individual counties and towns, to New York and still further south; but none was to be procured. In the urgency of extreme distress, congress undertook to borrow six thousand pounds, a little more than twenty-five thousand dollars, "for the use of America," to be applied to the purchase of gunpowder for what was now for the first time called THE CONTINENTAL ARMY.

CHAP. XXXVII 1775. June.

In the arrangement of its committees and the distribution of business, it still sought to maintain a position, adverse alike to a surrender of liberty and to a declaration of independence; its policy was an armed defence, while waiting for a further answer from the king. On Wednesday the seventh of June, one of its resolutions spoke of "the Twelve United Colonies," Georgia being not yet included; and the name implied an independent nation; but on the eighth, it tardily recommended to Massachusetts not to institute a new government, but to intrust the executive power to the elective council, "until a governor of the king's appointment would consent to govern the colony according to its charter." For a province in a state of insurrection and war, a worse system could hardly have been devised. It had no unity, no power of vigorous action; it was recommended because it offered the fewest obstacles to an early renewal of allegiance to the British crown.

The twelfth of June is memorable for the contrast between the manifest dispositions of America and of the British representatives at Boston. On that day, Gage, under pretence of proclaiming a general pardon to the infatuated multitude, proscribed by name Samuel Adams and John Hancock, reserving them for condign punishment, as rebels and traitors, in terms which included as their abettors not only all who should remain in arms about Bos-

CHAP. XXXVII 1775. June 12. ton, but every member of the provincial government and of the continental congress. In the same breath he established martial law throughout Massachusetts, while vessels cruised off Sandy Hook to turn to Boston the transports which were bound with four regiments to New York. He also called upon the British secretary of state to concentrate at Boston fifteen thousand men, of whom a part might be hunters, Canadians, and Indians; to send ten thousand more to New York; and seven thousand more, composed of regular troops with a large corps of Canadians and Indians, to act on the side of Lake Champlain. "We need not be tender of calling upon the savages," were his words to Dartmouth; some of the Indians, domiciled in Massachusetts, having strolled to the American camp to gratify curiosity or extort presents, he pretended to excuse the proposal which he had long meditated, by falsely asserting that the Americans "had brought down as many Indians as they could collect."

On that same day the congress of New York, which had already taken every possible step to induce the Indians not to engage in the quarrel, had even offered protection to Guy Johnson, the superintendent, if he would but leave the Six Nations to their neutrality, and had prohibited the invasion of Canada, addressed to the merchants of that province the assurance, "that the confederated colonies aimed not at independence," but only at freedom from taxation by authority of parliament. On that same twelfth of June, the general congress made its first appeal to the people of the twelve united colonies by an injunction to them to keep a fast on one and

1775. June 12.

the same day, when they were to recognise "king George the Third as their rightful sovereign, and to look up to the supreme and universal superintending Providence of the great Governor of the world, for a gracious interposition of heaven for the restoration of the invaded rights of America, and a reconciliation with the parent state." Every village, every family, whether on the seaside or in the forest, was thus summoned to give the most solemn attestation of their desire to end civil discord, and "regard the things that belong to peace."

Measures were next taken for organizing and paying an American continental army, to be enlisted only till the end of the year, before which time a favorable answer from the king was hoped for. Washington, Schuyler, and others were deputed to prepare the necessary rules and regulations. It was also resolved to enlist ten companies of expert riflemen, of whom six were to be formed in Pennsylvania, two in Maryland, and two in Virginia.

June 15.

Then on the fifteenth day of June, it was voted to appoint a general. Thomas, of Maryland, nominated George Washington; and as he had been brought forward "at the particular request of the people in New England," he was elected by ballot unanimously.

Washington was then forty-three years of age. In stature he a little exceeded six feet; his limbs were sinewy and well proportioned; his chest broad; his figure stately, blending dignity of presence with ease. His robust constitution had been tried and invigorated by his early life in the wilderness, his habit of occupation out of doors, and his rigid temperance; so

CHAP. XXXVII June 15. that few equalled him in strength of arm or power of endurance. His complexion was florid; his hair dark brown; his head in its shape perfectly round. His broad nostrils seemed formed to give expression and escape to scornful anger. His dark blue eyes, which were deeply set, had an expression of resignation, and an earnestness that was almost sadness.

At eleven years old, left an orphan to the care of an excellent but unlettered mother, he grew up without learning. Of arithmetic and geometry he acquired just knowledge enough to be able to practise measuring land; but all his instruction at school taught him not so much as the orthography or rules of grammar of his own tongue. His culture was altogether his own work, and he was in the strictest sense a self-made man; yet from his early life he never seemed uneducated. At sixteen he went into the wilderness as a surveyor, and for three years continued the pursuit, where the forests trained him, in meditative solitude, to freedom and largeness of mind; and nature revealed to him her obedience to serene and silent laws. In his intervals from toil, he seemed always to be attracted to the best men, and to be cherished by them. Fairfax, his employer, an Oxford scholar, already aged, became his fast friend. He read little, but with close attention. Whatever he took in hand, he applied himself to with care; and his papers, which have been preserved, show how he almost imperceptibly gained the power of writing correctly; always expressing himself with clearness and directness, often with felicity of language and grace.

When the frontiers on the west became dis-

CHAP. XXXVII 1775. June 15.

turbed, he at nineteen was commissioned an adjutant-general with the rank of major. At twenty-one he went as the envoy of Virginia to the council of Indian chiefs on the Ohio and to the French officers near Lake Erie. Fame waited upon him from his youth; and no one of his colony was so much spoken of. He conducted the first military expedition from Virginia, that crossed the Alleghanies. Braddock selected him as an aide, and he was the only man who came out of the disastrous defeat near the Monongahela, with increased reputation, which extended to England. The next year, when he was but four and twenty, "the great esteem" in which he was held in Virginia, and his "real merit," led the lieutenant governor of Maryland to request that he might be "commissionated and appointed second in command" of the army designed to march to the Ohio; and Shirley, the commander in chief, heard the proposal "with great satisfaction and pleasure," for "he knew no provincial officer upon the continent to whom he would so readily give it as to Washington." In 1758 he acted under Forbes as a brigadier, and but for him that general would never have been able to cross the mountains.

Courage was so natural to him, that it was hardly spoken of to his praise; no one ever at any moment of his life discovered in him the least shrinking in danger; and he had a hardihood of daring which escaped notice, because it was so enveloped by superior calmness and wisdom.

He was as cheerful as he was spirited, frank and communicative in the society of friends, fond of the fox-chase and the dance, often sportive in his let-

CHAP. XXXVII 1775. June. ters, and liked a hearty laugh. This joyousness of disposition remained to the last, though the vastness of his responsibilities was soon to take from him the right of displaying the impulsive qualities of his nature, and the weight which he was to bear up, was to overlay and repress his gaiety and openness.

His hand was liberal; giving quietly and without observation, as though he was ashamed of nothing but being discovered in doing good. He was kindly and compassionate, and of lively sensibility to the sorrows of others; so that if his country had only needed a victim for its relief, he would have willingly offered himself as a sacrifice. But while he was prodigal of himself, he was considerate for others; ever parsimonious of the blood of his countrymen.

He was prudent in the management of his private affairs, purchased rich lands from the Mohawk Valley to the flats of the Kanawha, and improved his fortune by the correctness of his judgment; but as a public man he knew no other aim than the good of his country, and in the hour of his country's poverty, he refused personal emolument for his service.

His faculties were so well balanced and combined, that his constitution, free from excess, was tempered evenly with all the elements of activity, and his mind resembled a well ordered commonwealth; his passions, which had the intensest vigor, owned allegiance to reason; and, with all the fiery quickness of his spirit, his impetuous and massive will was held in check by consummate judgment. He had in his composition a calm, which gave him in moments of highest excitement the power of self-control, and enabled him to excel in patience, even when he had most cause for disgust. Washington was offered a command when there was little to bring out the unorganized resources of the continent but his own influence, and authority was connected with the people by the most frail, most attenuated, scarcely discernible threads; yet vehement as was his nature, impassioned as was his courage, he so restrained his ardor, that he never failed continuously to exert the attracting power of that influence, and never exerted it so sharply as to break its force.

In secrecy he was unsurpassed; but his secrecy had the character of prudent reserve, not of cunning or concealment.

His understanding was lucid, and his judgment accurate; so that his conduct never betrayed hurry or confusion. No detail was too minute for his personal inquiry and continued supervision; and at the same time he comprehended events in their widest aspects and relations. He never seemed above the object that engaged his attention, and he was always equal, without an effort, to the solution of the highest questions, even when there existed no precedents to guide his decision.

In this way he never drew to himself admiration for the possession of any one quality in excess, never made in council any one suggestion that was sublime but impracticable, never in action took to himself the praise or the blame of undertakings astonishing in conception, but beyond his means of execution. It was the most wonderful accomplishment of this man that placed upon the largest theatre of events, at the head of the greatest revolution in human affairs, he

CHAP. XXXVII 1775. June. never failed to observe all that was possible, and at the same time to bound his aspirations by that which was possible.

A slight tinge in his character, perceptible only to the close observer, revealed the region from which he sprung, and he might be described as the best specimen of manhood as developed in the south; but his qualities were so faultlessly proportioned, that his whole country rather claimed him as its choicest representative, the most complete expression of all its attainments and aspirations. He studied his country and conformed to it. His countrymen felt that he was the best type of America, and rejoiced in it, and were proud of it. They lived in his life, and made his success and his praise their own.

Profoundly impressed with confidence in God's Providence, and exemplary in his respect for the forms of public worship, no philosopher of the eighteenth century was more firm in the support of freedom of religious opinion; none more tolerant, or more remote from bigotry; but belief in God and trust in His overruling power, formed the essence of his character. Divine wisdom not only illumines the spirit, it inspires the will. Washington was a man of action, and not of theory or words; his creed appears in his life, not in his professions, which burst from him very rarely, and only at those great moments of crisis in the fortunes of his country, when earth and heaven seemed actually to meet, and his emotions became too intense for suppression; but his whole being was one continued act of faith in the eternal, intelligent, moral order of the universe. Integrity was so completely the law of his nature, that a planet would sooner have shot from its sphere, than he have departed from his uprightness, which was so constant, that it often seemed to be almost impersonal. CHAP. XXXVII 1775. June

They say of Giotto, that he introduced goodness into the art of painting; Washington carried it with him to the camp and the cabinet, and established a new criterion of human greatness. The purity of his will confirmed his fortitude; and as he never faltered in his faith in virtue, he stood fast by that which he knew to be just; free from illusions; never dejected by the apprehension of the difficulties and perils that went before him, and drawing the promise of success from the justice of his cause. Hence he was persevering, leaving nothing unfinished; free from all taint of obstinacy in his firmness; seeking, and gladly receiving advice, but immovable in his devotedness to right.

Of a "retiring modesty and habitual reserve," his ambition was no more than the consciousness of his power, and was subordinate to his sense of duty; he took the foremost place, for he knew from inborn magnanimity, that it belonged to him, and he dared not withhold the service required of him; so that, with all his humility, he was by necessity the first, though never for himself or for private ends. He loved fame, the approval of coming generations, the good opinion of his fellow-men of his own time, and he desired to make his conduct coincide with their wishes; but not fear of censure, not the prospect of applause, could tempt him to swerve from rectitude, and the praise which he coveted, was the sympathy of that moral sentiment which exists in every human breast, and goes forth only to the welcome of virtue.

CHAP. XXXVII 1775. June.

There have been soldiers who have achieved mightier victories in the field, and made conquests more nearly corresponding to the boundlessness of selfish ambition; statesmen who have been connected with more startling upheavals of society; but it is the greatness of Washington, that in public trusts he used power solely for the public good; that he was the life, and moderator, and stay of the most momentous revolution in human affairs, its moving impulse and its restraining power. Combining the centripetal and the centrifugal forces in their utmost strength and in perfect relations, with creative grandeur of instinct he held ruin in check, and renewed and perfected the institutions of his country. Finding the colonies disconnected and dependent, he left them such a united and well ordered commonwealth as no visionary had believed to be possible. So that it has been truly said, "he was as fortunate as great and good."

This also is the praise of Washington; that never in the tide of time has any man lived who had in so great a degree the almost divine faculty to command the confidence of his fellow-men and rule the willing. Wherever he became known, in his family, his neighborhood, his county, his native state, the continent, the camp, civil life, the United States, among the common people, in foreign courts, throughout the civilized world of the human race, and even among the savages, he, beyond all other men, had the confidence of his kind.

Washington saw at a glance the difficulties of the position to which he had been chosen. He was appointed by a government which, in its form, was one of the worst of all possible governments in time of peace, and was sure to reveal its defects still more plainly in time of war. It was inchoate and without an executive head; the several branches of administration, if to be conducted at all, were to be conducted by separate, ever changing, and irresponsible committees; and all questions of legislation and of action ultimately decided by the one ill organized body of men, who, in respect of granted powers, were too feeble even to originate advice. They were not the representatives of a union; they alone constituted the union of which, as yet, there was no other bond. One whole department of government, the judicial, was entirely wanting. So was, in truth, the executive. The congress had no ability whatever to enforce a decree of their own; they had no revenue, and no authority to collect a revenue; they had none of the materials of war; they did not own a cannon, nor a pound of powder, nor a tent, nor a musket; they had no regularly enlisted army, and had even a jealousy of forming an army, and depended on the zeal of volunteers, or of men to be enlisted for less than seven months. There were no experienced officers, and no methods projected for obtaining them. Washington saw it all. He was in the enjoyment of fame; he wished not to forfeit the esteem of his fellow-men; and his eye glistened with a tear, as he said in confidence to Patrick Henry on occasion of his appointment: "This day will be the commencement of the decline of my reputation."

But this consideration did not make him waver. On the sixteenth of June, he appeared in his place in congress, and after refusing all pay beyond his ex-

CHAP. XXXVII 1755. June. penses, he spoke with unfeigned modesty: "As the congress desire it, I will enter upon the momentous duty, and exert every power I possess in their service, and for the support of the glorious cause. But I beg it may be remembered by every gentleman in the room, that I this day declare, with the utmost sincerity, I do not think myself equal to the command I am honored with."

The next day, the delegates of all the colonies resolved unanimously in congress "to maintain and assist him, and adhere to him, the said George Washington, Esquire, with their lives and fortunes in the same cause."

By his commission, he was invested with the command over all forces raised or to be raised by the United Colonies, and with full power and authority to act as he should think for the good and welfare of the service; and he was instructed to take "special care that the liberties of America receive no detriment."

Washington knew that he must depend for success on a steady continuance of purpose in an imperfectly united continent, and on his personal influence over separate and half-formed governments, with most of which he was wholly unacquainted; he foresaw a long and arduous struggle; but a secret consciousness of his power bade him not to fear; and whatever might be the backwardness of others, he never admitted for a moment the thought of sheathing his sword or resigning his command, till his work of vindicating American liberty should be done. To his wife he unbosomed his inmost mind: "I hope my undertaking this service is designed to answer some good purpose. I rely confidently on that Providence, which has heretofore preserved and been bountiful to me." CHAP. XXXVII 1775. June.

His acceptance at once changed the aspect of affairs. John Adams, looking with complacency upon "the modest and virtuous, the amiable, generous, and brave general," as the choice of Massachusetts, said: "This appointment will have a great effect in cementing the union of these colonies." "The general is one of the most important characters of the world; upon him depend the liberties of America." All hearts turned with affection towards Washington. This is he who was raised up to be not the head of a party, but the father of his country.

CHAPTER XXXVIII.

PRESCOTT OCCUPIES BREED'S HILL.

JUNE 16–17, 1775.

CHAP. XXXVIII. 1775. June. THE army round Boston, of which Washington in person was soon to take command, was "a mixed multitude," as yet, "under very little discipline, order, or government." The province of Massachusetts had no executive head, and no unity even in the military department. Ward was enjoined to obey the decisions of the committee of safety, whose directions were intercepted on their way to him by the council of war. Thus want of confidence multiplied the boards to which measures were referred, till affairs wore an aspect of chaos. The real strength of the forces was far inferior to the returns. There were the materials for a good army in the private men, of whom great numbers were able bodied, active, and unquestionably brave, and there were also officers worthy of leading such men. But by a vicious system of recruiting, commissions were given to those who raised companies or regiments; and many had crowded themselves into place from love of rank or pay, without experience, spirit, or military capacity. This also led to the engagement of unsuitable men; and in some cases to false muster-rolls. In nearly every company, many were absent with or without leave. No efficient discipline or proper subordination was established. For tents, canvas and sails, collected from the seaport towns, had furnished a small but insufficient supply, and troops were quartered in the colleges and private houses. There was a great want of money and of clothing; of engineers, but above all, of ammunition. The scanty store of powder was reserved almost exclusively for the small arms, and used with great frugality. "Confusion and disorder reigned in every department, which in a little time must have ended either in the separation of the army, or fatal contests with one another."

Of the soldiers from the other colonies, the New Hampshire regiments only had as yet been placed under the command of Ward. The arrival of Greene quieted a rising spirit of discontent, which had threatened to break up the detachment from Rhode Island; but some of their captains and many subalterns continued to neglect their duty, from fear of offending the soldiers, from indolence, or from obstinacy. Of the men of Connecticut, a part were with Spencer at Roxbury; several hundred at Cambridge with Putnam, the second brigadier; who was distinguished for bold advice, alertness, and popular favor; and was seen constantly on horseback or on foot, working with his men or encouraging them.

The age and infirmities of Ward combined to increase the caution which the state of the camp made imperative. He was unwilling to hazard defeat, and

CHAP. XXXVIII. 1775. June. inclined to await the solution of events from the negotiations of the continental congress. It was sometimes even suggested that the Americans could never hold Cambridge, and that they had better go back and fortify on the heights of Brookline. "We must hold Cambridge," was Putnam's constant reply, and he repeatedly but vainly asked leave to advance the lines to Prospect Hill. Yet the army never doubted its ability to avenge the public wrongs; and danger and war were becoming attractive.

The British forces gave signs of shame at their confinement and inactivity. "Bloody work" was expected, and it was rumored that they were determined, as far as they could, to lay the country waste with fire and sword. The secretary of state frequently assured the French minister at London, that they would now take the field, and that the Americans would soon tire of the strife. The king of England, who had counted the days necessary for the voyage of the transports, was "trusting soon to hear that Gage had dispersed the rebels, destroyed their works, opened a communication with the country," and imprisoned the leading patriots of the colony.

The peninsula of Boston, at that time connected with the main land by a very low and narrow isthmus, had at its south a promontory then known as Dorchester Neck, with three hills, commanding the town. At the north lay the peninsula of Charlestown, in length not much exceeding a mile; in width, a little more than a half mile, but gradually diminishing towards the causeway, which kept asunder the Mystic and the Charles, where each of those rivers meets an arm of the sea. Near its northeastern termination rose the round smooth acclivity of Bunker Hill, one hundred and ten feet high, commanding both peninsulas. The high land then fell away by a gradual slope for about seven hundred yards, and just north by east of the town of Charlestown, it re-appeared with an elevation of about seventy-five feet, which bore the name of Breed's Hill. Whoever should hold the heights of Dorchester and Charlestown would be masters of Boston.

About the middle of May, a joint committee from that of safety and the council of war, after making a careful examination, recommended that several eminences between the camp and Charlestown should be cccupied, and that a strong redoubt should be raised on Bunker Hill. The advice was to be followed at the earliest day, after obtaining adequate supplies of artillery and powder. But delay would have rendered even the attempt impossible.

Gage, with the three major generals, was forming a plan for extending his lines over Charlestown. To that end, Howe was to land troops on the point; Clinton in the centre; while Burgoyne was to cannonade from the causeway. The operations, it was believed, would be very easy; and their execution was fixed for the eighteenth of June.

This design became known in the American camp, and such was the restless courage of the better part of the officers, such the confidence of the soldiers, that it seemed to justify a desire to anticipate the movement. Accordingly, on the fifteenth of June, the Massachusetts committee of safety informed the council of war,

CHAP. XXXVIII. 1775. June. that in their opinion, Dorchester heights should be fortified; and they recommended unanimously to establish a post on Bunker Hill. Ward, who was bound to comply with the instructions of his superiors, proceeded to execute the advice.

The decision was so sudden, that no fit preparation could be made. The nearly total want of ammunition rendered the service desperately daring; in searching for an officer suited to such an enterprise, the choice fell on William Prescott, of Pepperell, colonel of a regiment from the northwest of Middlesex, who himself was solicitous to assume the perilous June 16. duty; and on the very next evening after the vote of the committee of safety, a night and day only in advance of the purpose of Gage, a brigade of one thousand men was placed under his command.

Soon after sunset, the party composed of three hundred of his own regiment, detachments from those of Frye and of Bridge, and two hundred men of Connecticut, under the gallant Thomas Knowlton, of Ashford, were ordered to parade on Cambridge common. They were a body of husbandmen, not in uniform, bearing for the most part no other arms than fowling pieces which had no bayonets, and carrying in horns and pouches their stinted supply of powder and bullets. Langdon, the president of Harvard college, who was one of the chaplains to the army, prayed with them fervently; then, as the late darkness of the midsummer evening closed in, they marched for Charlestown in the face of the proclamation, issued only four days before, by which all persons taken in arms against their sovereign, were threatened under martial law with death by the cord as rebels and traitors. Prescott and his party were the first to give the menace a defiance. For himself, he was resolved "never to be taken alive."

CHAP. XXXVIII. 1775. June 16.

When with hushed voices and silent tread, they and the wagons laden with intrenching tools had passed the narrow isthmus, Prescott called around him Richard Gridley, an experienced engineer, and the field officers, to select the exact spot for their earth works. The committee of safety had proposed Bunker Hill; but Prescott had "received orders to march to Breed's Hill." Heedless of personal danger, he obeyed the orders as he understood them; and with the ready assent of his self-devoted companions, who were bent on straitening the English to the utmost, it was upon the eminence nearest Boston, and best suited to annoy the town and the shipping in the harbor, that under the light of the stars the engineer drew the lines of a redoubt of nearly eight rods square. The bells of Boston had struck twelve before the first sod was thrown up. Then every man of the thousand seized in his turn the pickaxe and spade, and they plied their tools with such expedition, that the parapet soon assumed form, and height, and capacity for defence. "We shall keep our ground," thus Prescott related that he silently revolved his position, "if some screen, however slight, can be completed before discovery." The Lively lay in the ferry, between Boston and Charlestown, and a little to the eastward were moored the Falcon, and the Somerset, a ship of the line; the veteran not only set a watch to patrol the shore, but bending his ear to catch every sound, twice repaired to the margin of the water, where he heard the drowsy

June 17.

CHAP. XXXVIII. 1775. June 17. sentinels from the decks of the men of war still cry: "All is well." Putnam also during the night came among the men of Connecticut on the hill; but he assumed no command over the detachment.

The few hours that remained of darkness hurried away, but not till the line of circumvallation was already closed. As day dawned, the seamen were roused to action, and every one in Boston was startled from slumber by the cannon of the Lively playing upon the redoubt. Citizens of the town, and British officers, and tory refugees, the kindred of the insurgents, crowded to gaze with wonder and surprise at the small fortress of earth freshly thrown up, and "the rebels," who were still plainly seen at their toil. A battery of heavy guns was forthwith mounted on Copp's Hill, which was directly opposite, at a distance of but twelve hundred yards, and an incessant shower of shot and bombs was rained upon the works; but Prescott, whom Gridley had forsaken, calmly considered how he could best continue his line of defence.

At the foot of the hill on the north was a slough, beyond which an elevated tongue of land, having few trees, covered chiefly with grass, and intersected by fences, stretched away to the Mystic. Without the aid of an engineer, Prescott himself extended his line from the east side of the redoubt northerly for about twenty rods towards the bottom of the hill; but the men were prevented from completing it "by the intolerable fire of the enemy." Still the cannonade from the battery and shipping could not dislodge them, though it was a severe trial to raw soldiers, unaccustomed to the noise of artillery. Early in the day, a private was killed and buried. To inspire confidence, Prescott mounted the parapet and walked leisurely backwards and forwards, examining the works and giving directions to the officers. One of his captains, perceiving his motive, imitated his example. From Boston, Gage with his telescope descried the commander of the party. "Will he fight?" asked the general of Willard, Prescott's brother-in-law, late a mandamus councillor, who was at his side. "To the last drop of his blood," answered Willard. As the British generals saw that every hour gave fresh strength to the intrenchments of the Americans, by nine o'clock they deemed it necessary to alter the plan previously agreed upon, and to make the attack immediately on the side that could be soonest reached. Had they landed troops at the isthmus as they might have done, the detachment on Breed's Hill would have had no chances of escape or relief.

The day was exceedingly hot, one of the hottest of the season. After their fatigues through the night, the American partisans might all have pleaded their unfitness for action; some left the post, and the field officers, Bridge and Brickett, being indisposed, could render their commander but little service. Yet Prescott was dismayed neither by fatigue, nor desertion. "Let us never consent to being relieved," said he to his own regiment, and to all who remained; "these are the works of our hands, to us be the honor of defending them." He consented to despatch repeated messengers for reënforcements and provisions; but at the hour of noon no assistance had appeared. His men had toiled all the night long, had broken their fast only with what they had brought

CHAP. XXXVIII. 1775. June 17.

in their knapsacks the evening before, had, under a burning sky, without shade, amidst a storm of shot and shells, continued their labor all the morning, and were now preparing for a desperate encounter with a vastly superior force; yet no refreshments were sent them, and during the whole day they received not even a cup of cold water, nor so much as a single gill of powder. The agony of suspense was now the greater, because no more work could be done in the trenches; the tools were piled up in the rear, and the men were waiting, unemployed, till the fighting should begin.

The second messenger from Prescott, on his way to the head-quarters at Cambridge, was met by Putnam, who was hastening to Charlestown. The brigadier seems to have been justly impressed with the conviction, that the successful defence of the peninsula not only required reënforcements, but that intrenchments should be thrown up on the summit of Bunker Hill. He, therefore, rode up to the redoubt on Breed's Hill, where he did not appear again during the whole day, and asked of Prescott, "that the intrenching tools might be sent off." It was done, but of the large party who took them away, few returned; and the want of a sufficient force, and the rapid succession of events, left Putnam no leisure to fortify the crown of the higher hill.

Far different was the scene in Boston. To finished and abundant equipments of every kind, the British troops, though in number hardly more than five thousand effective men, added experience and exact discipline. Taking advantage of high water, the Glasgow sloop of war and two floating batteries had

CHAP. XXXVIII. 1775. June 17.

been moored, where their guns raked the isthmus of Charlestown. Between the hours of twelve and one, by order of General Gage, boats and barges, manned by oars, all plainly visible to Prescott and his men, bore over the unruffled sheet of water from Long Wharf to Moulton's Point in Charlestown, the fifth, the thirty-eighth, the forty-third, and the fifty-second regiments of infantry, with ten companies of grenadiers, ten of light infantry, and a proportion of field artillery, in all about two thousand men. They were commanded by Major General Howe, who was assisted by Brigadier General Pigot. It was noticed that Percy, pleading illness, let his regiment go without him. The British landed under cover of the shipping, on the outward side of the peninsula, near the Mystic, with a view to outflank the American party, surround them, and make prisoners of the whole detachment.

The way along the banks of the river to Prescott's rear lay open; he had remaining with him but about seven or eight hundred men, worn with toil and watching and hunger; he knew not how many were coming against him; his flank was unprotected; he saw no signs of reënforcements; the enemy had the opportunity to surround and crush his little band. "Never were men placed in a more dangerous position." But Howe, who was of a sluggish temperament, halted on the first rising ground, and sent back for more troops. The delay cost him dear.

When Prescott perceived the British begin to land on the point east by north from the fort, he made the best disposition of his scanty force, ordering the train of artillery with two field pieces, and the

CHAP. XXXVIII. 1775. June 17.

Connecticut forces under Knowlton, "to go and oppose them."

At about two hundred yards in the rear of the still unfinished breastwork, a fence of posts with two rails, set in a low stone wall, extended for about three hundred yards or more towards the Mystic. The mowers had but the day before passed over the meadows, and the grass lay on the ground in cocks and windrows. There the men of Connecticut, in pursuance of Prescott's order, took their station. Nature had provided "something of a breastwork," or a ditch had been dug many years before. They grounded arms and made a slight fortification against musket balls by interweaving the newly mown grass between the rails, and by carrying forward a post and rail fence alongside of the first, and piling the fresh hay between the two. But the line of defence was still very far from complete. Nearer the water the bank was smooth and without obstruction, declining gently for sixty or eighty yards, where it fell off abruptly. Between the rail fence and the unfinished breastwork, the space was open and remained so; the slough at the foot of the hill guarded a part of the distance; nearly a hundred yards were left almost wholly unprotected.

Brooks, afterwards governor of Massachusetts, one of Prescott's messengers, had no mode of reaching head-quarters but on foot. Having performed the long walk, he found the general anxious and perplexed. Ward saw very clearly the imprudence of risking a battle for which the army was totally unprepared. To the committee of safety which was in session, the committee of supplies expressed its concern at the "expenditure of powder;" "any great consumption by cannon might be ruinous;" and it is a fact that the Americans—with companies incomplete in number, enlisted chiefly within six weeks, commanded, many of them, by officers unfit, ignorant, and untried, gathered from four separate colonies, with no reciprocal subordination but from courtesy and opinion—after collecting all the ammunition that could be obtained north of the Delaware, had in the magazine for an army, engaged in a siege and preparing for a fight, no more than twenty-seven half barrels of powder, with a gift from Connecticut of thirty-six half barrels more.

CHAPTER XXXIX.

BUNKER HILL BATTLE.

June 17, 1775.

CHAP. XXXIX 1775. June 17. Ward determined, if possible, to avoid a general action. Apprehending that, if reinforcements should leave his camp, the main attack of the British would be made upon Cambridge, he refused to impair his strength at head-quarters; but he ordered the New Hampshire regiments of Stark, stationed at Medford, and of Reed, near Charlestown neck, to march to Prescott's support.

When word was brought that the British were actually landing in Charlestown, the general regarded it as a feint, and still refused to change his plan. But here the character of New England shone out in its brightest lustre. The welcome intelligence that the British had actually sallied out of Boston, thrilled through men, who were "waiting impatiently to avenge the blood of their murdered countrymen." Owing to the want of activity in Ward, who did not leave his house during the whole day, all was confusion; but while the bells were ringing and the drums

1775. June. 17.

beating to arms, officers who had longed for the opportunity of meeting the British in battle, soldiers who clung to the officers of their choice with constancy, set off for the scene of battle, hardly knowing themselves whether they were countenanced by the general, or the committee of safety, or the council of war; or moved by the same impetuous enthusiasm which had brought them forth on the nineteenth of April, and which held "an honorable death in the field for the liberties of all America preferable to an ignominious slavery."

The veteran, Seth Pomeroy of Northampton, an old man of seventy, once second in rank in the Massachusetts army, but now postponed to younger men, heedless of the slight, was roused by the continuance of the cannonade, and rode to Charlestown neck; there, thoughtful for his horse, which was a borrowed one, he shouldered his fowling-piece, marched over on foot, and amidst loud cheers of welcome, took a place at the rail fence.

Joseph Warren also, after discharging his duty in the committee of safety, resolved to take part in the battle. He was entreated by Elbridge Gerry not thus to expose his life. "It is pleasant and becoming to die for one's country," was his answer. Three days before, he had been elected a provincial major-general. He knew perfectly well the defects of the American camp, the danger of the intrenched party, and how the character of his countrymen and the interests of mankind hung in suspense on the conduct of that day. About two o'clock he crossed Bunker Hill, unattended, and with a musket in his hand. He stood for a short time near a cannon at the rail

CHAP. XXXIX 1775. June 17. fence in conversation with Putnam, who declared a readiness to receive his orders; but Warren declined to assume authority, and passed on to the redoubt, which was expected to be the chief point of attack. As soon as he arrived there Prescott proposed that he should take the command; but he answered as he had done to Putnam: "I come as a volunteer, to learn from a soldier of experience;" and in choosing his station he looked only for the place of greatest danger and importance.

Of the men of Essex who formed Little's regiment, full a hundred and twenty-five hastened to the aid of Prescott; Worcester and Middlesex furnished more than seventy from Brewer's regiment, and with them the prudent and fearless William Buckminster, of Barre, their lieutenant colonel. From the same counties came above fifty more, led by John Nixon, of Sudbury. Willard Moore, of Paxton, a man of superior endowments, brought on about forty of Worcester county; from the regiment of Whitcomb, of Lancaster, there appeared at least fifty privates, but with no higher officers than captains. Not more than six light field pieces were brought upon the ground; but from defective conduct and want of ammunition, even these were scarcely used. A few shot were thrown from two or three of them; as if to mark the contrast with the heavy and incesssant cannonade of the British.

At the rail fence there were, as yet, but the Connecticut men, whom Prescott had detached. The two field pieces had been deserted by the artillerymen. After the British had landed, and just before they advanced, a party of New Hampshire levies arrived,

1775. June 17

led on by Colonel John Stark, who, next to Prescott, brought the largest number of men into the field. When they came to the isthmus, which was raked by cannon, Dearborn, one of his captains who walked by his side, advised a quick step. "Dearborn," replied Stark, "one fresh man in action is worth ten fatigued ones;" and he marched leisurely across Charlestown neck, through the galling fire of cannon shot, which buzzed about them like hail. Of quickest perception, resolute in decision, the rugged trapper was as calm as though he had been hunting in his native woods. At a glance upon the beach along Mystic river, "I saw there," he related, "the way so plain, that the enemy could not miss it." While some of his men continued the line of defence by still weaving grass between the rails, others, at his bidding, leaped down the bank, and with stones from adjacent walls, on the instant threw up a breastwork to the water's edge. Behind this, in the most exposed station that could have been selected, where a covered boat, musket proof, carrying a heavy piece of cannon, if it had been towed up the channel, could have taken them on the side and instantly dislodged them, he posted triple ranks of his men; the rest knelt or lay down. The time allowed him no opportunity of consulting with Prescott; they fought independently; Prescott to defend the redoubt, Knowlton and Stark, with Reed's regiment, to protect its flank. These are all who arrived before the beginning of the attack; and not more than a hundred and fifty others of various regiments, led by different officers or driven by their own zeal, reached the battle ground before the retreat. From first to last, Putnam took an active interest in

CHAP. XXXIX 1775. June 17. the expedition, and the appointment of Prescott to its command, was made with his concurrence. Without in the least interfering with that command, he was now planning additional works on Bunker Hill, now mingling with the Connecticut troops at the rail fence, now threatening officers or men who seemed to him dilatory or timid, now at Cambridge in person or by message, earnestly demanding reënforcements, ever busily engaged in aiding and encouraging, here and there, as the case required. After the first landing of the British, he sent orders by his son to the Connecticut forces at Cambridge, "that they must all meet and march immediately to Bunker Hill to oppose the enemy." Chester and his company ran for their arms and ammunition, and marched with such alacrity that they arrived at the battle ground before the day was decided.

While the camp at Cambridge was the scene of so much confusion, Howe caused refreshments to be distributed abundantly among his troops. The reinforcements which he had demanded, arrived, consisting of several more companies of light infantry and grenadiers, the forty-seventh regiment, and a battalion of marines. "The whole," wrote Gage, "made a body of something above two thousand men;" "about two thousand men and two battalions to reinforce him," wrote Burgoyne; "near upon three thousand," thought very accurate observers, and a corps of five regiments, one battalion, and twenty flank companies, more than seventy companies must, after all allowances, be reckoned at two thousand five hundred men, or more. It comprised the chief strength of the army.

Not till the news reached Cambridge of this second landing at Charlestown, was Ward relieved from the apprehension, that the main body of the British would interpose themselves between Charlestown and Cambridge. Persuaded of the security of the camp, and roused by the earnest and eloquent entreaties of Devens, of Charlestown, himself a member of the committee of safety, Ward consented to order reinforcements; among them his own regiment, but it was too late.

CHAP. XXXIX 1775. June 17.

The whole number of Americans on the ground at that time, including all such as crossed the causeway seasonably to take part in the fight, according to the most solemn assurances of the officers who were in the action, to the testimony of eye witnesses, to contemporary inquirers, and to the carefully considered judgment of Washington, did not exceed one thousand five hundred men.

Nor should history forget to record that, as in the army at Cambridge, so also in this gallant band, the free negroes of the colony had their representatives. For the right of free negroes to bear arms in the public defence was, at that day, as little disputed in New England as their other rights. They took their place not in a separate corps, but in the ranks with the white man, and their names may be read on the pension rolls of the country, side by side with those of other soldiers of the revolution.

Two days after the massacre at Lexington, Gage had threatened, that if the Americans should occupy Charlestown heights, the town should be burned. Its inhabitants, however, had always been willing that the threat should be disregarded. The time for the

CHAP. XXXIX 1775. June 17. holocaust was now come. Pretending that his flanking parties were annoyed from houses in the village, Howe sent a boat over with a request to Clinton and Burgoyne to burn it. The order was immediately obeyed by a discharge of shells from Copp's Hill. The inflammable buildings caught in an instant, and a party of men landed and spread the fire; but from the sudden shifting of the wind, the movements of the assailants were not covered by the smoke of the conflagration.

At half past two o'clock, or a very little later, General Howe not confining his attack to the left wing alone, advanced to a simultaneous assault on the whole front from the redoubt to Mystic river. In Burgoyne's opinion, "his disposition was soldier-like and perfect." Of the two columns which were put in motion, the one was led by Pigot against the redoubt; the other by Howe himself against the flank, which seemed protected by nothing but a fence of rails and hay easy to be scrambled over, when the left of Prescott would be turned, and he would be forced to surrender on finding the enemy in his rear.

As they began to march, the dazzling lustre of a summer's sun was reflected from their burnished armor; the battery on Copp's Hill, from which Clinton and Burgoyne were watching every movement, kept up an incessant fire, which was seconded by the Falcon and the Lively, the Somerset and the two floating batteries; the town of Charlestown, consisting of five hundred edifices of wood, burst into a blaze; the steeple of its only church became a pyramid of fire; and the masts of the shipping, and the heights of the

British camp, the church towers, the housetops of a populous town, and the acclivities of the surrounding country were crowded with spectators, to watch the battle which was to take place, in full sight on a conspicuous eminence, and which, as the English thought, was to assure the integrity of the British empire, as the Americans believed, was to influence the freedom and happiness of mankind.

1775. June 17.

As soon as Prescott perceived that the enemy were in motion, he commanded Robinson, his lieutenant colonel, the same who conducted himself so bravely in the fight at Concord, and Henry Woods, his major, famed in the villages of Middlesex for ability and patriotism, with separate detachments to flank the enemy; and they executed his orders with prudence and daring. He then went through the works to encourage and animate his inexperienced soldiers. "The redcoats will never reach the redoubt," such were his words, as he himself used to narrate them, "if you will but withhold your fire till I give the order, and be careful not to shoot over their heads." After this round, he took his post in the redoubt, well satisfied that the men would do their duty.

The British advanced in line in good order, steadily and slowly, and with a confident imposing air, pausing on the march to let their artillery prepare the way, and firing with muskets as they advanced. But they fired too soon, and too high, doing but little injury.

Incumbered with their knapsacks, they ascended the steep hill with difficulty, covered as it was with grass reaching to their knees, and intersected with walls and fences. Prescott waited till the enemy

CHAP. XXXIX 1775. June 17. had approached within eight rods as he afterwards thought, within ten or twelve rods as the committee of safety of Massachusetts wrote, when he gave the word: "Fire." At once from the redoubt, and breastwork, every gun was discharged. Nearly the whole front rank of the enemy fell, and the rest to whom this determined resistance was unexpected, were brought to a stand. For a few minutes, fifteen or ten, who can count such minutes! each one of the Americans completely covered while he loaded his musket, exposed only while he stood upon the wooden platform or steps of earth in the redoubt to take aim, fought according to his own judgment and will; and a close and unremitting fire was continued and returned, till the British staggered, wavered, and then in disordered masses retreated precipitately to the foot of the hill, and some even to their boats.

The column of the enemy which advanced near the Mystic under the lead of Howe, moved gallantly forward against the rail-fence, and when within eighty or one hundred yards, displayed into line, with the precision of troops on parade. Here, too, the Americans, commanded by Stark and Knowlton, cheered on by Putnam, who like Prescott bade them reserve their fire, restrained themselves as if by universal consent, till at the proper moment, resting their guns on the rails of the fence, they poured forth a deliberate, well directed, fatal discharge. Here, too, the British recoiled from the volley, and after a short contest, were thrown into confusion, and fell back till they were covered by the ground.

Then followed moments of joy in that unfinished redoubt, and behind the grassy rampart, where New

England husbandmen, so often taunted with cowardice, beheld veteran battalions shrink before their arms. Their hearts bounded as they congratulated each other. The night watches, thirst, hunger, danger, whether of captivity or death, were forgotten. They promised themselves victory.

CHAP. XXXIX

1775. June 17.

As the British soldiers retreated, the officers were seen by the spectators on the opposite shore, running down to them, using passionate gestures, and pushing them forward with their swords. After an interval of about fifteen minutes, during which Prescott moved round among his men, encouraging them and cheering them with praise, the British column under Pigot rallied and advanced, though with apparent reluctance, in the same order as before, firing as they approached within musket shot. This time the Americans withheld their fire till the enemy were within six or five rods of the redoubt, when, as the order was given, it seemed more fatal than before. The enemy continued to discharge their guns, and pressed forward with spirit. "But from the whole American line, there was," said Prescott, "a continuous stream of fire," and though the British officers were seen exposing themselves fearlessly, remonstrating, threatening, and even striking the soldiers to urge them on, they could not reach the redoubt, but in a few moments gave way in greater disorder than before. The wounded and the dead covered the ground in front of the works, some lying within a few yards of them.

On the flank also, the British light infantry again marched up its companies against the grass fence, but could not penetrate it. "Indeed," wrote some of the survivors, "how could we penetrate it? Most of

CHAP. XXXIX 1775. June 17. our grenadiers and light infantry, the moment of presenting themselves, lost three-fourths, and many, nine-tenths of their men. Some had only eight or nine men in a company left, some only three, four, or five." On the ground where but the day before the mowers had swung the scythe in peace, "the dead," relates Stark, "lay as thick as sheep in a fold." Howe for a few seconds was left nearly alone, so many of the officers about him having been killed or wounded; and it required the utmost exertion of all, from the generals down to the subalterns, to repair the rout.

At intervals the artillery from the ships and batteries was playing, while the flames were rising over the town of Charlestown, and laying waste the places of the sepulchres of its fathers, and streets were falling together, and ships at the yards were crashing on the stocks, and the kindred of the Americans, from the fields and hills around, watched every gallant act of their defenders. "The whole," wrote Burgoyne, "was a complication of horror and importance beyond any thing it ever came to my lot to be witness to. It was a sight for a young soldier, that the longest service may not furnish again."

"If we drive them back once more," cried Prescott, "they cannot rally again." To the enduring husbandmen about him, the terrible and appalling scene was altogether new. "We are ready for the red-coats again," they shouted, cheering their commander, and not one of them shrunk from duty.

In the longer interval that preceded the third attack, a council of officers disclosed the fact, that the ammunition was almost exhausted. Though

Prescott had sent in the morning for a supply, he had received none, and there were not fifty bayonets in his party. A few artillery cartridges were discovered, and as the last resource the powder in them was distributed, with the direction, that not a kernel of it should be wasted.

CHAP. XXXIX

1775. June 17.

CHAPTER XL.

THE RESULT OF BUNKER HILL BATTLE.

June 17, 1775.

CHAP. XL. 1775. June 17. The royal army, exasperated at retreating before an enemy whom they had professed to despise, and by the sight of many hundreds of their men who lay dead or bleeding on the ground, prepared to renew the engagement. While the light infantry and a part of the grenadiers were left to continue the attack at the rail-fence, Howe concentrated the rest of his forces upon the redoubt. Cannon were brought to bear in such a manner as to rake the inside of the breastwork, from one end of it to the other, so that the Americans were obliged to crowd within their fort. Then the British troops, having disencumbered themselves of their knapsacks, advanced in column with fixed bayonets. Clinton, who from Copp's Hill had watched the battle, at this critical moment, and without orders, pushed off in a boat, and put himself at the head of two battalions, the marines and the forty-seventh, which seemed to hesitate on the beach as if uncertain what to do. These formed the extreme left of the British, and advanced from the south; the fifth, the thirty-eighth, and forty-third battalions formed the centre, and attacked from the east; on their right was the fifty-second with grenadiers, who forced the now deserted intrenchments.

The Americans within the redoubt, attacked at once on three sides by six battalions, at that time numbered less than seven hundred men. Of these some had no more than one, none more than three or four rounds of ammunition left. But Prescott's self-possession increased with danger. He directed his men to wait till the enemy were within twenty yards, when they poured upon them a deadly volley. The British wavered for an instant, and then sprang forward without returning the fire. The American fire slackened, and began to die away. The British reached the rampart on the southern side. Those who first scaled the parapet were shot down as they mounted. Major Pitcairn fell mortally wounded, just as he was entering the redoubt. A single artillery cartridge furnished powder for the last muskets which the Americans fired. For some time longer they kept the enemy at bay, confronting them with the butt end of their guns, and striking them with the barrels after the stocks were broken. The breastwork being abandoned, the ammunition all expended, the redoubt half filled with regulars and on the point of being surrounded, and no other reinforcements having arrived, at a little before four, Prescott gave the word to retreat. He himself was among the last to leave the fort; escaping unhurt, though with coat and waistcoat rent and pierced by bayonets, which he parried with his sword. The men, retiring through

CHAP. XL. 1775. June 17. the sallyport or leaping over the walls, made their way through their enemies, each for himself, without much order, and the dust which rose from the dry earth now powdered in the sun, and the smoke of the engagement, gave them some covering. The British, who had turned the north-eastern end of the breastwork, and had likewise come round the angle of the redoubt, were too much exhausted to use the bayonet against them with vigor, and at first the parties were so closely intermingled as to interrupt the firing; it also appeared that a supply of ball for the artillery, sent from Boston during the battle, was too large for the field-pieces which accompanied the detachment.

The little handful of brave men would have been effectually cut off, but for the unfailing courage of the provincials at the rail fence and the bank of the Mystic. They had repulsed the enemy twice; they now held them in check, till the main body had left the hill. Not till then did the Connecticut companies under Knowlton, and the New Hampshire soldiers under Stark quit the station, which they had "nobly defended." The retreat was made with more regularity than could have been expected of troops, who had been for so short a time under discipline, and many of whom had never before seen an engagement. Trevett and his men drew off the only field-piece that was saved. Pomeroy walked backwards, facing the enemy and brandishing his musket till it was struck and marked by a ball. The redoubt, the brow of Bunker Hill, and the passage across the Charlestown causeway, were the principal places of slaughter.

Putnam, at the third onset, was absent, "employed

in collecting men" for a reinforcement, and was encountered by the retreating party on the northern declivity of Bunker Hill. Acting on his own responsibility, he now for the first time during the day assumed the supreme direction. Without orders from any person, he rallied such of the fugitives as would obey him, joined them to a detachment which had not arrived in season to share in the combat, and took possession of Prospect Hill, where he encamped that very night.

Repairing to head-quarters, Prescott offered with three fresh regiments to recover his post. But for himself he sought neither advancement, nor reward, nor praise, and having performed the best service, never thought that he had done more than his duty. It is the contemporary record, that during the battle "no one appeared to have any command but Colonel Prescott," and that "his bravery could never be enough acknowledged and applauded." The camp long repeated the story of his self-collected valor, and a historian of the war, who best knew the judgments of the army, has rightly awarded the "highest prize of glory to Prescott and his companions."

The British were unable to continue the pursuit beyond the isthmus. They had already brought their best forces into the field; more than a third of those engaged lay dead or bleeding, and the survivors were fatigued, and overawed by the courage of their adversaries. The battle put an end to all offensive operations on the part of Gage.

The number of the killed and wounded in his army was, by his own account, at least one thousand and fifty-four. Seventy commissioned officers were wounded, and thirteen were slain. Of these, there

CHAP. XL. 1775. June 17. were one lieutenant colonel, two majors, and seven captains. For near half an hour there had been a continued sheet of fire from the provincials; and the action was hot for double that period. The oldest soldiers had never seen the like. The battle of Quebec, which won half a continent, did not cost the lives of so many officers as the battle of Bunker Hill, which gained nothing but a place of encampment.

Sir William Howe who was thought to have been wounded was untouched; though his white silk stockings were stained from his walking through the tall grass, red with the blood of his soldiers. That he did not fall was a marvel. The praises bestowed on his apathetic valor, on the gallantry of Pigot, on the conduct of Clinton, reflected honor on the untrained farmers, who though inferior in numbers, had required the display of the most strenuous exertions of their assailants, before they could be dislodged from the defences which they had had but four hours to prepare.

The whole loss of the Americans amounted to one hundred and forty-five killed and missing, and three hundred and four wounded. The brave Moses Parker, of Chelmsford, was wounded and taken prisoner; he died in Boston jail. Major Willard Moore received one severe wound at the second attack, and soon after another, which he felt to be mortal; so bidding farewell to those who would have borne him off, he insisted on their saving themselves, and remained to die for the good cause, which he had served in council and in arms. Buckminster was dangerously wounded, but recovered. The injury to Nixon was so great that he suffered for many months, and narrowly escaped

CHAP. XL. 1775. June 17.

with his life. Thomas Gardner, a member of congress from Cambridge, was hastening with some part of his regiment to the redoubt, but as he was descending Bunker Hill, he was mortally wounded by a random shot. His townsmen mourned for the rural statesman, to whom they had unanimously shown their confidence; and Washington gave him the funeral honors due to a gallant officer. Andrew McClary, on that day unsurpassed in bravery, returning to reconnoitre, perished by a chance cannon ball on the isthmus.

Just at the moment of the retreat, fell Joseph Warren, the last in the trenches. In him were combined celerity, courage, endurance, and manners which won universal love. He opposed the British government, not from interested motives, nor from resentment. A guileless and intrepid advocate of the rights of mankind, he sought not to appear a patriot; he was one in truth. As the moment for the appeal to arms approached, he watched with joy the revival of the generous spirit of New England's ancestors; and where peril was greatest, he was present, animating not by words alone, but ever by his example. His integrity, the soundness of his judgment, his ability to write readily and well, his fervid eloquence, his exact acquaintance with American rights and the infringements of them, gave authority to his advice in private, and in the provincial congress. Had he lived, the future seemed burdened with his honors; he cheerfully sacrificed all for his country, and for freedom. Sorrow could now no more come nigh him, and he went to dwell in men's memories with Hampden.

His enemies recognised his worth by their ex-

CHAP. XL. 1775. June 17.

ultation at his fall. By his countrymen, he was "most sincerely and universally lamented;" his mother would not be consoled. His death, preceded by that of his wife, left his children altogether orphans, till the continent, at the motion of Samuel Adams, adopted them in part at least as its own. The congress of his native state, that knew him well, and had chosen him to guide their debates, and recently to high command in their army, proclaimed to the world their "veneration for Joseph Warren, whose memory is endeared to his countrymen, and to the worthy in every part and age of the world, so long as virtue and valor shall be esteemed among men."

The reports of the generals show the opinions in the two camps after the battle. "The success," wrote Gage to Dartmouth, "which was very necessary in our present condition, cost us dear. The number of killed and wounded is greater than our forces can afford to lose. We have lost some extremely good officers. The trials we have had, show the rebels are not the despicable rabble too many have supposed them to be, and I find it owing to a military spirit encouraged among them for a few years past, joined with uncommon zeal and enthusiasm. They intrench, and raise batteries; they have engineers. They have fortified all the heights and passes around this town; which it is not impossible for them to annoy. The conquest of this country is not easy; you have to cope with vast numbers. In all their wars against the French, they never showed so much conduct, attention, and perseverance, as they do now. I think it my duty to let your lordship know the true situation of affairs."

On the other hand, Ward, in a general order, expressed thanks to "the officers and soldiers who behaved so gallantly at the late action in Charlestown;" and in words which expressed the conviction of the American camp, he added, "we shall finally come off victorious, and triumph over the enemies of freedom and America." Washington, as he heard the narrative of the events of the day, was confirmed in his habitual belief that the liberties of America would be preserved. "Americans will fight," wrote Franklin on the occasion, to his English friends; "England has lost her colonies for ever." CHAP. XL. 1775. June 17.

END OF VOL. VII.

BANCROFT'S HISTORY.

A History of the United States,

FROM THE

DISCOVERY OF THE AMERICAN CONTINENT.

BY GEORGE BANCROFT.

Vols. I. to VI. 8vo.

PUBLISHED BY LITTLE, BROWN AND COMPANY,

112 Washington Street, Boston.

THE publishers invite the attention of the readers of the present volume of Mr. Bancroft's History of the United States to the first six volumes of the work, "the distinguished merits of which have been gratefully acknowledged by his countrymen." A glance at the following Table of Contents will indicate the special topics treated in these volumes; and as to the manner of treatment, the readers of the new volume will not need any recommendation to induce them to peruse the others, if they have not already done so.

CONTENTS OF VOLUME I.

CHAPTER I. Early Voyages. — French Settlements.
II. Spaniards in the United States.
III. England takes possession of the United States.
IV. Colonization of Virginia.
V. Slavery. — Dissolution of the London Company.
VI. Restrictions on Colonial Commerce.
VII. Colonization of Maryland.
VIII. The Pilgrims.
IX. Extended Colonization of New England.
X. The United Colonies of New England.

CONTENTS OF VOLUME II.

CHAP. XI. The Restoration of the Stuarts.
XII. Massachusetts and Charles II.
XIII. Shaftesbury and Locke legislate for Carolina.
XIV. The Colonies on the Chesapeake Bay.
XV. New Netherlands.
XVI. The People called Quakers in the United States.
XVII. James II. consolidates the Northern Colonies.
XVIII. The Result thus far.

CONTENTS OF VOLUME III.

CONTENTS OF VOLUME IV.

CONTENTS OF VOLUME V.

CONTENTS OF VOLUME VI.

www.ingramcontent.com/pod-product-compliance
Lightning Source LLC
LaVergne TN
LVHW021138110826
845150LV00005B/1056

9781425549329